Abortion in the American Imagination

Abortion in the American Imagination

Imagination

Before Life and Choice, 1880–1940

KAREN WEINGARTEN

Rutgers University Press

NEW BRUNSWICK, NEW JERSEY, AND LONDON

LIBRARY OF CONGRESS CATALOGING-IN-PUBLICATION DATA

Weingarten, Karen, 1980–
    Abortion in the American Imagination : Before Life and Choice, 1880–1940 /
Karen Weingarten.
        pages   cm. — (American Literatures Initiative)
Includes bibliographical references and index.
    ISBN 978-0-8135-6530-9 (hardback)
    ISBN 978-0-8135-6529-3 (pbk.)
    ISBN 978-0-8135-6539-2 (e-book)
    1. American literature—History and criticism. 2. Abortion in literature. I. Title.
PS169.A28W45   2014
810.9'355—dc23
                                                                    2013040900

A British Cataloging-in-Publication record for this book is available
from the British Library.

Copyright © 2014 by Karen Weingarten

Visit our website: http://rutgerspress.rutgers.edu

Manufactured in the United States of America

THE
AMERICAN
LITERATURES
INITIATIVE

A book in the American Literatures Initiative (ALI), a collaborative
publishing project of NYU Press, Fordham University Press, Rutgers
University Press, Temple University Press, and the University of Virginia
Press. The Initiative is supported by The Andrew W. Mellon Foundation.
For more information, please visit www.americanliteratures.org.

For CJF

CONTENTS

ACKNOWLEDGMENTS

The support of many colleagues and friends made this book possible, and I am grateful for their belief in me and my work. I owe particular thanks to the institutional support I received from Queens College, City University of New York, and from the PSC-CUNY Research Foundation, whose grants made much of my summer work and travel possible. I am also thankful to the Woodrow Wilson Women's Studies Fellowship, which funded this project at an early stage. I hope the fellowship will be available to many more young scholars in women, gender, and sexuality studies. I am grateful for the help of several archives and libraries, including the Wertheim Room at the New York Public Library and especially the support of Jay Barksdale, the Sophia Smith Archives at Smith College, the UCLA film and television archive, the Margaret Herrick Library at the Academy of Motion Picture Arts and Sciences, the Performing Arts Library at the New York Public Library, and the library at the New York Academy of Medicine. An earlier version of chapter 2, "The Inadvertent Alliance of Anthony Comstock and Margaret Sanger," was published in *Feminist Formations* 22, no. 2 (Summer 2010): 42–59, and a shorter version of chapter 3 was published as "Bad Girls and Biopolitics: Abortion, Popular Fiction, and Population Control" in *Literature and Medicine* 29, no. 1 (Spring 2011): 81–103. My expanded discussion of abortion rhetoric in Edith Wharton's *Summer*, which I briefly touch on here in chapter 1, was published as "Between the Town and the Mountain: Abortion and the Politics of Life in Edith Wharton's *Summer*" in *Canadian Review of American Studies* 40, no. 3 (Autumn 2010): 351–72. The editors of all three journals and the anonymous reviewers gave me invaluable advice and insight that ultimately helped shaped the entire manuscript. They were examples of how peer review works at its very best.

Ultimately, I owe the biggest thanks to individual people who guided me along the way. I couldn't ask for better colleagues and friends at Queens College. Amy Wan, Gloria Fisk, Kevin Ferguson, Jason Tougaw, Caroline Hong, Carrie Hintz, Talia Schaffer, Steven Kruger, and Glenn Burger either read pieces of the manuscript or gave me invaluable advice along the way. I've also been fortunate to work with Andrea Walkden, Annmarie Drury, Sian Silyn Roberts, Veronica Schanoes, Seo-Young Chu, Nicole Cooley, Kimiko Hahn, Ryan Black, John Weir, Harold Schechter, Hugh English, and Miles Grier at Queens College. I am grateful to have such a welcoming and supportive work environment. Outside of Queens, I can't say enough to express my gratitude and appreciation for the members of my writing group, Lauren Klein, Sarah Blackwood, and Kyla Schuller. I could not wish for a smarter and more dedicated group of writing friends. I also owe many thanks to David Kazanjian, Hildegarde Hoeller, and David Reynolds for helping me at various stages along the way. My dear friend and colleague Diana Colbert isn't alive to see this book in print, but my conversations with her echo in its pages. My community of academic friends, now scattered across North America, has also been invaluable to this process. There are so many people to thank, but in particular Karen Weiser, Lily Saint, Heather Latimer, and Rebekah Sheldon are models for me of intelligence, kindness, and political commitment to making the world a smarter, more thoughtful place. Dale Bauer's and the anonymous reader's comments on the manuscript in its later stages were also invaluable and made this book better. Katie Keeran at Rutgers University Press has been a model editor. I owe her innumerable thanks for bringing this project to fruition. Finally, at the end stages of this project, where detail matters, I am grateful for the careful attention provided by Tim Roberts and Carol Sickman-Garner.

My family, spread across the Atlantic, on the other coast, and up north in Canada, has cheered me on and only occasionally pestered me with the question, "So when will that book be done?" I am so grateful for their love and support. I also owe so much to many friends who cheered me up and cheered me on. Joanna Sondheim, Laura Davis, Tali Horowitz, Olivia deBree, MK Babcock, Arielle DePaolo, Solvej Schou, Lilla Töke, and Aman Gill deserve a special thank you for their love and support. For Ansel I have a special thank you for helping focus and distract me in equal measures. Finally and most importantly, I cannot thank Corey Frost enough. With wisdom, love, and amazing editorial skills, he talked me through difficult moments in this project and always believed in me. I could not ask for a better partner and friend.

ABORTION IN THE AMERICAN IMAGINATION

Introduction

It is . . . no wonder that the debate about abortion should refuse to settle into a single voice.
—BARBARA JOHNSON, "APOSTROPHE, ANIMATION, AND ABORTION"

Visually almost indistinguishable from mint yet even stronger smelling and tasting than the average leaves from a peppermint plant, pennyroyal, a member of the mint family, is an obscure herb that is rarely used today. Along with savin, tansy, thyme, aloes, and various tree barks, pennyroyal was often advertised in various nineteenth-century guides as a possible abortifacient.[1] If taken in too large a dose, it was also known to cause death. In Sarah Orne Jewett's *The Country of the Pointed Firs*, pennyroyal is described as the favorite herb of Mrs. Todd, her town's renowned herbalist, who takes every opportunity to pick a good batch as she travels through the outskirts of her small community in rural Maine. Mrs. Todd remains quiet about her work, and the novel has only the most oblique references to abortion. Mrs. Todd, for example, is "incommunicative" about her reasons for stopping during a journey to pick some boughs "of a rare shrub which she valued for its bark."[2] Only a reader knowledgeable in common nineteenth-century abortifacients might connect the mysterious bark to the visitors who come "at night as if by stealth" to Mrs. Todd's door, seeking help for their ailments and receiving "whispered directions."[3] While there are a handful of sensational dime novels in the nineteenth century that were explicitly produced to scandalize, most novels, like Jewett's, had only elliptical references to abortion.[4] By the first few decades of the twentieth century, American authors latched onto abortion as a complicating plot device, and the number of novels, short stories, plays, and poems that openly discuss abortion proliferated.

Among the earliest works with representations of abortion is Eugene O'Neill's 1914 one-act play *The Abortion*, which would never be performed in his lifetime and which was only rescued from extinction because the typescript was preserved in the Library of Congress. The play conforms to popular conceptions of abortion at the time as it reveals that the death of a young working-class woman was the result of her illegal abortion. In 1916 director Lois Weber produced the silent film *Where Are My Children?*, which features a villainous abortionist, a reckless woman who has one abortion after another, and her husband, who remains unaware of his wife's practice until the film's end, when in response he cries, "Where are my children?" Soon after his plea, we see an image of the supposedly unborn children with angel wings ascending to heaven. The early twentieth century also saw the emergence of abortion in fiction. Edith Wharton's 1917 novel *Summer*—discussed in chapter 1—is one of the first novels that explicitly mentions abortion and depicts an abortionist in the malevolent caricature of the time. In 1924 Dorothy Parker published "Mr. Durant" in *American Mercury*, a popular literary journal that featured some of the most prominent early twentieth-century writers; the story describes a married middle-class man's idle affair that ends with his mistress's abortion. Three years later, Ernest Hemingway's 1927 short story "Hills like White Elephants," first published in his collection *Men without Women*, follows a conversation between an older man and his mistress as he attempts to convince her to obtain an illegal abortion.

This short list covers only a small subset of the works that appeared between 1900 and 1939 that mention abortion and abortionists.[5] *Abortion in the American Imagination* posits that because the early twentieth century marked a formative period for abortion discourse, examining the era's representations of abortion provides insight into how the issue is framed today. Early twentieth-century American writers for the first time risked discussing abortion openly in fictional works, even if it meant the threat of censorship. This book brings together a broad range of texts and archival materials: it examines abortion rhetoric in popular early twentieth-century novels, as well as works now considered canonical; it looks at letters, journals, and periodicals to contextualize key figures in the antiabortion movement, like Margaret Sanger and Anthony Comstock; and it tracks newspaper articles that sensationalized abortionists such as the infamous Madame Restell. By bringing these texts together, this book aims to show how the use of the terms *life* and *choice* is caught in liberal American ideals of individuality, autonomy, and self-responsibility, which work to obscure abortion's entanglement in larger questions about race, eugenics, economics, biopolitics, and, of course, gender. By tracing how antiabortion rhetoric was used to delineate the contours of the ideal American citizen, the book constructs a discursive genealogy of one of the most intractable issues in the United States today. As A. Cheree Carlson has argued, rhetoric not only mirrors social conditions but is "also an intensely practical art of effecting change in one's social world."[6] *Abortion in the American Imagination* treats literary texts as rhetorical entities that both reflect their milieu and produce social realities, new discourses, and competing narratives.

In Floyd Dell's 1923 novel *Janet March*, the wealthy and forward-thinking Janet has an abortion after a quick love affair that led to her first sexual experience. Conflicted about her decision to have an abortion, she longs for her experience to be represented within the novels she reads. She thinks, "why weren't there things like [abortions] in novels—oh yes, there were dreadful things enough in novels, but they only happened to poor girls—ignorant and reckless girls—."[7] For Janet, finding her experience represented within the pages of novels would have legitimized her decision. Instead, she realizes that several of her friends are likely to have had abortions but refused to discuss their circumstances, and in novels, only "ignorant and reckless girls" had premarital sex and suffered the consequences. With her observation, Janet, a young, white, upper-middle-class woman, points to the discursive power of novels in their ability to shame women into believing that abortion is an irresponsible and contemptible choice. Taking this analysis even further, novels and other forms of popular culture have the potential not only to represent but also to create material realities. Laura Doyle elegantly articulates this point when she writes, "For [racial patriarchy] capitalizes on that connection between words and acts, bodies and texts, while denigrating the words of those who protest."[8] Even if Janet and her friends, who are for the most part wealthy and white, are having premarital sex and abortions, because their actions are not reflected in the cultural productions consumed by their peers, they can be effectively hidden and erased.

As chapter 3, which focuses on the popular novel, discusses in more detail, novels—and other forms of mass media—can enforce social behavior and beliefs even more powerfully than laws themselves. Within a disciplinary society they become one tactic for naturalizing experiences and creating the material conditions that shape our actions and beliefs. I chose to focus on the novels, films, and cultural artifacts studied in this book because they produce a discourse that was at times in conversation with, and at times in opposition to, early twentieth-century discussions about abortion that were more often than not presented through the terms of liberalism—even if only to critique them. I thus read these works as theoretical pieces that are in dialogue with the political and cultural norms of their time. Lisa Duggan has claimed that liberalism is successful because it both organizes human activity in terms of race, gender, sexuality, nationality, ethnicity, and religion and also intentionally obscures the connections between these categorizations. This way of arranging human life then becomes naturalized, as do the divisions between the categories. By reading cultural productions for their theoretical contributions, the obfuscations generated by liberalism can be denaturalized because they reveal how, for example, nationality and religion are connected or, in the example used most commonly in this book, how gender, sexuality, and race are tied to reproduction. The passage of time is especially effective in denaturalizing cultural productions and the material work they do in their contemporary moment. Janet might worry that because her sexual experience and subsequent abortion are only represented in novels by characters that are reckless and ignorant, that means that she too is irresponsible and reprehensible. However, almost a hundred years later, the cultural work of her reading material becomes more transparent. While twenty-first-century feminists have already critiqued the 2007 films *Juno* and *Knocked Up* for their refusal to acknowledge abortion as a legitimate response to an unwanted pregnancy, I imagine that fifty years from now, feminist scholars will be able to tell us even more about how those films generated a materiality that was implicitly accepted by most of us.

Scholars such as Rebecca Walkowitz and Douglas Mao have called for readings of modernist texts that go beyond aesthetic classification.[9] *Abortion in the American Imagination* responds to this call by reading popular novels classified as "low art" alongside canonical works seen as having achieved literary distinction. It seeks to trace a conversation about abortion through a range of texts circulating in the early twentieth century that sought to participate in, extend, and challenge the ways Americans viewed and discussed women's reproductive issues. I borrow Michael Trask's use of the terms *modernism* and *modernity* in literary history, which he views as a way to intervene "in the assessment of the intellectual and sexual cultures of the period more broadly."[10] Similarly, when I refer to modern or modernist novels, I do not necessarily point to an aesthetic movement with innovative forms—even though some of the texts studied here are considered canonical modernist texts through this definition. Doyle has argued that experimental modern novels "push narrative language to *its* outlying borders . . . thus exposing, and in some moments surpassing, the racial and gendered linguistic and literary borders of the flesh."[11] While experimental fiction might allow the printed page to push normative assumptions and reveal relationships— to denaturalize, to use Duggan's term—I also argue in the following pages that some rather unexperimental novels from the same era can do the same work when read against their grain. Like Trask, I see the modernity of the early twentieth century, even in its more conventional forms, as allowing for an experimentation with representing taboo sexualities in new—and at times daring—ways. For this reason, I find early twentieth-century literature, a body of work that has often been referred to as chronologically modernist, compelling for the study of gendered lives: while it does not present a unified view of abortion, it does allow for new ways—theoretical ways—to think about the relationships among sexuality, economy, politics, and life. Dana Seitler posits that modernity is characterized by both progress and loss, and both have led to anxieties concerning the new and the real or imagined world we may have lost.[12] In many ways, this description aptly captures the rhetoric of abortion in early twentieth-century America. Continuing Seitler's argument about modernity, I suggest that, in part, abortion became a contentious issue in the United States because it became enmeshed in anxieties about change and progress and that those anxieties are generated and circulated by the cultural productions of the time.

Liberalism, Biopolitics, and Modernity

Kristin Luker's groundbreaking book on abortion politics argues that the abortion controversy is so bitter because "the two sides share almost no common premises and very little common language."[13] Yet by studying how the liberal individual serves as a foundational figure in abortion rhetoric, extending from the mid-nineteenth century to today, I aim to deconstruct the rhetoric of life and choice to demonstrate how the terms are intimately bound to each other and to an American liberalism that upholds individual freedom and rights over all. This book will often invoke a critique of liberalism, a term with a contested and confused history. Simply defined, liberalism "signifies an order in which the state exists to secure the freedom of individuals on a formally egalitarian basis."[14] In other words, liberalism serves as the basis for American democracy and social relations through the establishment of the

Lockean assumption that rights and freedom are natural and, further-more, that the primary and most basic building block of human society is the autonomous individual.

Twentieth- and twenty-first-century feminists have long engaged critiques and defenses of liberalism, from Martha Nussbaum's support of liberalism as fundamentally protecting "spheres of choice," to Car-ole Pateman's "radical liberalism," which emphasizes autonomy and the will to consent (but still critiques masculinist tendencies of liberal-ism),[15] to Saba Mahmood's work, which detaches the concept of agency from Western and progressive politics. To generalize, Nussbaum cri-tiques feminists for not acknowledging that liberalism itself has a long and diverse history and notes that in fact it would be more accurate to speak of *liberalisms* when we discuss the term. Yet, despite the differ-ences among the liberalisms of Kant, Mill, Hume, Smith, and Rawls—to name just some of the key figures who have created divergent strands of liberalism—most feminist scholars, whether writing in support or in critique of the ideology, can agree on some basic tenets. For example, Nussbaum, Mahmood, and Jane Mansbridge all agree that an emphasis on the individual and his (or, less often, her) autonomy lies at the center of liberal philosophy. Whether they agree or disagree with the tenets of liberalism they summarize, all three thinkers contend that at its core liberalism emphasizes the autonomous, self-reliant, individual citizen whose singular rights must be protected above all. This definition is the one I rely on when evoking "liberalism" in this book.

This book's critique of liberalism is influenced by Wendy Brown's *States of Injury*, which demonstrates a fundamental paradox within lib-eralism: while it advances the cause of the individual and his natural rights, it also places primary importance on the familial unit and a gen-dered division of labor. The father mirrors the sovereign in the family unit and should bear responsibility for the women and children in his care. Women in this model are thus effectively excluded from citizen-ship. Extending this critique, I am particularly interested in how liber-alism binds even the seemingly starkest of oppositions such as pro-life and pro-choice supporters. Both groups have historically advanced their causes by invoking individual rights and by emphasizing the importance of family structures and responsibilities. I contend that using liberalism as a basis for securing access to abortion (or any other right) ensures the exclusion of some other marginalized group. As Brown suggests, "the gendered terms of liberal discourse solicit the production of a bourgeois feminism that emancipates certain women to participate in the terms of masculinist justice without emancipating gender as such from those terms."[16] In other words, certain women might have the right to abortion if they can afford the procedure, if they can obtain permission from a spouse, if they can wait twenty-four hours after their initial appointment. Similarly, by claiming the individuality of the fetus and its right to life, the rights of the woman carrying the pregnancy must necessarily be elided. Liberalism thus serves to protect and shield, but its protection is premised on recognizing only certain forms of life and only under certain conditions.

Brown's feminist critique of liberalism in part builds on Foucault's theories of biopolitics, which this book also relies on. As Penelope Deutscher has written, Foucauldian biopolitics lend themselves to an analysis of how power is gendered, and how it genders, because Foucault's theories often explicitly describe sexual differentiation as a tool within biopolitics. Deutscher notes that in two different interviews Foucault even used abortion laws as an example of his theories on power.[17] Beginning in chapter 1, readers will notice that I also draw on Giorgio Agamben's somewhat different account of biopolitics. One key difference between these two theories is that Agamben doesn't see the political preoccupation with controlling life—and those who are deemed worthy of livable lives—to be a modern phenomenon. However, as I'll discuss in the first chapter, the control of abortion and women's reproduction, while perhaps not exclusive to the modern world, became a more acute interest in modernity.

Agamben is also mostly silent on the issue of gender and sex, yet he figures as a major theoretical support throughout this work. Deutscher speculates that his silence might be because the fetus doesn't fit into his examples of life on the threshold (the comatose, the internee, the *Muselmann*). In chapters 1, 3, and 5, I'll expand on this feminist reading of Agamben's concept of bare life to include the pregnant woman, particularly one who seeks an abortion. In other words, women's reproductive bodies, I'll argue, fit neatly into Agamben's category of life on the threshold, even though his own work ignores them. I'll show how in many early twentieth-century novels it is not the fetus who figures on the threshold of life, but rather the accidentally pregnant woman who is in danger of dehumanization once she is designated as the container for a future child. And, as chapter 1 in particular elaborates, this new view of women's bodies not only emerged with modernity but also intensified as reproductive technologies, such as the sonogram, allowed us to visualize the fetus as a developing human.

Doyle's groundbreaking *Bordering on the Body* was one of the first books to argue for reading modern fiction alongside eugenics to understand how together they form a discourse about racially and sexually differentiated bodies. "Modern mother figures give birth to racial plots," Doyle writes,[18] and continuing with that observation she convincingly demonstrates how modern experimental fiction emerged out of the same material conditions that gave rise to the eugenics movement and modernism. *Abortion in the American Imagination* follows Doyle's example by similarly situating literary texts alongside racial and gendered ideologies to understand how new narratives about abortion emerged in the late nineteenth and early twentieth centuries; yet what I add to her matrix is the biopolitical project of life management in order to show how abortion rhetoric managed women's lives. The stories I examine in chapter 1 suggest that with modernity came a new interest in controlling women's reproduction, and that interest was in part shaped by the establishment of new forms of biopolitics.

Alys Eve Weinbaum's work in *Wayward Reproductions* also makes a case for modernity's new relationship to reproduction. By carefully tracing the etymology of the word *reproduction* Weinbaum demonstrates how the term itself only gained its contemporary association with procreation in modern times.[19] In part, her project aims to show how by the nineteenth century discourses of reproduction were almost always racially charged, and by proving this argument she also posits that reproduction should be viewed as tied to issues traditionally placed outside of "women's issues" and the domestic realm. This move is by no means a critique of feminist theory and feminist studies of domesticity. On the contrary, Weinbaum's work seeks to broaden the categories of feminist inquiry and to demonstrate its fundamental connection to nation-state formation, racial discourses, and class construction. Similarly, *Abortion in the American Imagination* argues that the abortion controversy is rooted in political issues that are often defined as "masculine": economy, autonomy, racism, and political life. While some of the works discussed in the following chapters had explicitly feminist motivations, many others were authored by men with no feminist intentions (or even awareness). In many cases these works were chosen because their silence on the issue of gender reveals how abortion rhetoric was bound to numerous tentacles of political life.

Economies of Choice

Since *Roe v. Wade* legalized abortion in 1973 it has been under relentless attack. In many states antiabortion activists have successfully lobbied for the passage of laws that force women to have ultrasounds before consenting to pregnancy, to obtain parental approval if they are under a certain age, to wait twenty-four to forty-eight hours for an abortion after their initial appointment requesting one, and to listen to information about how abortion may harm them—even if this "information" has no scientific basis. Such laws, antiabortion proponents claim, are for the protection of women. Their logic paternalistically argues that women who seek abortion don't realize the psychological harm they might be imposing on themselves, and thus they need strictures in place to warn them. Missing from this conversation, until recently, is a discussion about what happens to women who are refused abortion—because they discover their pregnancy too late, don't have access to health care and insurance, or are turned away because of medical complications.[20] The economic repercussions of having a child are enormous, particularly for women who are already in a difficult financial position. The antiabortion position claims, on one hand, that women don't understand enough about reproduction to make the decision to have an abortion on their own, yet on the other hand it claims that women are irresponsible if they have children without the financial and social support to raise that child successfully. As chapter 4 will continue to argue, the outlawing of abortion functions to strip women of economic power in a capitalist society founded on liberal tenets. If abortion is inaccessible, then women without the economic means to seek it are denied control of their reproductive lives. This effectively ensures that they are also demarcated as not responsible enough, not autonomous enough, and not self-reliant enough, and thus full citizenship can be denied them.

Meridel LeSueur's 1939 novel *The Girl* recognizes the economic complexity of women's reproduction. The eponymous girl, who is never named, lives a harsh life surrounded by prostitutes and criminals. Her lover is a professional thief, and her roommate has sex when she needs to pay the rent. When the girl finds herself pregnant, both her lover and her friend Clara insist that she needs to have an abortion. They take a long view of her situation, recognizing that a child must be fed and supported. Clara tells the girl, "if you got a kid you got to get rid of it. . . . What will you feed it? Be sensible and take an aspirin."[21] Butch, her lover, is even more blunt: "Nobody cares a rap in hell what happens to you, might as well get that first as last. Get rid of it. I could do it myself with a pair of scissors, there's nothing to it."[22] Poor, jobless, and without family support, when the girl goes to seek assistance, she speaks to a social worker who coaxes her to tell her story under the pretence of trust. Later, when the social worker leaves the room, the girl steals her file and reads:

The girl is maladjusted, emotionally unstable, and a difficult problem to approach. A most unfortunate situation. A change of environment would be helpful, with continuous casework follow-up, to inspire poise and educational interests should be encouraged as a solution. In our opinion there should be a referral to a psychiatric clinic if she shows indications of further or aggravated mental and emotional disturbance. She should be tested for sterilization after her baby is born. In our opinion sterilization would be advisable.[23]

Sterilizing working-class and single pregnant women after they gave birth was, unfortunately, a common practice for many decades in the United States. Johanna Schoen, for example, has researched how common it was to label single woman who had children out of wedlock unstable, mentally ill, or maladjusted.[24] Applying such descriptions to young women meant that they could be stripped of all rights, and particularly reproductive rights, because they were deemed unfit to act within a liberal society. *The Girl* exposes this contradiction because its protagonist decides to carry her pregnancy to term and raise her daughter within a supportive and welcoming community of women. Its end provides a rather utopic alternative to the economic and political oppression faced by disenfranchised women like the girl, but it still successfully critiques the economic contradictions inherent within capitalism for women's reproductive rights. Since financial resources are needed to manage reproduction (especially when access to abortion and most forms of birth control is outlawed), women without those resources are deemed, as the girl was, "maladjusted, emotionally unstable, and a difficult problem." Because of these labels, judges, social workers, doctors, and other institutional workers in positions of power are legitimized in stripping such women of any agency they may have remaining through invoking infantilizing laws or, worse, sterilization. In this way the outlawing of abortion also effectively worked to economically disenfranchise women.

While abortion was stigmatized in the mid-nineteenth century, it was legal in most states until women reached quickening, the moment when the woman could feel the fetus move, which often occurs after the fourth month of pregnancy. In the 1860s and 1870s, however, movements led by social reformers and the American Medical Association began a campaign to completely outlaw abortion, state by state. By the 1880s every single state had a law criminalizing abortion. *Abortion in the American Imagination* takes this moment as its starting point to find an answer to the question: How did early twentieth-century literature, film, and popular culture contribute to a narrative about abortion that still resonates today? In this sense, my work on abortion in the early twentieth-century United States contributes to the growing body of scholarship that seeks to understand abortion beyond the terms of life and choice. By looking at different rhetorical flashpoints in American literary history, the project reveals how abortion ethics and practices complicate what we mean by *life*, *choice*, and *rights*. The texts examined here provide new key words for framing abortion discourse, such as *biopolitics*, *liberalism*, *eugenics*, *economics*, and *capital*, which I argue must be integrated into twenty-first-century conversations about abortion.

Chapter 1 focuses on the biopolitical characteristics of abortion to argue that the late nineteenth century's emergent interest in abortion's morality corresponded with a biopolitical shift in the United States.[25] In other words, bodies—particularly female and raced bodies—became the metaphorical ground for merging conversations about politics, biology, and medicine, allowing for new laws to be passed that legislated what was once thought to be private and beyond the law. The chapter examines how this shift was represented and circulated in various sensational news stories, novels, and short stories from the era. Chapter 2 examines liberalism's role in abortion politics by comparing the social reform projects of Anthony Comstock—the conservative reformer who crusaded to rid society of all "pornographic" material, including information about birth control and abortion—and Margaret Sanger—the birth control activist. While their two projects seem diametrically opposed, I demonstrate how both Sanger and Comstock promoted antiabortion arguments by invoking the self-reliant, autonomous liberal citizen who, if properly disciplined and contained, should "naturally" find herself repulsed by abortion. I then demonstrate how this ideology circulated through F. Scott Fitzgerald's *The Beautiful and Damned* and short stories and articles in Sanger's journal *Birth Control Review*. While chapter 2 also touches on how Sanger's ideology was shaped by the emerging American eugenics movement, chapter 3 spends more time discussing how eugenics influenced abortion rhetoric in the early twentieth century. By focusing on three best-selling novels from the era—Christopher Morley's *Kitty Foyle*, Viña Delmar's *Bad Girl*, and Sinclair Lewis's *Ann Vickers*—I connect the stigmatization of abortion to the eugenics movement, which generated a philosophy of how "good" or eugenic girls should behave. Chapters 4 and 5 shift away from eugenics to emphasize the liberal undertones of the antiabortion movement by unpacking the economic motivations of abortion's illegality. Chapter 4 studies

Theodore Dreiser's *An American Tragedy*, William Faulkner's *As I Lay Dying*, and Agnes Smedley's *Daughter of Earth* to show how each novel theorizes abortion as always tied to an economy that values the liberal and privileged male citizen to the exclusion of women. Finally, chapter 5 continues this argument by placing William Faulkner's *The Wild Palms* in a theoretical conversation with Hannah Arendt's *The Human Condition* and Agamben's *State of Exception*; Faulkner's novel, I argue, critiques modern society's valuation of production for the sake of production, including the reproduction of children. This chapter challenges so-called pro-life politics in antiabortion discourse by suggesting that the movement's blanket valuation of life is rooted in a capitalist ethics that demands reproduction for its own sake—and with no respect for the end product: the child. Through reading these representations of abortion in literary and other cultural texts from the early twentieth century, I provide additional conceptual frameworks to illuminate the ways in which abortion engages issues beyond the individual, family, and state.

The history of abortion in the United States has been documented by historians, rhetoricians, and political scientists such as Kristin Luker, James Mohr, Leslie Reagan, Rosalind Petchesky, Janet Brodie, and Nathan Stormer.[26] Historians seem to agree that while abortion was often presented in the mainstream media as a practice pursued only by defiled, indigent, and unconscionable women, it was in fact most often used as a means to limit family size by middle-class and wealthy women who could actually afford its high costs. Chapter 4 in particular looks at some novels that examine this economic contradiction, such as Agnes Smedley's *Daughter of Earth*, but many other short stories and novels also confront the economic implications of abortion. Dorothy Parker's "Mr. Durant" tells the story of a working-class girl seduced and impregnated by her boss, who then seeks an abortion for her; and in Edith Summers Kelly's *Weeds* the protagonist tries to self-abort when she fears that her impoverished rural life will be completely engulfed by childrearing if she were to have another child. Taken as a whole, the representation of abortion in many of these stories reflects and contributes to the conversations that were taking place about abortion in American society; therefore, to discuss these representations is also to discuss the history—rhetorical and material—of the practice. The work of this book is not purely representational, however. While many novels of the era reflect popular sentiments about abortion, others resist the common discourse and participate in creating alternate narratives. Sinclair Lewis's *Ann Vickers*, for example, has a fraught relationship to abortion as it presents a narrative that is sympathetic to the social conditions of working-class women, while Langston Hughes's "Cora Unashamed" openly portrays abortion as a racial issue that divides a predominantly white southern town.

I started this project with a firm belief in the importance of free and unrestricted access to abortion. My commitment to that belief stands as strong as ever. If anything, as I embarked on my archival and literary research, I became even more convinced that abortion should not be a moral issue in American politics. Many Americans, even those who consider themselves pro-choice or supportive of abortion, take for granted that abortion is a political issue. As I hope this work will demonstrate, this perspective didn't always exist. Through examining cultural productions that incorporate abortion politics in their plots and premises, the following chapters will show, in part, how abortion came to be viewed as a moral issue rather than as a medical practice free from juridical or ethical inscriptions. As the first chapter will describe in more detail, I chose early twentieth-century texts as the site for my research because they reflect the new biopoliticization of abortion, as well as other new anxieties about women's reproduction. By examining the moment when abortion is first represented in popular and literary productions, the project aims to trace a genealogy of abortion that might begin the work of revealing how abortion came to be viewed as such a taboo topic in our contemporary moment.

1 / The Biopolitics of Abortion as the Century Turns

There are many good people who are denied the supreme blessing of children. . . . But the man or woman who deliberately foregoes these blessings, whether from viciousness, coldness, shallow-heartedness, self-indulgence, or mere failure to appreciate aright the difference between the all-important and the unimportant,—why, such a creature merits contempt as hearty as any visited upon the soldier who runs away in battle, or upon the man who refuses to work for the support of those dependent upon him, and who tho able-bodied is yet content to eat in idleness the bread which others provide.
—THEODORE ROOSEVELT, FROM A 1905 SPEECH DELIVERED BEFORE THE NATIONAL CONGRESS OF MOTHERS

"Cora Unashamed," first published in 1936 in Langston Hughes's collection *The Ways of White Folks*, is focalized through Cora Jenkins, the eponymous protagonist, who is a black woman in a predominantly white southern town.[1] Cora works for the Studevants, a white family that "treats her like a dog"[2] and that, in a postslavery era, "thought they owned her, and they were probably right: they did."[3] When Cora's daughter dies of whooping cough, she develops a strong bond with Jessie, the Studevants' youngest daughter, who was born the same year as her own daughter. And when Cora learns of Jessie's pregnancy—a consequence of her premarital love affair with a newly immigrated Greek man—she is the only character who believes that Jessie has nothing to be ashamed of. Cora insists to Jessie's mother that it's "no trouble having a baby you want. I had one."[4] But Mrs. Art Studevant orders her to shut up and shuts her out from Jessie's life: Jessie is not a poor black woman, but a white woman from a wealthy and recognized family, and wanting a baby is not enough reason to have one outside of marriage. Although Jessie's boyfriend is willing to marry her, the narration informs us, "Mrs. Art had ambitions which didn't include the likes of Greek ice-cream makers' sons." And although Cora reassures Jessie that "there ain't no reason why you can't marry . . . you both white. Even if he is a foreigner, he's a right nice boy,"[5] Willie Matsoulos, the Greek boy, is not quite white enough for Jessie's mother. Instead Mrs. Art arranges a visit to Kansas City, presumably for an Easter shopping trip, but when they return, Jessie is no longer pregnant. A few days later, Jessie dies. Soon after her death Mrs. Studevant begins a campaign "to rid the town of objectionable tradespeople and questionable characters"[6] and forces Willie Matsoulos and his family to leave town. By convincing her Woman's Club that Matsoulos had been selling tainted ice cream, Mrs. Studevant classifies the family among the objectionable and questionable.

Hughes's story argues an important point: disciplining middle- and upper-class white women not to reproduce with black and immigrant men is a key reason why abortion restrictions emerged in the late nineteenth century. In "Cora Unashamed," Jessie's abortion holds no disciplining power over Cora. In fact, it has the opposite effect. During Jessie's funeral, Cora is so traumatized by her death and its tragic circumstances that she condemns Jessie's family and names the cause of Jessie's death: an abortion. Even if everyone in the town of Melton knew why Jessie died, no white person would have dared to speak it in public. Mrs. Studevant explains her daughter's illness when they returned from Kansas City as a bad case of indigestion, and her neighbors quietly accept the lie. Cora, however, as the story's title suggests, refuses to feel shame. She is unashamed by her own illegitimate pregnancy, by Jessie's premarital love affair, and even at the end by what led to Jessie's death. Ultimately, this lack of shame is what causes her to lose her position in the Studevant home as she shames them in public.

However, it is ultimately not Cora who performs the shaming. When Mrs. Studevant begins the process of forcing the Greek immigrant family to leave her town, she makes clear what she finds so terrifying about her daughter's pregnancy. Marriages brought about by unintended pregnancies were not uncommon in the early twentieth century. While there may have been talk about why a child came less than nine months after a wedding, the child would still be given "legitimate" status in the eyes of the community. Yet for Mrs. Studevant, the pregnancy and marriage were threatening not because they suggested that her daughter engaged in premarital sex but because they signified a destabilization of racial and class boundaries. By forcing her daughter to have an abortion she attempts to reify racial and reproductive norms and her view of the impermeable lines of her social position. The story demonstrates how the outlawing of abortion in the late nineteenth century effectively demonized the practice as something "bad" girls do: girls who engage in illicit sexual practices with the wrong kinds of boys. Thus it works to discipline women into normative sexual practices by positioning them against women like Jessie.

However, the story does more. Even as it demonstrates the powerful disciplining forces of biopolitics on the white population in the story, it also reveals the privilege of being allowed into the norm. For Cora and her parents, as the only black family in town, have to live on "the edge of Melton," known to the community as "the Jenkins niggers," who just "manage to get along."[7] Cora is not quite subject to the disciplining forces of her society, a point emphasized when she learns of her pregnancy: "Cora didn't go anywhere to have her child. Nor try to hide it. . . . There were no Negroes in Melton to gossip, and she didn't care what the white people said. They were in another world."[8] Quite literally living on the margins of her society, Cora is almost—but not quite—outside the confines of disciplinary law. Importantly, because Melton does not have a population of African Americans, she cannot be subject to their codes of normalization, and so she lives an in-between sort of life—not quite legible yet not quite bare. The price she pays for this condition is the price of laboring: "There was something about the teeth in the trap of economic circumstances that kept her in their power practically all her life—in the Studevant kitchen, cooking; in the Studevant parlor, sweeping; in the Studevant backyard, hanging clothes."[9] Like Hannah Arendt's model of society in ancient Greece, Cora is excluded from *bios*, or a politically recognized life, because she exists under the suffocating and endless conditions of labor. Her laboring can only produce more labor and more opportunities for consumption. Building on this theory, the story has an interesting twist: the Studevants are also trapped in a mirroring cycle of labor. Even as their white bodies provide them legibility through the law, they must also labor—literally through the labor women's bodies endure during childbirth—to ensure that their whiteness is maintained so that their bodies can cling to that legibility. It is precisely this precarious cycle (precarious because it can be unhitched with such a small shove) that positions them not far from Cora's edge, even as they live a life of privilege.

For Agamben the figure of bare life is central to modern biopolitics.[10] He argues that since World War I, with the sudden emergence of large numbers of refugees, the connection between nationality and birth could no longer be clearly made; the refugee breaks "the continuity between man and citizen, *nativity* and *nationality*."[11] This broken connection means that the very claims of national sovereignty then waver, threatening the nation-state's controlling and regulative measures. However, as this link breaks, nation-states "become greatly concerned with natural life, discriminating within it between a so-to-speak authentic life and a life lacking every political value," a bare life.[12]

In *Homo Sacer* Agamben picks up the term *biopolitics* and argues that its ultimate fruition can be seen in the camp—and in his prime example, the concentration camps of Nazi Germany. Key to Agamben's conception of biopolitics is that it "is the original activity of sovereign power."[13] This understanding of biopower differs significantly from Foucault's formulation, in which the emergence of biopolitics is tied to the emergence of the liberal Western European and American state in the eighteenth and nineteenth centuries. For Agamben, modern politics has only more explicitly revealed the bind between sovereign power and biopolitics because of the rise of fascism in the early twentieth century and the concentration camp. Additionally, entering into Agamben's discussion is the figure of bare life, which marginally exists in Foucault's writings. The concept of bare life comes from Aristotle's distinction between *bios*—a qualified life that is recognized by the law and that has full protection under that law—and *zoe*—a life that is stripped to the mere biological functions of living.[14] While bare life resembles *zoe*, it is also a more complicated conception of *zoe* because what distinguishes a biopolitical state is that it has brought *zoe* into its political sphere while at the same excluding it from full recognition within that sphere. Thus Agamben maintains that bare life exists in a state of inclusionary exclusion; sovereignty rests on recognizing bare life in order to point to qualified life, while at the same time insisting that bare life cannot have full political participation and protection. It is then through this political negotiation that all human life is managed and brought to the precarious position of potentially existing between *zoe* and *bios*. And it is through this negotiation that the sovereign exception is also made into the rule of law. Because bare life both threatens sovereignty and also subtends that sovereignty, the state of emergency becomes the rule of law. In this way life and law become bound together so that the processes of normalization that Foucault describes as integral in his conception of biopolitics are no longer at work. Instead it is the exception that regulates and controls and exposes us all to the risk of bare life. This concept of bare life is helpful for understanding antiabortion discourses that link outlawing the practice to defending the sacredness of life.

Heather Latimer notes that "the reproductive body is a blank spot in Agamben's definition of bare life."[15] Latimer argues that the fetus gives the pregnant woman's body legibility, even when the woman herself is considered an outcast. Reading contemporary film and fiction, Latimer complicates Agamben's analysis of bare life by casting the fetus "as the ultimate symbol of hope in a time of terror"[16] and shows how the figure of the fetus plays a key role in the state of exception's configuration. However, in "Cora Unashamed," as in the novels and stories discussed further in this chapter, the fetus often works conversely to mark how precariously close women's reproductive bodies are to bare life. As I'll argue further, it is precisely this precariousness on which national identity rests in the early twentieth-century texts I discuss. In other words, the fetus often comes to mark a kind of death for the woman, as it signals the impoverishment and loss of hope that is about to come. In Hughes's short story, Jessie's mother is willing to risk her daughter's death by an illegal abortion because her pregnancy already marks a kind of death within the logic of white citizenship. Because if a baby were born, her mother and her mother's community would not consider it white enough, Jessie and her Greek lover threaten the national order of white citizenship for the inhabitants of the small, predominantly white town. Thus once Jessie is pregnant—illegitimately, according to her mother—she, like Cora and like the Greek family, is relegated to bare living. First her abortion and then her death work to ensure that the white norms for citizenship within the town can continue onward for the time being.

Feminist theorists have eloquently explained how reproduction is tied to the construction of both race and nation. As Alys Eve Weinbaum writes, focusing on the period shortly after the end of the Civil War: "Although miscegenation law again stabilized the holdings of white property owners, this time rather than ensuring that a mother's blackness rendered her children salable (like her own body), the legal apparatus attended to the complicated task of investing white blood with value—rendering whiteness a rare inalienable commodity—and then arresting its circulation in the body politic."[17] In a related line of argument, Cheryl Harris argues that in the era after the Civil War whiteness became a form of property as a means to protect it and distinguish its status from other racialized identities. Harris shows how whiteness was turned into a sacrosanct possession and given the same status as property—the right to which was one of the most protected laws in the United States.[18] Similarly, as I'll demonstrate throughout this chapter, abortion became outlawed in the United States as a reaction to the shifting racial demographics of the nation. If whiteness was a form of property, then laws needed to be constructed to protect this new form of ownership. Women's bodies, and especially white women's bodies, were seen as in need of protection and control because they determined the inheritance of whiteness and the maintenance of its legitimacy and purity. Thus, by passing antiabortion laws, laws that were primarily aimed at regulating white women, these women were disciplined into viewing their bodies as national vessels of reproduction and believing that disrupting this process was against the nation-state and their race.[19] Worse, by not adhering to national discourse that mandated what was reproductively permissible, they would commit a crime against their own bodies as they risked being designated bare life.

Through the process of prohibiting abortion and setting limits on women's reproductive options, and particularly white women's options, "white blood" is imbued with value—as something that cannot be lost or let loose, that must be contained and managed because it is now precious and under threat of contamination. This management of life is one of the cornerstones of biopolitics and explains how reproduction is keenly tied not only to the formation of national identity but also to the figure of bare life, which works to uphold a precariously formed nation-state. This point is key to the theoretical investigations of my argument, which seeks to understand how race, reproduction, and biopolitics are always tied together in abortion discourse. "Cora Unashamed" critiques the connection among race, nation, and reproduction because it exposes the white anxiety of interracial mixing. While the story could be read as antiabortion—Jessie dies of the abortion her racist mother forced her to have—it could also be read as critiquing the ways in which white women are disciplined not to reproduce with "nonwhite" men through the threat of bare life. Thus it also critiques the normalizing mechanisms of biopolitics. However, by generating this critique, it points to how imbuing white blood with value adheres to liberal values of individualism as it gives rise to an identity politics founded on racial difference. Mrs. Art Studevant forces her daughter to have an abortion because she must maintain the demarcation between whites and foreigners, which upholds her own individualized and privileged identity as a white woman within the norms of a world organized through biopolitics and the threat of bare life. This chapter expands this argument to show how biopolitics and abortion became enmeshed in the late nineteenth century so that by the early twentieth century biopolitics became one of the organizing forces of abortion rhetoric.

The 1871 Trunk Mystery

The late nineteenth century saw the emergence of antiabortion laws that were entrenched in anxieties about whiteness and citizenship, which by the early twentieth century would be immersed in biopolitical norms that dictated how white, middle-class women should govern their reproductive bodies, as Hughes's short story demonstrates. Along these lines, the sociologists Nicola Beisel and Tamara Kay's "Abortion, Race, and Gender in Nineteenth-Century America" examines how the influx of Irish immigrants around the turn of the century led to anxieties about maintaining a predominantly Anglo-Saxon American citizenry, which in turn, they argue, led to the outlawing of abortion in the late nineteenth century.[20] Additionally, Leslie J. Reagan, in her important historical examination of the years when abortion was a crime (1867 to 1973), begins by suggesting this same argument. She documents how "antiabortion activists pointed out that immigrant families, many of them Catholic, were larger and would soon outpopulate native-born white Yankees and threaten their political power." A little later in her introduction she adds, "Regular physicians won passage of new criminal abortion laws because their campaign appealed to a set of fears of white, native-born, male elites about losing political power to Catholic immigrants and to women."[21] However, this line of thought linking the outlawing of abortion to race is never brought up again in the text as she focuses more on the implications of the antiabortion laws, particularly in Chicago. Similarly, historians of abortion briefly comment on the link between abortion and eugenic epistemologies but never fully develop the significance of antiabortion regulation and racial demarcations.[22] Taking an approach closer to my own, Nathan Stormer's work focuses on how eugenic discourse in abortion politics works through biopolitical technologies that are closely tied to formation of memory about what constitutes "normal" bodies. His emphasis on the role of Foucauldian biopolitics is key for understanding how life is managed through the production of reproductive norms. Yet what must also be added to this formulation is a theory of how life is constituted and, more important, how the law grants certain lives legibility through the exclusion of other bodies, which are more often than not gendered. The Trunk Mystery, which sensationalized New York in the summer of 1871, illustrates this argument because it shows how abortion discourse was beginning to be viewed through the biopolitical organization of bare life.

On a hot day in late August of that year, a porter moving luggage to the platform of a train bound to Chicago from New York City noticed a fetid smell emanating from a small trunk. He notified the station's baggage master, who confirmed that the trunk had an "intolerable stench" and decided to break open its lock to reveal the contents.[23] Inside the two men found the body of a young woman, obviously dead for some time. Her body had been contorted into a position few people still living could have managed, in order to fit into a trunk that was two and a half feet long by one and a half feet deep. She was completely naked, and the only mark of violence was a bruised abdomen; an autopsy later confirmed that this was the result of an abortion. In the weeks that followed article after article commented on her youth, her attractive appearance, and her long blond hair and blue eyes. The case of the mysterious woman became an immediate sensation in the New York metro area as police investigators sought to discover her identity and the identity of her abortionist. The *New York Times*, leading in the story's spread, called it a "trunk mystery," which soon became the story's identifying headline.[24]

The *New York Times*'s presentation of the Trunk Mystery made explicit these ties among antiabortion sentiments, racism, and life politics. The man accused of performing the abortion was Dr. Jacob Rosenzweig, a Jewish doctor who also went by the name of Ascher and who denied knowing the victim and giving her the abortion throughout the trial that found him guilty and sentenced him to seven years in prison. The *New York Times* hungrily worked to construct a case that depicted Rosenzweig as a foreign, greedy, and corrupt monster, who should both be excluded from national citizenship and demarcated in terms resembling Agamben's definition of bare life. An article published as his trial was about to begin provided what was claimed to be a "sketch" of the man. Describing him as a "fat, coarse, and sensual-looking fellow, without any traces of refinement in person or manners," it then added that he "does not bear the faintest appearance of the educated physician." The article also reported that he claimed to be a Russian, but that "his voice has the twang of a German Jew."[25] In order to demonstrate this "twang," it presented an extensive quotation from him, although it gave little context for when Rosenzweig might have given this information to a reporter: "These other fellows are all humpugsh; they bromish to do someting vot they don't do. I poshitively do all operashunsh widout any danger, and as sheap as anybody." If those details did not scare readers by emphasizing his foreignness, the article ends by declaring that "the corpse-like faces to be seen peering through [his] bedroom blinds are enough to horrify the stoutest-hearted passer-by." In creating this caricature of Rosenzweig, the *New York Times* contributed to an emerging campaign in the United States to criminalize abortion while associating the practice with foreigners and so-called dysgenic individuals who threatened the welfare of white, middle-class Americans. Further, by

FIGURE 1. Illustration of the opened trunk from *The "Great Trunk Mystery" of New York*, the dime novel that loosely fictionalizes the story.

affiliating Rosenzweig with "corpse-like faces," the newspaper worked to connect him to death and to those living only in the margins of legibility. The *Times* also embraced the American Medical Association's interest in merging the management of health, which itself is implicated in the governing of life, with federal and state laws regulating access to such procedures as abortion. By the beginning of the twentieth century, as the rest of this chapter will demonstrate, the themes running through the Trunk Mystery—the innocent, white, and feminized victim; the evil and foreign abortionist; and the intersection between life politics and law— would be fully embraced in American abortion rhetoric. Together these strands depict an emergent abortion politics steeped in the management of life and tied to an anxiety about American national identity.

Arguably, the Trunk Mystery captivated New Yorkers because when the victim was finally identified, by interviewing doctors who identified the woman by scars and dentistry, she was revealed to be Alice Augusta Bowlsby, a white and attractive woman who easily fit the model of an abortion victim and an idealized white, feminized American citizen. In fact, the story of the Trunk Mystery produced such a following that later that year an anonymous dime novel, which made little effort to disguise the details of the case, was published with embellishing details.[26] *The Great "Trunk Mystery" of New York City*, printed by the Philadelphia publishing house Barclay, emphasized the sensational details. Alice's body is emphatically described as "YOUNG AND BEAUTIFUL."[27] Her hair, we are told, "must have been as white as Parian marble," while her "every feature showed refinement and grace."[28] The novel situates Alice as "moving in respectable society, and having relatives in the highest circles,"[29] even as news articles portray a more working-class woman whose pregnancy was the result of an illicit love affair with a working-class man,[30] who, the *New York Times* deduces, barely made enough in a year as a mill worker to cover her abortion. In contrast, the novel exaggerates Rosenzweig's foreignness by only quoting him in broken dialect, by referring to him as a "monster" no fewer than three times,[31] and by excluding any information from the trial that might have cast doubt on whether he did indeed perform the abortion on Alice that led to her death. Additionally, the novel, with obvious disdain, reports that Rosenzweig's position as an abortionist "yielded him an income sufficient to supply him with all the comforts of life."[32] The novel goes on to describe the handsome-looking exterior of his home and its luxurious furnishings. Even Rosenzweig, as is clear from various declarations during his trial, understood at the time that he was being targeted because his identity as Jew and outsider positioned him as a threat to the reproductive imperatives of an idealized white America. In a statement to the police, Rosenzweig, explaining his innocence, declared, "These people know I am a Jew and believe me to be rich, and want to extract it from me by persecution. That is why I have been seized and incarcerated. I assure you, sir, I have never met or saw the trunkman in my life. I am, in fact, perfectly innocent."[33]

The close attention given to this case, and to other abortion-related cases, by the *New York Times*, as well as the paper's explicit push to convict and demonize Rosenzweig, ushered in a new era of abortion politics that embraced the state's new investment in life management. A year later New York State passed harsher laws condemning abortionists, making the practice a felony and punishable by up to twenty years in prison. It also contributed to the depiction of abortionists as evil, conniving, and un-American, if not German or Jewish. As Rosenzweig himself recognized: whether or not he actually provided women with abortions, he was being targeted as Jewish, foreign, and unworthy of any profit he made from his practice. His story, like almost every other story circulating about abortion at the time, constructed him as the villain—as barely human—in contrast to the moral (and always white) citizen who needed protection from American law. In this case, the white, pregnant woman's body was used quite literally to construct an idealized American identity based on a supposedly fragile woman who was in need of protection from the base elements threatening the stability of the nation.

The sensational story of the Trunk Mystery had all the elements of intrigue: a pretty girl, a mysterious death, a maliciously painted villain. While the *Times* had a financial interest in pursuing this story, which surely brought readers eager to follow the mystery to its end, it also brought together elements that would often color abortion stories—in fiction and the popular press—for the next fifty years. Lois Weber's 1916 silent film *Where Are My Children?*, which would not be released for almost forty years after the Trunk Mystery's conclusion, demonstrates the enduring caricatures of the case: the innocent and pretty working-class girl, the foreign and conniving abortionist, and the "heroic" efforts of the law to bring justice to "innocent" victims by eliminating abortion. The abortionist featured in the film, Dr. Herman Malfit, who provides abortions to the upper-middle-class socialites of the film, has a German-sounding name—even if it is flat-footedly expressed—and his widow's peak, dark features, and facial hair all link him to the depiction of Rosenzweig. Similarly, Edith Wharton's *Summer* portrays the abortionist that Charity visits as a German woman named Dr. Merkle. Both Dale Bauer and Jennie Kassanoff note that Dr. Merkle mispronounces newspaper as "noospaper," further hinting at her foreignness. Kassanoff also connects Dr. Merkle's name to the Latin root "*marc-*," which means "to decay" and "links her to racial decline."[34] The abortionist's office is described as lavishly decorated with expensive furniture and art. When Dr. Merkle enters, she wears gold chains and an expensive-looking black dress. Giving women abortions has obviously made her wealthy, and even though Charity leaves insisting that she does not want one, she still owes the doctor five dollars—a fee that Dr. Merkle refuses to waive even though Charity obviously cannot afford it.[35]

While *Where Are My Children?* and *Summer*, like the Trunk Mystery and the loosely fictionalized and sensationalized dime novel with the same name, contribute to the villainizing of abortionists as evil foreigners outside the law, they also depict the biopolitical link that was emerging between abortion as a medical practice and abortion as a political issue in the mid- to late nineteenth century. Both works, following in the tradition of the Trunk Mystery, view abortion as a practice introduced by those on the margins of society. In *Where Are My Children?* the protagonist is a lawyer intent on bringing legal justice and persecuting abortionists like the one his wife sought without his knowledge. The film already assumes a connection between the legal system and its reach into legislating medical practices. Its legal target is a foreigner who by the film's end unravels and is portrayed as a raging lunatic, who has already destroyed several white American families. *Summer* is subtler in weaving together the workings of law and body. Charity's adopted father, who by the end of the novel is her husband, is a lawyer, and his few speeches in the novel combine his legal vocation with his investment in the body politics of North Dormer. In *Summer*, however, as I will discuss later in this chapter, it is Charity's body—not that of the abortionist's—that is threatened with bare life once she becomes pregnant. This shift marks one of the key changes to abortion rhetoric in the early twentieth century.

The case of the Trunk Mystery reveals these developing links between medicine and law and between the management of life and the development of a national identity. The Trunk Mystery trial depended on the medicalization of Bowlsby's body as evidence for the crime. Not only were doctors brought in to prove that she was indeed Alice Augusta Bowlsby, but they had to demonstrate that she had died of an abortion using the physical markers revealed by her autopsy. The case, in other words, made explicit the new collusion between those who explicitly care for the biological needs of bodies and those who govern those bodies through the force of law. The trial, and the *Times* coverage of the trial, also placed much emphasis on distinguishing between the qualifications of the "certified" doctors who examined Bowlsby and the forged diploma that Rosenzweig held from a medical college in Philadelphia. This concern with official certification from an institution accredited by the American Medical Association (AMA) was fairly new. The AMA itself had only been founded in 1847, and it would take until the early twentieth century before both the law and the public would discredit any doctor not certified by the organization.[36] Also new was the AMA's attention to abortion. Prior to 1845 abortion before quickening was legal in New York, as it was in all the states. However, even New York's 1845 law provided contradictory language about whether abortion performed after quickening could be criminalized.[37] Nevertheless, by 1869 New York would lead the way in outlawing abortion in all stages of pregnancy.[38] The Trunk Mystery trial, while by no means the first to bring abortion to court, did demonstrate how abortion and reproduction, medicine and the body, sex and sexuality, were now all subjected to law in a biopolitical America.

The Biopolitics of Abortion in Nineteenth-Century America

As previously mentioned, in 1869 New York would pass harsher anti-abortion laws restricting abortion before quickening. Also in 1869, just a

FIGURE 2. Depiction of Dr. Rosenzweig from The "Great Trunk Mystery" of New York.

FIGURE 3. Screenshot from *Where Are My Children?* Dr. Malfit appears between the two women.

few years before the Trunk Mystery sensationalized New York, the spiritualist and free love advocate Andrew Jackson Davis published one of the only nineteenth-century novels that explicitly address abortion, even as its representation in his work spoke to a perspective that was slowly disappearing from American popular representations of the practice. *Tale of a Physician; or, The Seeds and Fruits of Crime* was a dime novel produced for popular tastes, and like many novels of its genre, its plot is disjointed and, for contemporary readers, at times difficult to follow. The appearance of two abortionists, Doctor Morte and Madame La Stelle, functions as a diversion from the main plot, and like other mainstream discussions of abortion at the time, the novel conflates infanticide with abortion. In fact, given popular sentiment, it is possible that abortion in the novel only refers to what twenty-first-century readers might consider late-term abortion, since abortion in the first trimester was still widely accepted at the time. Doctor Morte, whose name needs no explanation, and Madam La Stelle, whose name is an obvious play on the infamous New York abortionist Madame Restell, offer two services at their lying-in hospitals, "live and found" or "still and lost."[39] The latter refers to sheltering women during the end stages of their pregnancy, helping them give birth, and then finding homes for the infants (or possibly killing them), while the former refers to providing women abortions.

Doctor La Force Du Bois is the novel's reluctant protagonist, a physician interested both in emerging theories of eugenics and in ridding

American society of crime; his character thus embodies the biopolitical melding of law and medicine. He moves to New York to find his long-lost love and in the meantime embarks on a quest to reform abortionists, although he labels the crime "abortion and infanticide."[40] In a Comstock-like scheme (whose practices are described further in the next chapter), Du Bois asks his friend's niece, Miss Phoebe Milton, to disguise herself as a woman seeking abortion in order to ascertain from Madam La Stelle the reason behind her alleged crimes. Phoebe is shocked to learn that rather than being a villainous and hateful woman, Madam La Stelle is both forward thinking and intelligent: she believes that "all intercourse between the sexes when not mutual, whether in or out of marriage, are rapes and adulteries and nothing else," adding that it is not "any more right for a woman to have an unwelcome child than it is for a man to force one upon her."[41] Davis's description of La Stelle as protective of women's rights and providing abortions in order to achieve more equality between the sexes would be the most affirming portrait of a female abortionist in fiction for almost a hundred years.

In contrast, Dr. Morte's character conforms to how the popular media often represented abortionists, especially women like Madame Restell. His clinic is described as an

> unclean, wretched den where his crimes are committed. It is a
> back room on the second floor. A leprous moisture oozes from the
> walls and ceiling. Heavy curtains, fetid with filth, and covered with
> last year's spiders' webs, shut out the golden summer Sunday light
> of June. On the mantel, over the fireplace, were dirty plates and
> besmeared cups and saucers. An infectious, sickening atmosphere
> filled the room and almost suffocated the wretched patient.[42]

Doctor Morte's patient, Molly Ruciel, forced to have an abortion by her lover, who pays for the procedure, and by Doctor Morte, who physically harms her to bring her to the operating table, reproduces the story of Mary Rogers, whose case consumed the New York media when her body was found floating in the Hudson River.[43] Molly's portrayal as an innocent victim, who is forced into the abortion clinic, is also reflective of nineteenth-century attitudes toward women who sought abortion. Legally women in Molly's position would not have been held responsible if their case came to court; however, this lenience toward women who had abortions would change by the early twentieth century, and the patronizing pardon of women who sought abortions would also disappear from most popular novels.

Outside of fiction and at around the same time as the publication of *Tale of a Physician*, the biopoliticization of abortion was consciously advanced by the work of Horatio R. Storer, a physician and vocal member of the American Medical Association, who made it his mission to change American abortion law. In 1860, the year after the AMA passed its resolution condemning abortion in any stage of pregnancy, Storer published *On Criminal Abortion in America*, where he expounded on his claims for recognizing fetal life as fully individuated human life. Eight years later, in collaboration with Franklin Fiske Heard, Storer republished an updated edition of *On Criminal Abortion* with an added section on the legal aspects of abortion and retitled the volume *Criminal Abortion: Its Nature, Its Evidence, and Its Law*. This new volume makes explicit that abortion should no longer be a concern just of doctors and medical workers but must be taken up by the law. The addition of chapters by Heard does just that.

Storer's text makes his position clear: "By the MORAL LAW, THE WILFUL KILLING OF A HUMAN BEING AT ANY STAGE IS MURDER."[44] He argues against the "belief that the contents of the womb, so long as manifesting no perceptible sign of life, were but *lifeless* and *inert* matter: in other words, that, being, previous to quickening, a mere ovarian excretion, they might be thrown off and expelled from the system so coolly and as guiltlessly as those from the bladder and rectum."[45] He calls the fetus an independent unit, and he believes that to define it as living at one point or another is arbitrary.[46] According to him, the fetus from conception is "as [a] distinct and independent a nervous centre, self-existing, self-acting, living."[47] Interestingly, he uses the language of liberalism to define the individuality of the fetus, and to emphasize his point, he ignores that the fetus is actually dependent on a woman's body for life support. In Storer's language, the fetus now embodies the qualities of man in the Western world: he is autonomous, individuated, and self-reliant. Furthermore, Storer explains, "If there be life, then also the existence, however undeveloped, of an intellectual, moral, and spiritual nature, the inalienable attribute of humanity, is applied."[48] The fetus, according to Storer, also has a developed, enlightened nature from the moment of conception.[49] Storer, in other words, began the work that by the late twentieth century would mark abortion politics. While most representations of the fetus in the early twentieth century avoid this singularization of the fetus, Storer saw his mission as protecting the fetus from what he perceived as its bare life.[50] However, in turn, the pregnant woman who wanted to abort that fetus was subjected to a precarious existence.

Storer's position became popular with physicians in the American Medical Association, with clergy representing the more mainstream American religions, and eventually with government officials. In the late nineteenth century physicians began publishing articles in leading medical journals drawing the connection between abortion as a medical procedure and abortion as a procedure that needed to be controlled and punished by the state. Edward H. Parker, one such doctor, published an article in the *Transactions of the American Medical Association* in 1880 concluding that American courts needed to begin viewing abortion not as a crime against the woman—a position clearly seen in the trial for the Trunk Mystery— but as a crime against the fetus. In frustration he ends, "Nowhere does the destruction of the foetus come into consideration, so far as we can judge."[51] By 1905, in just a few decades, Parker's wish is fulfilled, and the law's position is almost entirely reversed. C. S. Bacon, also a medical doctor, writes in reference to the fetus that "the right to life is the most fundamental right of an individual and he should not be deprived of it no matter whether he be diseased, unconscious, worthless or for any reason whatever unless the State represented by its judicial officers decides that he has forfeited his life by his crimes and rendered its extinction necessary for the welfare of the State."[52] He then continues to explicitly depict the fetus as an individual protected by the constitution as he describes the fetus as "a separate being and not just part of the mother, not a pars viscerum like the ovary or appendix which she can do with as she pleases."[53] Or in another example that takes constitutional language to describe abortion, the Reverend Albert Biever, writing in the *New Orleans Medical and Surgical Journal* in 1908, proclaims, "Neither the intention of saving the mother's life nor even the intention of procuring baptism for the child whose life cannot be saved, justifies the physician to deprive the unborn offspring of a life to which it has a God-given right."[54]

As Stormer notes, Storer's emphasis on fetal life often slips to reveal other concerns. For example, he quotes Professor Simpson, in a speech to the British Medical Association given in August 1867 in Dublin: "If a woman with a deformed pelvis would go on putting herself in the way of becoming pregnant, she ought to be made to take the risks of the Caesarian, rather than be encouraged in her course by sacrificing the life of her child."[55] Earlier in his work, he proclaims "that medical men are the physical guardians of women and their offspring; from their position of peculiar knowledge necessitated in all obstetric matters to regulate public sentiment, and to govern tribunals of justice."[56] This paternalistic language reveals an entrenched chauvinism that both supports claims by historians like Leslie Reagan and Janet Brodie, who argue that nine-teenth-century antiabortion movements were motivated by fear that women were gaining too much authority in medical establishments, particularly gynecology and obstetrics, and also demonstrates a fierce commitment to the continuation of reproduction for the sake of repro-duction. For in agreeing with Professor Simpson, Storer makes clear that he believes that once a woman is pregnant, her primary responsibility is to ensure that the fetal life inside her has priority.[57] Unfortunately, Storer's vision did eventually become entrenched, as a new form of bio-politics emerged that would precisely privilege the protection of the fetus over the protection of the pregnant woman.

The Biopolitics of Abortion in Early Twentieth-Century America

The trial of the Trunk Mystery in 1871 occurred just as abortion was being framed according to a biopolitical logic. The incomplete infusion of abortion within biopolitics can be seen in how Alice Bowlsby was presented in the trial and the media. As both the Trunk Mystery and *Tale of a Physician* reflect, this was the era before women who sought abortions were persecuted and treated as criminals because they wished to end their pregnancies. The *New York Times* presented Bowlsby as an innocent victim of both the crime and her class in choosing only to represent the prosecution's depiction of her as "a young girl ruined and betrayed; a child of misfortune, she is stricken with the thought that every day brings her nearer to disgrace. . . . Remember, he said, what a struggle these unfortunate girls go through. Born in pov-erty and with an inheritance of beauty which is sometimes more ruinous than any gift that could be conferred on them. They are daily tempted by the scoundrels and rascals that surround them" (October 29, 1871). The piece goes on to describe Bowlsby as a victim of her circumstances (which she likely was), but in order to villainize Rosenzweig, the prosecution also dramatizes conditions to present Bowlsby as young (she was twenty-five), naïve, and completely undone by her circumstances. Rosenzweig, the uncul-tured Jew who seemingly profited from abortions, was the target of the court, the medical community, and New Yorkers who eagerly followed the case. Bowlsby's body was protected—and patronized—by the media, while Rosenzweig's was butchered and defiled.

By the second decade of the twentieth century, women were no longer free from the disciplining eyes of biopolitics. *Summer* presents a harsher picture of abortion in a culture organized by biopolitics. Charity, the novel's protagonist, encounters an abortionist as a means to bridge the novel's tension between the carefully defined laws of North Dormer, the town and Charity's adopted home, and the lawlessness of the Mountain, Charity's birthplace. When Charity marries Mr. Royall, her adoptive father and the town lawyer, her choice, if it can be called one, is between a life stripped of all rights that mark one as human and a livable life, one guarded and recognized by the law. Throughout the novel Charity compares herself with Julia, her friend's older sister, who also had an illicit romance and became pregnant, and reassures herself that she is not like Julia. In fact, her decision to flee the abortion clinic is partially based on the decision that she cannot end up like Julia; she must still act within the confines of a legible norm, even if she has transgressed it in other ways.

Julia exists for Charity as a warning of what her life might become if she allows herself to slip through the cracks of her society's disciplinary mechanisms. Julia physically appears only once in the novel, on the arm of Mr. Royall during the festivities by the Lake on the Fourth of July. With her own lover by her side, Charity sees Julia, "her white feather askew, and the face under it flushed with coarse laughter."[58] Julia, of course, has not escaped the disciplining technologies of early twentieth-century New England. She just rebelled against normative sexual behavior and thus fell into being labeled a whore, unmarriageable, and a threat, labels that are just as disciplining through their distribution of value. She remains for girls like Charity a reminder of the costs of transgressing taboos; when Charity contemplates what to do with her pregnancy, she asks herself, "Only—was there no alternative but Julia's? . . . In the established order of things as she knew them she saw no place for her individual adventure."[59] The order of things, Charity recognizes, places her extramarital pregnancy in the same category as Julia's, despite the fact that Charity persists in thinking her romance was one that started and ended in love. Still, despite Charity's condemnation, Julia lives an intelligible life. Later Charity realizes that even though Julia must have to earn her living in unnameable ways, her life is still recognized as human; she hangs on the bottom rungs of the hierarchy of life, but she is still on that rung, unlike Charity's mother, who lives on the lawless Mountain.

When Charity realizes that she can neither marry Harney, nor terminate her pregnancy, nor raise her child alone in North Dormer, she decides to live on the Mountain so she can "escape from all that hemmed her in and beset her."[60] She arrives at the Mountain, after an exhausting hike, just in time for her mother's funeral, a gruesome and pitiful event;

at first she is unable to recognize her relation to such a pathetic-looking figure. The description is one of the most haunting passages in Wharton's novel:

> A woman lay on it [a dirty mattress] but she did not look like a dead woman; she seemed to have fallen across her squalid bed in a drunken sleep, and to have been left lying where she fell, in her ragged disordered clothes. One arm was flung above her head, one leg drawn up under a torn skirt that left the other bare to the knee; a swollen glistening leg with a ragged stocking rolled down about the ankle.... She looked at her mother's face, thin yet swollen with lips parted in a frozen gasp above the broken teeth. There was no sign in it of anything human: she lay there like a dead dog in a ditch.[61]

She is abject, discarded: bare life.

When Charity escapes to the Mountain she encounters a gruesome landscape described as a "lifeless circle" populated with people whose movements mimic "the heads of nocturnal animals" and "herded together in passive promiscuity in which their common misery was the strongest link." Observing the starkness of the life around her, Charity comes to realize that "anything, anything was better than to add another life to the nest of misery on the Mountain."[62] Her refusal to have an abortion, and then her refusal to live on the Mountain, become a way of choosing a legible life in North Dormer as a means to distinguish herself from the bare life of the Mountain. In the novel's conception of bare life, Charity's decision means attempting to carve out an existence that breaks away from the herd; yet, the novel reveals, in terms similar to Agamben's theorization of the relation between bare life and sovereignty, the herd of the Mountain is precisely the ground through which North Dormer defines its sovereignty. (As Mr. Royall emphasizes, "The Mountain belongs to this township."[63]) Charity at first thinks that escaping to the Mountain might give her freedom from the law, as she describes it, to "begin life again among people to whom the harsh code of the village was unknown,"[64] but eventually she realizes that this lawlessness is even more suffocating than the law because where the "harsh code of the village" exists there in an even more encompassing form, with few exits. To move to the Mountain is to become a refugee.

Hannah Arendt describes the position of the refugee as "the scum of the earth." She sees the first decades of the twentieth century as verging on the brink of barbarism because the war displaced and expelled so many people from their homes. She writes, "The great danger arising from the existence of people forced to live outside the common world is that they are thrown back, in the midst of civilization, on their natural givenness, on their mere differentiation." She goes on to describe the refugee as only belonging to the human race as "animals belong to a specific animal species."[65] Arendt, writing about the First World War as a refugee of the next world war, sees the refugee as having the potential to act from a place of otherness that can radically undercut the displacement of human life to the margins, which occurred during World War I and again in World War II. However, the danger of this position, as she notes above, is complete disconnection from the civilized precisely as one is living within this civilization. It reduces the refugee to a category of the human, one that is allowed to remain on the outside, exterior to all other forms of human life.[66]

Charity hears her mother described for the first time in terms similar to the ones Arendt uses in the same conversation she overhears between Mr. Royall and Harney. As Mr. Royall explains to Harney how he retrieved Charity from the Mountain at the request of her imprisoned father, Harney asks whether Charity has a mother. "Oh, yes: there was a mother," Mr. Royall responds. "But she was glad enough to have her go. She'd have given her to anybody. They *ain't half human up there*. I guess the mother's dead by now, with the life she was leading."[67] As in Arendt's description of the refugee, Charity's mother, as seen through the eyes of Mr. Royall, is barely human because she is forced to live outside the common world. She lacks the quality that Mr. Royall believes marks women as women: protective mothering. By emphasizing that Charity's mother didn't care to keep her, Mr. Royall also dismisses her humanity and connection to civilization because she was willing to give up her child. Only once Charity is pregnant is she able to understand the conditions that forced her mother to give up her child. During the night she takes refuge on the Mountain, Charity "tried to picture to herself what her life would have been if she had grown up on the Mountain, running wild in rags, sleeping on the floor curled up against her mother, like the pale-faced children huddled against old Mrs. Hyatt, and turning into a fierce bewildered creature like the girl who had apostrophized her in such strange words. . . . What mother would not want to save her child from such a life?"[68] Like the refugee, Charity's mother gives up her daughter not because she is not human, but because she is not "allowed to partake in the human artifice" and is "thrown back on her natural givenness." Yet the novel, in a line of argumentation similar to Arendt's and Agamben's work, foregrounds Charity's mother's predicament and Charity's own predicament to emphasize the crisis of reproductive rights that exists in America, where the "illegitimately" pregnant woman loses not only her rights to motherhood but her rights to personhood. In other words, reproduction and the refusal to reproduce through abortion cannot exist outside a biopolitical regime that manages the gendered body.

While Wharton's novel might seem to be antiabortion, when read against the grain it also deconstructs the rhetoric of life as sacred by demonstrating how Charity's life and the life in her womb are interpellated through codes of living. Life is imbued with meaning when the law surrounds it and anoints it with subjectivity and individuality as a means of dividing those that count from those that do not. However, ultimately, as in contemporary abortion politics, this decision says less about whatever matter is granted the status of legible life and more about those doing the deciding and what that means in terms of how their lives count and have meaning. Thus, for example, at the end of the novel, when Mr. Royall finally "wins" Charity's hand in marriage and parental rights over her soon-to-be child, his life and law are granted the ultimate legitimacy and power, while Charity's will is defaced and deflated in exchange for recognition of her life and the life of the fetus.

Thus it is precisely when Charity recognizes her mother as bare life, a life that has been excluded not only from citizenship but also from any political recognition, that she understands the conditions that led to her pathetic state in life and death and she begins to see in her the possibility for humanness. She realizes, "after all, was her mother so much to blame? Charity, since that day [the day of Mr. Royall's conversation with her lover, Harney], had always thought of her as destitute of all human feeling; now she seemed merely pitiful."[69] This emotional comprehension of her mother's bare life as life potentially imbued with humanness interpellates Charity through the technologies of biopolitics. As she understands her mother as living on the cusp of recognizable human life, she also becomes a subject formed through the codes of North Dormer. And it is this understanding that leads her to feel not empowered, but acquiescent. When Mr. Royall feeds her on the way back from the Mountain, she feels the coffee flow through her veins and revive her; "she began to feel like a living being again; but the return to life was so painful that the food choked in her throat and she sat staring down at the table in silent anguish." Then later, back in his carriage, "she had only a confused sensation of slipping down a smooth irresistible current."[70] Mr. Royall offers her safety, warmth, food, and shelter—all the conditions of a livable life that will allow her to escape following her mother into the desolate and barely livable conditions of the Mountain. As Wendy Brown incisively describes, "Given a choice between rationalized, procedural unfreedom on one hand, and arbitrary deprivation, discrimination, and violence on the other, some, perhaps even most, women might opt to inhabit a bureaucratized order over a 'state of nature.'"[71] "Choice" is then not really an option, although Brown only alludes to the problems of this term. Charity, as she returns to the town with Mr. Royall, finds his voice "so strong and resolute that it was like a supporting arm about her. She felt resistance melting, her strength slipping away from her as he spoke."[72] As Charity has harshly learned, resistance does not lead to escape but to different entrapments that regulate her body and limit her movements. Marrying Mr. Royall just has its own price, one that she is painfully aware of and that makes her rejuvenation so agonizing. A livable life is also a compliant one, one subject to regulation and control under the terms of Mr. Royall and the town.

Summer exposes the fact that abortion rhetoric about the politics of life is never really about the life of the fetus or the "unborn child"; rather, it is about the limits of sovereignty, recognition, and agreement to the terms of containment and conditioning for the woman carrying that fetus. It is biopolitics at its extreme. For Charity, it is about recognizing that when we live in a state of exception,[73] the danger is in being banished to the outside, to those places where the law claims to not apply, but to which it actually points in order to uphold itself. In Summer this is the Mountain, a place of stark poverty, where human beings live on the threshold of what is recognizable as human. Thus the fetus exposes neither the limits of the human nor the precariousness of life, but rather the fetus is constructed as fully human in order to deface the body of the pregnant woman. When Charity becomes pregnant, her choices are no longer her own because whatever decision she makes is now in relation to her legibility in the state. She now produces for the state and within its conditions, and if she chooses to attempt transgression, either by escaping to the Mountain or by having an abortion or even by marrying her lover because of her pregnancy, she will either be stripped down to the bareness of humanity or be forever ridiculed and shunned for her position—in the novel's language, called "a whore." Her days of negotiating a space that allows her to literally meet her lover between the town and the Mountain are over once her body is marked as reproductive.

Summer only hints at Charity's physical—perhaps racial—difference. Dale Bauer eloquently reads this difference as a resistance to social

Darwinist thinking that categorized people through a eugenic logic. Critiquing previous readings of the novel that argue that Charity is a consequence of "bad blood" passed down by her mother, Bauer reads Charity's character as countering the numerous "scientific" studies of the early twentieth century that linked social demise to reproduction by people of "lower types."[74] The next two chapters explore further how antiabortion rhetoric functioned within the logic of both liberalism and eugenics and how both were tied to American national identity. As this chapter demonstrates, before that could happen abortion needed to be established not only as anti-American but as a practice that discarded those women to the unlivable margins of the nation-state. Whereas in the late nineteenth century popular fiction tended to portray women who sought abortions as victims who needed the state's guiding hand, by the early twentieth century women who sought abortions would be threatened with being discarded to a bare living. As the texts discussed in the following chapters demonstrate, national identity would come to rest on the precariousness of the reproductive body.

2 / The Inadvertent Alliance of Anthony Comstock and Margaret Sanger: Choice, Rights, and Freedom in Modern America

There's more than one kind of freedom. Freedom to and freedom from. In the days of anarchy, it was freedom to. Now you are being given freedom from. Don't underestimate it.

—MARGARET ATWOOD, *THE HANDMAID'S TALE*

This chapter seeks to trace a continuum between Anthony Comstock's moralizing jeremiads against "obscene acts" and Margaret Sanger's quest to legalize birth control, by demonstrating the ways in which both Comstock and Sanger used disciplining tactics that condemned abortion. Most important, this chapter demonstrates how Comstock and Sanger succeeded in criminalizing abortion, thus completing the task begun by the American Medical Association, which by the 1880s had managed to outlaw abortion in every American state.[1] Comstock's contribution to this juridical process worked by lumping abortion together with other "sexual crimes" and contributing to the misconception that abortion was primarily used by working-class and poor women. Sanger promoted birth control by separating it from the issue of abortion; she often portrayed birth control as a means to better the human race by emphasizing abortion's pernicious effects, thus paralleling Comstock's construction of abortion as degrading and destructive. While Sanger and Comstock initially appear to be working through different paradigms, the opposition between them is belied by the investment that both activists made in similar constructions of freedom and protection that subtend liberal *and* conservative ideologies.[2] Comstock's opposition to abortion mirrors Sanger's position because both are invested in constructing laws that interpellate subjects into individualizing and moralizing persons that if properly trained *should* be capable of self-control. Comstock's politics, traditionally seen as conservative, contain components of liberal ideology because they are invested in an individuated and self-controlled (male) subject. It is through laws concerned with rights that the emphasis on the individuated life becomes foregrounded; indeed, it is precisely through the emergence of rights-based laws that the concept of an entitled subject capable of self-regulation emerged, as well as the inverse concept of a subject incapable of self-control and therefore legally stripped of "choice."

Using rights-based discourse, or what is sometimes called "the right to choose," as a means to reenfranchise historically oppressed communities has a prominent but conflicted history in the United States. From Patricia Williams's work that asserts that rights granted through constitutional law are crucial in the fight to grant African Americans equal status in the United States to Wendy Brown's critiques of rights as embedded in a liberalism that establishes identity-based politics, the discussion of rights as a tool for remedying civil and social inequality has been heated. Much has also been written about the role of rights in granting women access to abortion and control over their bodies.[3] For example, Mary Poovey has argued that giving women the *right* to have an abortion maintains an individualistic attitude toward a procedure that should be based in community decision and with a community's support. In *Roe v. Wade*, while the Supreme Court decided that women had the freedom *to* make their own reproductive choices because the state granted individual privacy, the Court also granted women freedom *from* the potentially undue burden of pregnancy.[4] The slipperiness between freedom *from* and freedom *to* points to a tension in the foundations of American liberalism. Freedom *from* assumes what Kimberlé Crenshaw points to as a victims-based protectionist ideology; the Supreme Court is "protecting" women who without laws protecting abortion rights would fall prey to the potentially difficult conditions of an unwanted pregnancy even as the same law mandates that the individual woman has a right to control her own body.[5] Freedom *to* assumes an individuated private body that should not be subject to government interference. While Sanger and Comstock were both invested in outlawing abortion, the rhetoric they established for antiabortion arguments mirrors rights-based proabortion law and thus points to how proabortion policy in the United States has been so deftly undermined in the years following *Roe v. Wade*.

Beyond Rights?

In rehearsing rights rhetoric from the American civil rights movement, Kimberlé Crenshaw provides a nuanced picture of the critique of rights that emerged from the movement, but also the necessity for those rights.[6] Crenshaw recites the "Crits"[7] argument, which argues that rights discourse is often legitimated through a "victim's" perspective—the discourse doesn't address why crimes or oppressions are perpetuated, but rather looks at how the victim's experience is shaped. The problem with this framework is that "victims" need to prove their status, and as Crenshaw notes, in the decades following the height of the civil rights era this became harder to do as courts more narrowly defined what counted as an act of discrimination. However, Crenshaw doesn't advocate doing away with rights altogether, since she sees in rights the potential to envision society "as the way things ought to be." For her the legitimizing force of rights is in the actions they produce, not necessarily in the results.[8] Crenshaw's essay is anthologized in a collection that attempts to comment on the language of rights and provide an overview of where rights talk stands in contemporary culture. Sandwiched between an essay by Martin Chanock that argues that rights provide a *necessary* universalizing power, especially to formerly colonized cultures, and Thandabantu Nhlapo's work that fiercely argues against this universalizing paradigm, the anthology, entitled *Beyond Rights Talk and Culture Talk*, is not quite ready to go beyond either of these paradigms. The majority of the essays, some with good reason, still cling to the language of rights as providing crucial frameworks for activism.

However, Wendy Brown, in work that was published almost a decade before, presents a compelling argument for how and why we should go beyond rights. Brown is not actually interested in whether rights free subjects from repressive structures, but rather in how rights work to shape those subjects into identity-based individuals, thus pointing to the impossibility of the universal claims that much rights-oriented legislation posits. Brown sees bourgeois rights discourse as functioning through biopolitics by depoliticizing sectors of the social sphere such as the family and private property to make them seem naturalized. Through an extended reading of Karl Marx's "On the Jewish Question" Brown demonstrates how bourgeois rights reify the power from which the claim to rights supposedly liberates us.[9] Thus in Marx's example of the right to practice religion in the United States, that right naturalizes religion as inherently based in individual choice and, worse yet, as a form of property the individual then clings to as a way to demand individual freedom.[10]

If American regimes of biopolitics work to discipline subjects into perceiving themselves as rational individuals capable of self-regulation, then discourses of rights and choice function within this regime as tech-nologies that maintain the system and sediment its structures. As Lealle Ruhl suggests, "contemporary debates about birth control and fertility control are unique in their emphasis on *self*-control." She argues, "There are two aspects to the willed pregnancy: the individual dimension (a woman should be able to control and space her births) and a collec-tive dimension (which populations are bearing how many children)."[11] Ruhl puts forth a critique of birth control that assumes a self-managing individual; that women's reproductive functions, like almost all other components of the body, should be regulated and controlled; and that to do otherwise is to fail as a productive and responsible citizen. While Ruhl does not touch on how the rhetoric of rights and choice organizes discussions of birth control and abortion, I'd like to frame her argument with a brief overview of how abortion rights and choice are subtended by American legal theory and are crucial to the technologies that manage populations and demarcate identity.

While proabortion feminists have challenged granting abortion through the rhetoric of choice, little has been written on the critique of abortion as women's right. In fact, Drucilla Cornell has adamantly stressed the necessity of maintaining the right to abortion on the basis of psychoanalytic individuation. Arguing against the rhetoric of "choice" and control in proabortion discourse because it separates the self from the body as though women could prevent unwanted pregnancies simply through desire, Cornell argues for more emphasis on state-controlled abortion intervention through legislating rights. Using a Lacanian model of the body that is individuated and universal, Cornell perceives women as united through the ability to conceive.[12] Thus she argues for abortion rights on the basis of sexual difference—difference that sets up a binary between what constitutes the female versus the male. Cornell posits that abortion must be made legal as a means to establish bodily integrity for women. She cites testimonials of women who have under-gone illegal abortions and experienced a splitting of self as a result of the procedure. Although Cornell acknowledges that "bodily integrity always remains imaginary,"[13] she still insists that for a self to exist, this imaginary projection of being whole must be created. However, Cor-nell's language seems to effortlessly merge with exactly the rhetoric she argues against; recent antiabortion activists have conversely insisted that abortion must be outlawed because the procedure literally dismembers women, destroying their sense of self by stripping them of a function that defines them as women.[14] Thus Cornell's logic is slippery because it appeals to an unstable construction of women as reproductive bodies that can and do imagine themselves as whole only when access to abortion is made available.

Similarly, in a more recent argument, Ricki Solinger has defended abortion rights through critiquing the rhetoric of choice. Tracing the history of choice in abortion discourse, Solinger points to how the language of "choice" did not crop up until the early 1970s, primarily after the *Roe v. Wade* decision, which explicitly made abortion legal through granting women *the right to choose*. Solinger argues that choice became an easier way of selling abortion; it "became *the* way liberal and mainstream feminists could talk about abortion without mentioning the 'A-word.'"[15] Implicit in Solinger's arguments is a mourning for the language and power of rights, which, she suggests, would have the power to grant women access to abortion in a way that does not evoke market resources, competition, and individualism, as the politics of choice does. However, I often use the terms *rights* and *choice* interchangeably because I see them as equally implicated in individuating bodies and, more important, as creating a discourse of *responsibilization*; in other words, because both rights and choice are granted (and in fact, choice is often just depicted as one kind of right, as in *the right to choose*) based on assumptions of well-disciplined subjects, those subjects that exceed the norms of *responsibilization* also exceed the limits as recipients of the right to choice. Hence, Comstock can argue that certain bodies should be controlled at the expense of others, and, as I will demonstrate in the following sections, Sanger can argue that certain women should not be granted the right to self-control while the thrust of her argument is based in a rights and choice discourse.

Thus while Solinger's and Cornell's critiques of choice and defenses of rights are intriguing, both their arguments are too often based on false assumptions about the body, and as my discussion of Sanger and Comstock will show, their language can be easily co-opted to argue the opposite of their intentions. In a more convincing argument, Rosalind Petchesky also critiques the rhetoric of choice, but through a juridical discourse that makes no assumptions about bodily or legal integrity. In her preface to the revised 1990 edition of *Abortion and Women's Choice: The State, Sexuality, and Reproductive Freedom*, Petchesky stresses that the abortion debate must be taken outside the rhetoric of "individual choice" if we are to discuss abortion honestly within its implications for divisions of race, class, and gender.[16] Petchesky acknowledges that reproduction "is social and individual at the same time."[17] In a compelling

Marxist critique against the rhetoric of choice in abortion discourse, Petchesky points out that choice is problematically rooted in an individuated understanding of the body. She wonders whether feminists can construct language that neither denies women access to abortion nor exclusively frames it within liberal understandings of individuation. Abortion rights, Petchesky argues, "seeks access to a necessary service, but by itself it fails to address the social relations and sexual divisions around which responsibility for pregnancy and children is assigned. In real-life struggles, this limitation exacts a price, for it lets men and society neatly off the hook."[18] Furthermore, "choice" is a problematic framework in certain conditions, as in Petchesky's example of a Native American woman who may have been historically subjected to measures that attempt to regulate her fertility and is now being asked when she enters a clinic for prenatal testing whether she would like an abortion.

Mary Poovey extends the critique of the liberal notions of individuality on which abortion discourse is based. Poovey explains, "the abortion debate is about what it means to accept—or reject—the notion that there is a 'natural' basis for individual identity and therefore for individual rights and sexual identity."[19] For Poovey, the system of law that assigns us rights as individuals is problematic because it assumes that the existence of those rights precedes the existence of the law. Instead, she suggests that the law actually creates what it claims to recognize. She later points out, "In the mouths of anti-abortionists, 'choice,' 'privacy,' and 'rights' invert effortlessly into their opposites, precisely because, regardless of who uses them, these terms belong to a single set of metaphysical assumptions."[20] Those assumptions include the idea that there is some kind of preexisting truth underlying the law. This so-called truth changes, of course, depending on one's subject-position. As Lauren Berlant has argued, pro-life discourse has borrowed the language of rights to advance a belief that fetuses—and in fact the aims of national reproduction—"ought to have a politically protected right to natural development."[21] Thus, Petchesky, Poovey, and Berlant begin to contribute to a critique of abortion rights that like Brown's analysis demands that access to abortion be considered politically, as rooted in particularity and not as granted through the so-called universalizing discourse of rights.

Margaret Sanger's work and Anthony Comstock's work, while seemingly professing conflicting political paradigms, actually share a rights-based discourse that works to manage bodies and populations. Comstock's opposition to abortion mirrors Sanger's similar position, as I will show in the next section, because both are invested in constructing laws that interpellate subjects into individualizing and moralizing persons that if properly trained *should* be capable of self-control. As Michel Foucault argues:

> It was life more than the law that became the issue of political struggles, even if the latter were formulated through affirmations concerning rights. The "right" to life, to one's body, to health, to happiness, to the satisfaction of needs, and beyond all the oppressions or "alienations," the "right" to rediscover what one is and all that one can be, this "right"—which the classical juridical system was utterly incapable of comprehending—was the political response to all these new procedures of power which did not derive, either, from the traditional right of sovereignty.[22]

Foucault demonstrates that the language of "rights" as it emerges in biopolitical regimes actually functions to mold life rather than to preserve the sovereign's power. However, it is through laws concerned with rights that the issue of life—and always an individuated life—becomes foregrounded; in fact, it is precisely through the emergence of rights-based laws that the concept of an entitled subject capable of self-regulation emerged or, in the inverse example, of a subject incapable and therefore legally stripped of "choice." In the next section, I will explore how Comstock's politics are similarly invested in this biopolitical regulation and thus work to maintain an imagined (white) America.

While my abbreviated overview of rights discourse seems distant from early twentieth-century discussions of abortion politics, I intentionally began with this discussion in order to contextualize both Comstock's and Sanger's ideologies within a more current moment as a tactic to reveal the politics of historicizing. In other words, Brown's insistence that rights be seen within the local and particular will subtend my discussions of Comstock and Sanger to reveal how both successfully politicized abortion through liberal techniques of discipline that sought to appear depoliticized and universal.

Abortive Damnation and Family Values in *The Beautiful and Damned*

Premarital sex, free-flowing alcohol, reckless partying: the characters in F. Scott Fitzgerald's second novel, *The Beautiful and Damned*, engage in all the practices that would have outraged the late nineteenth- and early twentieth-century moral reformer Anthony Comstock and instigated him into disciplining action. When Fitzgerald named his protagonist and prime actor in these crimes Anthony Comstock Patch, he was making more than just a flat-footed ironic gesture. The fictional Anthony—named in the novel by his grandfather, Adam Patch, to honor the moral reformer—decides at a young age that his grandfather's path of moral righteousness leads to boredom and unhappiness. Therefore, he refuses to work, engages in licentious behavior with working-class girls (preferably older than he), and regularly spends his evenings consuming alcohol with friends. When he meets Gloria Gilbert he finds his match in carelessness and selfishness, and the two decide to marry to continue a life of debauchery together. At first, however, the marriage surprisingly straightens Anthony (who decides to drop Comstock from his name), and he worries about money, household chores, and taking care of his wife. The couple even tentatively discuss having children when they reach their three-year anniversary. However, a year into their marriage, after some of the initial thrill of the love affair has faded, Gloria discovers she is pregnant.[23] She confronts Anthony with her new state and asks him straightforwardly, "Do you want me to have it?"[24] Her question implies that there is choice and that she could easily reverse her condition, even though abortion was illegal at the time. Anthony responds nonchalantly, telling her that he's fine with whatever she chooses; he just insists that she make up *her* mind. He stresses, "See here, Gloria, I'm with you whatever you do, but for God's sake be a sport about it." She decides to seek advice from her friend Constance Merriam the next day;[25] while her decision to visit Constance does not reveal whether she has decided to abort her pregnancy, she does add, "it isn't that I'm afraid—of this or anything else. I'm being true to me, you know."[26] Her curt assessment already exposes her decision because the only qualities Gloria recognizes as "true" to her are her beauty and youth; bearing a child, she later reveals, would surely destroy these features.

The next day, after Anthony returns from a visit to his grandfather, he immediately asks Gloria about her pregnancy, and she happily tells him, "It's all right."[27] He asks for a second confirmation, and she emphasizes the point. She mysteriously tells him that the incident surprised her and leaves it at that. No mention of the pregnancy is made again in the novel. Yet the incident slowly shadows their relationship: in the same conversation Anthony begins lying to Gloria, a trend that will only be exacerbated as the novel continues, and they have a fight about Anthony's attempt to find a job and be more responsible. In an ironic twist on the stereotypical fight in a heterosexual marriage, Gloria reminds Anthony that he once believed that he couldn't "see why an American couldn't loaf gracefully."[28] It was this characteristic that attracted her to him. The issue is dropped shortly after, and Anthony continues his life of idleness, to Gloria's satisfaction. Yet the next chapter begins with more discontent. Anthony and Gloria wake up in bed, so disoriented from a night of inebriation they can barely recall how they got home. The arguments continue; the aimlessness intensifies; money is squandered. Then one day Anthony comes home to find Gloria asleep on the sofa with a child's doll in her arms, "her face as untroubled as a little girl's" and the doll serving as "a profound and infinitely healing balm to her disturbed and childish heart."[29] In the narrative's logic, Gloria and Anthony have one more moral sin to add to their already depraved life. Gloria's abortion (and Anthony's indifference to her action) finally undo the couple, leading them in the downward spiral that encompasses the next half of the novel: extramarital affairs, constant inebriation, spending beyond their means, and slowly being expelled from their social circles. The doll that Gloria clasps in her arms is a farewell to the life they could have had—a healing balm that is ultimately temporary because her childish heart will eventually be destroyed, turned into the "unclean woman" she becomes in the closing pages of the story. The novel follows a path Comstock once warned against: Gloria, unprotected by her family, loses her girlishness and innocence, the most tragic fate in Comstock's polemical tracts.

The eponymous Anthony Comstock is perhaps best known for his antiprostitution and antiobscenity reforms. In 1872, the US Congress, after pressure from his organization, the New York Society for the Suppression of Vice (NYSSV), and the Young Men's Christian Association (YMCA), passed what are now popularly known as the Comstock Laws,[30] banning all forms of "erotic" material from the distribution of pornography to the availability of contraception.[31] Even information about how to limit family size was deemed obscene under these laws, and Comstock himself volunteered to sort through the mail at the post office to seize any material that was suspect. Although Comstock never attacked access to abortion specifically, he classified abortion with all the other immoral acts and ideas that he saw corrupting American society.[32] The language of his act concerning abortion reads:

> Every obscene, lewd, lascivious, indecent, filthy or vile article, matter, thing, device, or substance; and—
> Every article or thing designed, adapted, or intended for producing abortion, or for any indecent or immoral use; and

Every article, instrument, substance, drug, medicine, or thing which is advertised or described in a manner calculated to lead another to use or apply it for producing abortion, or for any indecent or immoral purpose; and

Every written or printed card, letter, circular, book, pamphlet, advertisement, or notice of any kind giving information, directly or indirectly, where, or how, or from whom, or by what means any of such mentioned matters, articles, or things may be obtained or made, or where or by whom any act or operation of any kind for the procuring or producing of abortion will be done or performed, or how or by what means abortion may be produced, whether sealed or unsealed; and

Every paper, writing, advertisement, or representation that any article, instrument, substance, drug, medicine, or thing may, or can, be used or applied for producing abortion, or for any indecent or immoral purpose; and

Every description calculated to induce or incite a person to so use or apply any such article, instrument, substance, drug, medicine, or thing—

Is declared to be nonmailable matter and shall not be conveyed in the mails or delivered from any post office or by any letter carrier.[33]

Comstock explicitly engaged in a discourse of protection and a concern for freedom *from* harmful materials and practices. By deeming any abortion-related instruments and information "nonmailable," the law allows for breach of privacy because any suspect package or letter could be opened by a postal agent. Yet this violation of privacy is justified because it provides a freedom *from* "indecent" materials that could infiltrate innocent lives.

Comstock's response to the case of Cora Sammis in his book *Frauds Exposed* illustrates this point more precisely.[34] Here Comstock writes about Cora, a twenty-two-year-old woman from a middle-class home who sought an abortion after she became pregnant. Although Cora was engaged, both she and her fiancé agreed to seek an abortion before the marriage. Unfortunately, Cora died shortly after the procedure, and her abortionist was arrested and imprisoned. In response to the case Comstock laments "the anguish of the parent who wakes up to the knowledge that the beloved child is debauched."[35] Interestingly, Comstock decries Cora's abortion more than her death and contends that her parents' pain must come from knowing that their daughter had been led astray. In great detail he imagines how Cora's father must have felt as he received news that his daughter died of an abortion, and he urges his reader to aid in abolishing this daughter-destroying practice. Cora is portrayed as an innocent victim who fell into the hands of the wrong people and was thus defiled. Employing this logic, Comstock urges his readers to agree that young women like Cora must be protected and freed from the harmful agents that circulate unfettered in American society.

Comstock's encounter with the infamous New York abortionist Madame Restell[36] is another example of his relentless antiabortion pursuits. Comstock initially pursued Restell on a dare that he could not succeed in finding grounds for her arrest, despite the fact that the nature of her practice was an open secret. In 1886 Comstock went to Restell's home disguised as a man seeking to help his pregnant lover obtain an abortion. When Restell agreed to sell him an abortifacient, he arrested her and charged her with distributing illegal and obscene material. Before Restell's case came to trial she committed suicide, which stirred much controversy in the New York media. As the sociologist Nicola Beisel documents, most of the circulating papers condemned Restell, although the newspaper *World* also denounced Comstock for luring her to sell him an illegal product. In the words of the paper, "No matter what the wretched woman was who took her life with her own hand yesterday, *her death has not freed the world from* the last of detestable characters. Whatever she was *she had her rights.*"[37] The *World*'s representation of the case again points to an important tension in discourses of freedom. Although the editorial asserts that Restell had rights, which Comstock violated when he tricked her, it also contributes to Comstock's conviction that to rid the world of debased people like Restell is to free us *from* their dangerous influences.

The historian Janet Farrell Brodie notes that Comstock frequently passed moral judgment on women he deemed immodest. As Brodie explains it, Comstock viewed women who put effort into their appearance as seeming "too independent, not 'belonging' to any man."[38] Brodie traces Comstock's involvement in curtailing contraception access to his conflict with Victoria Woodhull, the nineteenth-century feminist and "free love" activist. According to Brodie, Comstock felt threatened by Woodhull because she was precisely the type of woman who refused to belong to any man and insisted on pursuing ambitions that were usually reserved only for men.[39] Comstock arrested Woodhull on charges of libel, only to face humiliation when the judge dismissed the case.[40] Soon after this setback, he began his aggressive campaign to outlaw access to abortion and contraception. Brodie argues that the proximity of these two events suggests that Comstock, after his failure in prosecuting Woodhull, became driven to root out the causes that he saw "ruining" women. Implicit in this new quest is Comstock's concern with containing female bodies that could potentially exceed what he views as the norm for family, reproduction, and sexuality.

Comstock's construction of these norms is tied to ensuring the hegemony of the middle-class family—a construction that in the late nineteenth century was built on the subservient positions of women and children. For his commitment to "respectability" *is* tied to a classed notion of family. For example, in his description of Cora Sammis he bemoans the loss of a daughter in "a respectable" family, one that went to church, that lived in a "quiet village on the eastern end of Long Island."[41] In other words, this family had all appearances of existing apart from the moral debauchery that Comstock had dedicated his life to eradicating. In this example, as in others, Comstock reveals that he is most intent on protecting the Christian, middle-class family from the seedy elements infiltrating society. Thus his polemic against open displays of sexuality in general becomes a technology for regulating and controlling the bodies that pose the greatest danger to hegemonic norms.

Worse yet is when people from a "good, upstanding home" are so polluted by lust and desire that they begin to embody the moral degradation of society, a slippage difficult to return from. As Comstock preaches: "Lust defiles the body, debauches the imagination, corrupts the mind, deadens the will, destroys the memory, sears the conscience, hardens the heart, and damns the soul. . . . Like a panorama, the imagination seems to keep this hated thing before the mind, until it wears its way deeper and deeper, plunging the victim into practices he loathes."[42] Comstock is focused not only on protecting society—and Christian families in particular—from debauchery but also on protecting individuals from themselves. He does not merely fear evil men (or women) who seduce innocent persons; he also depicts lust as affectively entering the bodies of seducers and turning them into something/someone they are not. "The victim," as Comstock reveals in the following pages, is most often a young man or woman from a "good" middle-class home, who becomes drawn in by more powerful forces to become the immoral debaucher he was never *intended* to be. *Frauds Exposed* makes clear that it views abortion, or the possibility of abortion, as one of those dangerous moments: once abortion is inflicted, the subject quite literally aborts her possibility for returning to the respectable positions of her birth. Thus Comstock's work is bent on preventing women from having access to abortion so that they can be protected and freed from becoming victims that act against their own best interests.

Procreative behavior is socialized to interpellate reproducing subjects into an ethic of *responsibilization* so that reproduction can be controlled through generating particularized knowledge about what constitutes responsible behavior.[43] This ideology is precisely what Comstock constructs to regulate sexuality and to tie it to a number of other "perverse" acts and discourses. By lobbying for laws that ban the distribution of "obscene" materials and the practice of abortion because innocent women will then be protected, Comstock's antiabortion measures not only outlaw abortion but also discursively frame women as potential victims that need discipline and security.

Comstock differs from Sanger because he refuses to allow for the possibility that women can be self-controlled citizens; for Comstock the ability to be responsible is tied to masculinity, which is why he only imagines how Cora's father felt after her death and why he finds women like Woodhull and Restell so threatening. In Comstock's world, men must be disciplined so that they can protect and rein in women. As Sally Shuttleworth writes about Victorian body politics:

> Notions of gender differentiation fulfilled the ideological role of allowing the male sex to renew their faith in personal autonomy and control. Unlike women, men were not prey to the forces of the body, the unsteady oscillations of which mirrored the uncertain flux of social circulation; rather they were their own masters—not automatons or mindless parts of the social machinery but self-willed individuals, living incarnations of the rational individualists and self-made men of economic theory.[44]

This worldview aptly describes Comstock's motivation to outlaw abortion: while men should be self-willed, rational, and individualist, women are incapable of attaining these traits because of the more "natural" conditions of their bodies and therefore must be given freedom *from* the harmful elements in society. Therefore, despite Comstock's critiques of "Liberals," his ideologies are ultimately embedded in a liberal construction of the state and societal structures that discipline citizens—albeit only male ones—to be self-controlling individuals. Yet a key point to understanding Comstock's investment in male autonomy, and what Shuttleworth overlooks, is that the autonomous, self-willed man is also a classed construction that works to discipline middle-class men into seeing themselves according to class. Depicting men as autonomous and self-willed already imagines them as having a certain degree of disposable income or job security. When Comstock imagines the dismay Cora's father must have felt after learning about his daughter's abortion, he appeals to a middle-class man who has the luxury of constructing a rational and individualist identity because of his class status.[45]

Comstock's writings put forth that abortion, because it is keenly tied to both procreative behavior and presumably control, becomes a linchpin of responsibilization. Antiabortion laws function not only to prevent the practice but to construct a knowledge about how subjects should behave according to certain gender norms—through what is defined as "responsible" behavior—as a means of disciplining and controlling the body-as-machine, the individual, and the demarcation of populations—to deem which bodies and populations are "deserving" of responsibility and which ones need to be regulated and enclosed. In other words, law functions as judgment, but it also produces subjectivity. For Comstock, a society that allows abortion is a society in demise because it demonstrates men's lack of control and women's exposure to lustful forces. It both disallows men the freedom *to* and impedes women's freedom *from*. However, more important, his texts become technologies of discipline through their distribution of knowledge about the supposed inherent evil of abortion and their attempts to interpellate a middle-class American into their disciplinary apparati.[46]

Like Gloria and Anthony in *The Beautiful and Damned*, the debased person in Comstock's tracts performs "obscene" acts because "he doesn't know better," which then lead him or her onto a sinful path that soon becomes difficult to correct. Both *The Beautiful and Damned* and *Frauds Exposed* view abortion, or the possibility of abortion, as one of those slippery moments: because Gloria and Anthony seem to make their decision so lightly, like Cora Sammis, they quite literally abort their possibility for returning to the respectable positions of their birth. For Comstock and for Fitzgerald's characters, the abortion is then a mark of demise because it demonstrates a lack of control and a giving in to the lustful forces at large. Even if Gloria and Anthony sail away toward financial freedom in the closing pages of the novel, the narrative clarifies that their actions throughout the novel have made it impossible for them to now be free *from* the destructive forces of Western culture.[47]

The House Built on Sands

While much has been documented about Sanger's investment in eugenics and birth control, relatively little has been written about her fluctuating stance on abortion. Sanger's more ambivalent positions are often elided; relatively little attention is paid to the element of her rhetoric that is compatible with neither contemporary mainstream feminist arguments nor antiracist nationalisms.[48] Her work elicits either stringent criticism for its racism or effusive praise for its efforts in legalizing contraception. Some of Sanger's strongest antiabortion claims were published in the *Birth Control Review*, which began its run in February 1917 as a simply formatted periodical to be used as a political tactic in the quest to legalize birth control. In its first few issues, the journal mainly published polemical essays by known birth control activists like Havelock Ellis and Elizabeth Stuyvesant, as well as desperate letters from women seeking birth control help (only as a means to demonstrate the dire situation), but at the start of its second year it broadened its publication scope to include short stories and poetry and eventually added disturbing photo essays depicting dysgenic "types" overrun with children.

From the start, the journal was clearly invested in promoting the politics of eugenics; almost every issue mentions eugenics or has an article featuring the topic. Anna Blount, a frequent contributor to the journal, captures its eugenic philosophy best when she writes, "God speed the day when the unwilling mother, with her weak, puny body, her sad, anaemic, unlovely face, and her despondent whine, will be no more. In that day we shall see a race of American thoroughbreds, if not the superman."[49] Essays like Blount's made explicit that the *Review* was invested in a eugenics-like policy that would "improve" the conditions of all Americans and eventually eliminate "undesirable" citizens through preventing or reducing their ability to reproduce. However, Sanger also distanced herself from eugenicists who argued that woman's first duty is to reproduce for the state. In February 1919, in an article entitled "Birth Control and Racial Betterment," she strongly states that if eugenics is to succeed it must rely on birth control and change its position on voluntary motherhood. She writes that birth control activists contend that woman's first duty is not to the state, as eugenicists believed, but "that her duty to herself is her first duty to the state."[50] She continues to insist that birth control is the necessary foundation for eugenics, and in an elaborate gesture she ends with a compelling metaphor, arguing, "Eugenics without Birth Control seems to us a house builded upon sands. It is at the mercy of the rising stream of the unfit. It cannot stand against the furious winds of economic pressure."[51] As Sanger's language suggests, one of the *Review*'s most strident goals was to irrevocably link the issues of birth control and eugenics through its emphasis on a freedom *from* politics. Here Sanger stresses that eugenics, and hence the betterment of American citizenry, is doomed to fail unless there is a freedom *from* uncontrolled reproduction. Yet elsewhere, Sanger also insists on the necessity that women have freedom *to* control their reproductive capacities so that they can have freedom *from* abortion.

Sanger's most explicit antiabortion stance came in an article she wrote early in the journal's run, starkly titled, "Birth Control or Abortion?" (December 1918). Sanger opens her article by associating abortion with working-class women; she argues that wealthy and middle-class women have discovered how to limit family size and to be voluntary mothers, while more working-class women are denied "the knowledge of the safe, harmless, scientific methods of Birth Control" and thus limit their families "by means of abortion."[52] Sanger's disciplining tone, her juxtaposition of birth control as rational and safe with abortion as dangerous and volatile, is the main focus of the article. She proceeds with a scientific explanation of conception, clinically describing how pregnancy occurs, and then explicitly states, "When scientific means are used to prevent this meeting, and thereby to limit families, one is said to practice Birth Control."[53] She cites a doctor to prove that abortion risks women's health, potentially causing "hemorrhage, retention of an adherent placenta, sepsis, tetanus, perforation of the uterus . . . sterility, anemia, malignant diseases, displacements, neurosis, and endometritis." In case this long list would not scare readers enough, Sanger adds that the "hundreds of thousands of abortions performed in America each year are a disgrace to civilization." Birth control, she argues, means "health and happiness—a stronger, better race," while abortion "means disease, suffering, death." She ends by rhetorically asking, "*Birth Control or Abortion—which shall it be?*" clearly stating that the division between the two is definitive and complete.[54] Her logic, ultimately, depends on maintaining populations demarcated by class positions that are so well controlled they discipline themselves.

In 1920 Sanger republished an expanded version of this *Birth Control Review* essay in *Woman and the New Race*, retitling it "Contraceptives or Abortion?" Here she further elaborates her belief that women with disposable incomes were already practicing birth control, while working-class women could only resort to abortion if unwanted pregnancy occurred.

She again stresses that abortion is "abnormal" and "dangerous,"[55] but she adds in this version that "the woman who goes to the abortionist's table is not a criminal but a martyr—a martyr to the bitter, unthinkable conditions brought about by the blindness of society at large" because she has to sacrifice "what is highest and holiest in her—her aspirations to freedom, and her desire to protect the children already hers."[56]

In both versions of her essay, Sanger assumes that if working-class women, like wealthy and middle-class women, had access to birth control, then they would have the freedom to act responsibly and to prevent the demise of civilization by ceasing to reproduce what she views as defective children. However, in the later version, she also constructs a politics of victimization that turns working-class women into martyrs who expose themselves to the evils of abortion because the law gives them no choice. Sanger supposes that if given access to birth control, women would no longer seek abortion, and she uses wealthy and middle-class women as examples of this argument, even though recent historians of abortion have demonstrated that it was primarily white, middle-class women who sought abortion.[57] If the historical data are correct, her description of the working-class woman as martyr could only have been constructed to produce a disciplining and patronizing effect: if women want to actualize the middle-class values of self-control and freedom, which Sanger explicitly alludes to in the previous quotation, they must distinguish between birth control and abortion. Her writing, although it seems to be addressing the conditions of a working-class population, actually functions as a disciplining tactic for middle-class women as a means to differentiate them from the victims of abortion. In other words, her logic implies that working-class women need freedom *from* abortion because they need the protection of law, supposedly to protect them from the harm of abortion, while to be a wealthier woman means to know how to access the freedom *to* reproduce according to one's own self-will.

In her autobiography, Sanger describes two trips she took, to Germany in 1920 and to Russia thirteen years later, to promote birth control and to learn about new contraceptive methods she might export back to the United States. In both countries she discovers that abortion rather than birth control is the primary means to prevent unwanted children. When she questions a German doctor about his choice to perform abortions rather than offer women contraceptives, he replies, "We will never give over the control of our numbers to the women themselves. What, let them control the future of the human race? With abortions it is in our hands; we make the decisions, and they must come to us."[58] To Sanger's horror, she finds that most German doctors she meets have a similar response. Sanger's dismayed reaction to German birth control policy is rooted not only in their use of abortion rather than contraception but in the lack of control women have over their reproductive lives. The doctor clearly tells Sanger that reproduction is too important to allow women to make their choices and that thus it must be regulated by male doctors and the state, which denies women any option but abortion. Her conversation with the German doctor functions as evidence for her that while birth control provides women with the freedom to control their reproduction, abortion strips them of that right. Her visit to Russia, more than ten years later, reveals a similar opinion about abortion but also demonstrates Sanger's more complicated eugenics-based position.

In Russia, as in Germany, Sanger documents a concern with population decline and a concerted government effort to encourage people to reproduce more. Sanger meets with Dr. Kaminsky, secretary of the Commissariat of Public Health, and questions him about whether Russia has a policy to "control families." She adds, "I know you have much freedom for women and a fine technique for abortions. . . . Four hundred thousand abortions a year indicate women do not want to have so many children."[59] Dr. Kaminsky evasively responds to Sanger not by addressing Russia's abortion policy, but by simply insisting that Russia desires an increase of population in both skilled and unskilled workers. In fact, Dr. Kaminsky's emphasis on Russia's desire to increase its labor pool suggests that he was informing Sanger that his country refused to engage in a birth control policy based on eugenics. Thus, in assessing Russia's population growth, Sanger writes:

> I considered Russia's situation very serious. . . . Unless she looked
> ahead and educated her people in the problems which arose out of
> population, within two generations she would find herself with the
> same differential birth rate then existing in England and the United
> States. It would, however, have much more tragic consequences
> since it would lower the augmentation of the capable, skilled, shock
> troops of industry, the idealists and active, selfless workers, and
> would multiply from the bottom unskilled, ignorant, dull-witted
> workers, the superstitious element which even the greatest efforts
> of a Soviet dictatorship running at top speed could not pull up and
> out of their evolutionary environment.[60]

Here Sanger reveals her belief that a country with only an abortion policy cannot properly practice eugenics and will thus be left with a degenerate population. In her analysis of the situation in Germany and Russia, her antiabortion position rests on desiring more control for women so that they have the freedom to prevent pregnancy. At the same time, she maintains that as long as abortion is legal or accessible, then women will not learn to be self-controlled, and unwanted pregnancies will continue to occur, leading to the demise of the population. Implicit in her analysis is that with abortion as the only means to limit family size, people will remain uneducated and unregulated as the "dull-witted" workers reproduce while perhaps occasionally seeking abortion, a practice Sanger calls "a cruel method of dealing with the problem because abortion, no matter how well done, is a terrific nervous strain and an exhausting physical hardship."[61]

Ellen Chesler argues that Sanger dissociated abortion from contraception to make her arguments for legalizing birth control more palatable to contemporary legislators.[62] Chesler argues that Sanger took this position because "in respectable circles, illegal abortion was universally condemned as primitive, dangerous, and disreputable."[63] As Joan M. Jensen has shown, the evolution of Sanger's position can be seen in "Family Limitation,"[64] a pamphlet that provided information for women about contraception, sex, and, in the early days of its publication, abortion. Initially printed in 1914, the pamphlet went through several revisions, including one in 1921 that expurgated information about abortion techniques. From the first to the ninth editions, Sanger advised women in the early stages of an unwanted pregnancy to take quinine to "restore the menses." However, she warns that this procedure might not work past the first month of gestation and that women further along should consult a doctor.[65] By the tenth edition Sanger had omitted this advice. Jensen contends that this shift in position is reflective of Sanger's move to more right-wing politics from her earlier socialist-inflected stance. As institutionalized support for birth control from radical organizations waned, Sanger strategically approached middle-class suffrage organizations and other liberal feminists for financial and political support. Additionally, "Family Limitation" faced threats from postal censors, who under the 1873 Comstock Act deemed the material obscene and inappropriate for public circulation. Jensen argues that the combination of political changes and personal hardship pushed Sanger to revise the tenth edition of "Family Limitation" so that no references to abortion, either direct or oblique, were included.[66] Jensen views these edits as purely pragmatic: Sanger needed a new source of funding, and she found one most readily in a more conservative middle class.

Was Sanger's view rooted in sheer pragmatism? A closer look at Sanger's writings on abortion, including her personal letters to friends and political associates, reveals a more complicated position. These writings suggest that her stance on abortion changed as she became more concerned with medical issues, health, and what was then popularly called dysgenics—the passing on of negative traits to progeny. In a letter to her friend and activist ally Marie Stopes,[67] Sanger reveals her ambivalent feelings about abortion. She confides to Stopes that she understands that women resort to seeking abortion out of desperation, but she also stresses her firm belief that once contraception is legal and accessible, the necessity for abortion will be eliminated.[68] Thus she justifies her condemnation of abortion as a practice that will soon become null if her efforts succeed.[69]

By the time she started publishing the *Birth Control Review,* Sanger was intent on putting forth her antiabortion position, and her tactics were so forceful that it is difficult to consider them merely an attempt to please an antiabortion public. In November 1917 Sanger wrote a letter to the editor at *Medical World* expressing her dismay that the American Medical Association approved of laws that allowed women access to abortion if continuation of pregnancy would severely impact their health. Sanger angrily wrote that "abortion laws were broad enough to allow in such cases a 'duly licensed physician' to perform an abortion in order to save the life of either the women or the child. It all seemed such a chaotic state to me—that it was perfectly legal to go thru the sufferings of an abortion, but illegal to prevent conception."[70] This was a position she would put forth in many of her arguments against abortion in the *Birth Control Review.* Furthermore, she widely publicized stories about the "dangers" of abortifacients; she believed that if a woman did not successfully abort her pregnancy using these drugs, the fetus would be negatively impacted, and the woman had a high chance of giving birth to an infant with defects.[71] She continually stressed that her opposition to abortion was based on health factors, citing statistics (often miscalculated) about the number of women who died during or after the procedure.[72] Thus she emphasizes that if she sought to outlaw abortion, it was only for women's own protection because her goal was to grant them freedom *from* the dangerous effects of abortion.

In reading Sanger's work, Ruhl points out that Sanger's fight to legalize birth control rests on two separate platforms: On the one hand she argues that until birth control is accessible, women cannot be free and equal citizens. Birth control is a feminist issue. Yet, on the other hand, she stresses that birth control is necessary to prevent overpopulation, especially since "dysgenic types" tended to produce the most children.[73] Ruhl notes the slipperiness between these two positions; one demands that women have the freedom *to* control their bodies, whereas the other argues for the medical management of "unfit" women and their reproductive functions. Subtending these positions, Ruhl sees Sanger putting forth an argument about responsibility: women "need to uphold their end of the bargain of reproductive freedom: contraception in exchange for a guarantee to act 'responsibly' where reproductive decisions are concerned. . . . To act responsibly means to conform to an essentially middle-class, educated, and scientifically oriented worldview."[74] Sanger's contradictory programs point to the slipperiness of the language of rights, choice, and control. Rights and choice are *granted* to individuals when they can prove themselves to be responsible citizens, abiding by certain normative conditions. And as demonstrated most clearly by current federal abortion laws that set age limits on who can responsibly seek an abortion without a guardian's permission and that force women to view fetal ultrasounds so that decisions can be *responsibly* made, the discourse of self-control itself disciplines subjects into normative categories. In Sanger's writings, abortion comes to represent irresponsible and reckless behavior, meant to highlight how the use of contraception can construct a self-controlled woman, one who can responsibly choose when pregnancy occurs. Sanger is invested in constructing a birth control discourse that both manages and disciplines bodies. Furthermore, Sanger appeals to class status in her constructions of familial and reproductive norms. Subjects *should* be properly interpellated, and if they refuse to be, then they are abnormal and need to be managed, or they pose a threat to the supposedly well-managed, properly demarcated American.

Tools of Reproduction

In September 1919 the *Birth Control Review* published two works of fiction, an unusual move in a journal with limited space that normally dedicated itself to political writings. The African American playwright Mary Burrill published a one-act play (on "Negro Life," the subtitle informs) entitled "They That Sit in Darkness," and Angelina Weld Grimké,[75] also a playwright but here a fiction writer, published "The Closing Door," a short story that would be serialized in two issues of the *Review*. While not advertised as such, this issue seems to focus on African American life in the South, also including an essay by Chandler Owen, coeditor of the African American periodical the *Messenger*. Owen's essay, titled "Women and Children of the South," looks primarily at African American women in the South, arguing that the reason they marry early and have large families is because they have few outlets for pleasure, and so marriage and sex are taken up as distractions and amusements.[76] Owen compares these women with African American women living in northern cities, who, he argues, are more educated and have fewer children. While not definitively making any claims, Owen's article, filled with statistical figures, seems to suggest that northern women should be reproducing more and that poor southern women need to learn their birth control secrets.

Burrill's play, written especially for the *Birth Control Review*, has a similarly flat-footed message. The play centers on Malinda Jasper, mother to eight living children, some with obvious physical ailments like withered limbs. The younger children are described as "a crest-fallen, pathetic looking little group—heads unkempt, ragged, undersized, underfed."[77] Pinkie, one of the older daughters, has already left home after she became pregnant out of wedlock. From the start of the play, Malinda is portrayed as an exhausted, overworked mother who can barely support her children. Her husband is forced to work all day to bring in a barely sufficient wage. Her eldest daughter, Lindy, plans to enroll in Tuskegee, a life-long dream of hers since an encounter with Booker T. Washington when she was a small child. The play is framed by a visit from Elizabeth Shaw, a visiting nurse and the only character who doesn't speak in the constructed African American dialect written for Malinda and her children. Elizabeth comes to urge Malinda to stop working, warning that otherwise she will face death; tired from giving birth to more than eight children in almost as many years and frantically trying to support them, Malinda is portrayed as sick and weak. Malinda explains her hard luck by accusing God of punishing her, but Elizabeth pleads with her to stop having children. Malinda replies: "But whut kin Ah do—the chillern *come!*"[78] She has no ability to control her reproduction and no means, according to the story, of seeking this information. When Malinda pleads with Elizabeth to give her birth control, Elizabeth responds, "I wish to God it were lawful for me to do so! My heart goes out to you poor people that sit in darkness, having year after year, children that you are physically too weak to bring into the world."[79]

By the end of the play, Malinda is unable to survive her life's hardship and dies, leaving Lindy to care for her siblings and give up her dream of Tuskegee. Burrill's play neatly fits into the *Birth Control Review*'s political agenda: it portrays working-class and poor women as having little choice and control over their lives as a result of their inability to become voluntary mothers. It depicts an overworked mother with dysgenic children, a paradigm Sanger often described in her arguments for birth control. Sanger believed, like many eugenicists, that the more children poor women had, the more likely those children would have physical and mental disabilities. Like Shaw's essay, Burrill's play argues that large families were the underlying cause of poverty, ignorance, and sickness. Given the context of Shaw's and Burrill's work, Grimké's contribution is surprising in its more complex handling of racism and reproduction. "The Closing Door" opens on a false note of happiness and freedom, so much so that the race of the characters is at first only alluded to in the subtext. Agnes, the protagonist, is described as Spanish or Italian looking, as though she has been thoroughly assimilated into a white culture that has accepted her or is on the verge of accepting her. Jim Milton, her husband, is described as a brown, attractive giant, also an ambiguously raced description. At the start of the story, Agnes and Jim are a content middle-class couple, who are able to live comfortably and even put some money aside. The narrative, however, soon develops a more formidable tone, beginning with the narrator Lucy's pessimistic foreshadowing of the end of Jim and Agnes's ephemeral happiness.

Laura Dawkins and Joyce Meier ground Grimké's writings in the era of the Harlem Renaissance, when black writers were both claiming a space for their writing and growing more aware of the crippling and inescapable nature of American racism. Meier writes that Grimké's work reflects "the reality of the black woman who refused participation in a racist and patriarchal system by refusing motherhood."[80] In her essay Meier doesn't address "The Closing Door," but a play that Grimké wrote and produced in 1915 called *Rachel*. In it Rachel refuses to become a mother after she realizes the racist and disabling conditions under which she would have to raise her children. The play depicts her metaphorically denying the birth of her future children, and as a result many critics accused the play of advocating the genocide of African Americans.[81] Dawkins, however, reads the figure of infanticide at the hands of the black mother as a means of asserting black women's agency. She writes that Grimké, and other black women writers of the era, "suggested that the Victorian maternal ideal was an instrument of oppression rather than a source of spiritual motherhood, trapping the black mother in an inevitable martyrdom."[82] Thus infanticide, according to Dawkins, should be read metaphorically, as a means of subversion and an assertion of agency. While this framework provides a compelling reading and echoes the retelling of Margaret Garner's story in Toni Morrison's *Beloved*, I'd like to add to Dawkins's analysis a critique of choice that challenges her commitment to agency and that will be further elaborated through my reading of the story.

The trope of happiness frames "The Closing Door." As the story opens, Lucy, the narrator, describes Agnes and Jim as the only truly happy people she has ever met. Happiness, of course, resonates as integral in the United States' founding document, which declares the country's independence; all Americans should have the right not only to life and liberty but also to the pursuit of happiness. In the picture Lucy presents, Agnes and Jim seem to have all three. However, when Agnes finds out she is pregnant, she is overjoyed with the news, but she tells Lucy, "I'm—I'm just a little afraid, I believe . . . there's—such—a thing—as being—*too* happy,—*too* happy."[83] Her happiness, then, is mediated by the fear that she somehow doesn't have the right to happiness, or at least this much happiness; this questioning is the beginning of her realization that as a black woman, given the rampant racism in the United States, her lasting happiness is ultimately an impossibility. As the story unfolds, it becomes clear that Agnes's happiness is indeed predicated on forgetting certain aspects of her existence. For example, when her brother Joe comes up to visit, he describes the weariness he felt as a result of riding in segregated Jim Crow cars as he made his way through the South to visit Agnes in the North. Agnes responds with a sudden awareness and admits, "I'd forgotten. I've been away so long."[84] From this moment in the story Agnes is forced to begin remembering what it means to live as a black American.

Joe has come to tell Jim the truth behind his brother Bob's death; he also wants to warn Jim that Agnes must not find out what happened. As he explains the story behind Bob's horrific lynching, he begins by telling Jim, Lucy, and the hidden Agnes, "You don't know, I suppose, that there is an unwritten law in the South."[85] This unwritten law, Jim explains, states that all blacks must step off the sidewalk when a white person approaches, and if they refuse to obey, retribution will be enacted—a violent disciplining. Saidiya Hartman explains this paradigm as "the burdened individuality of freedom." She contends that "the nascent individualism of the freed designates a precarious autonomy since exploitation, domination, and subjection inhabit the vehicle of rights."[86] In other words, or using Joe's words, it was not the law that was subjugating blacks, as when slavery was legal pre-1865; it was the "unwritten law" that ensured that the freedom of American blacks was regulated through various means (lynching being one) so that this freedom was always "precarious" and dependent on the whims of a white hegemony. Thus Hartman, like Grimké's story, asserts that the separation between slavery and freedom is more tenuous and less definite.

Agnes unravels after eavesdropping on Joe's news and spends the rest of her pregnancy in bed. She laments to Jim and Lucy her naïveté in mistakenly believing that she could have been happy, could have lived out her dream of motherhood. She cries that she is "an instrument of reproduction!—a colored woman—doomed!—cursed!—put here!—willing or unwilling! For what?—to bring children here—men children—for the sport—the lust—of possible orderly mobs—who go about things—in an orderly manner—on Sunday mornings!"[87] When her child is born, she expresses surprise that he is not dead, suggesting that she may have taken unsuccessful steps to ensure a stillbirth or abort the pregnancy. She refuses to touch the baby or be near him; in fact, the only times she touches her son are in her two attempts to kill him. Her second attempt is successful, and she kills the baby by smothering him. As Agnes's cries demonstrate, she sees herself through the lens of a white world that views her solely through her ability to reproduce. However, she is no longer enslaved, so her children have no material value in terms of producing wealth for the slave owner. Still, as she points out, her children, and specifically her male children, will be used to maintain white supremacy through their denigration and manipulation in a white world. The power relation she perceives is not all that dissimilar to the one that existed during slavery, where slave owners abused and denigrated their slaves to maintain a rigid hierarchy. The difference in the situation that Agnes points to is that the hierarchy is no longer inscribed in law, but through unspoken social relations.

While I agree with Dawkins's reading that in Grimké's story "black motherhood serves as a paradigm for maternal loss and pain,"[88] the story should also be read as revealing Agnes's inability to exert choice in a society that has reinscribed the status quo of slavery through a new social code. Like Linda's decision to have children with a man she does not love as a means to resist a man she detests in Harriet Jacobs's *Incidents in the Life of a Slave Girl*, Agnes's decision to kill her child is ironically both a means to assert control and an acquiescence to the fact that neither she nor her child will have control, or the access to choice, given their social conditions. Thus her action is in recognition that she is not a liberal citizen. If she tried to practice self-control, it would be precisely to give in to the conditions of the state. Or as Linda might have described it: Agnes's infanticide is a reckless action in response to a condition where choice and freedom are impossible to attain.

Daylanne English, contributing toward a scholarship on black women's playwriting in the early twentieth century, points to how Grimké's fiction posits a critique of "the ways that social Darwinist and eugenic thinking is at best irrelevant, and at worst both morally and scientifically backward—given the racial injustice, white hegemony, and racial terrorism of the 1910s and 1920s."[89] Grimké's open dismissal of eugenic thought is striking given that her stories were published in the *Birth Control Review*, a self-proclaimed eugenicist publication.[90] However, as English also notes, Grimké's writings were seen as contributing to a critique of black oppression, particularly as it affected middle-class and wealthy African Americans. She argues that Grimké's play *Rachel*, which is narratively similar to "The Closing Door," demonstrates how, "as long as black women are not free both to control and to express their sexuality and fertility, they will be oppressed; as long as black men are at risk of being lynched, they will be oppressed."[91] Thus, Sanger likely envisioned Grimké's stories as constructing a mirroring eugenicist genealogy for blacks, one where the "best" African Americans were encouraged to reproduce to help their race and where those African Americans should have "choice" when it came to controlling their reproduction.[92] Yet Grimké's story is slippery because it ultimately performs the opposing critique by exposing how the rhetoric of "choice" is always problematic because it is *given*. In other words, it demonstrates how individual control is always embedded in larger social forces that shape *who* has "choice" and what that choice contains. Similarly, then, it returns us to the language of abortion rhetoric, both in the ways it is discussed today and in Comstock's and Sanger's writing, and reveals how just as "choice" claims to open up opportunities, it also has the power of exclusion. And in fact, almost by necessity, the rhetoric of choice in abortion discourse always marginalizes certain populations just as it grants others access.

First Encounter: Final Thoughts

Sanger's first encounter with Comstock occurred in 1913, after Sanger had published several columns in the *Call*, a popular New York socialist daily. Her column, "What Every Girl Should Know," gave women information on topics ranging from menstruation to masturbation and was one of the first explicit sex manuals for women written by a woman. Comstock banned its circulation for several weeks, citing it for containing obscene material. However, after relentless protests calling for First Amendment rights, the publication was resumed.[93] Later Comstock prosecuted her husband, William Sanger, for distributing materials related to birth control. However, during the trial Comstock fell ill with pneumonia, and eleven days later he died. In her autobiography Sanger attributes his death to William Sanger's release. She writes, "There was a terrific demonstration in Court which made the three judges turn pale & gave Comstock a shock from which he never recovered."[94] She writes about his death and her husband's acquittal with a triumphant glee that points to how strongly she perceived Comstock as a major opponent in her fight to legalize birth control. After all, her perception was not inaccurate, because the Comstock Laws of 1873 inscribed some of her major legal constraints. Yet, despite this apparent opposition, this chapter argues that Comstock and Sanger in some ways depended upon a similar ideology.

Margaret Sanger's and Anthony Comstock's works, while seeming to profess conflicting political paradigms, actually share a discourse based on individuated freedoms that works to manage bodies and populations. Both Sanger and Comstock were committed to outlawing abortion by employing two intertwined ideologies. First, they argue that middle-class values are a foundation for the betterment of the race. In Comstock's logic, if abortion were outlawed, then (middle-class) families, and specifically daughters, would be protected and preserved. In Sanger's logic, if access to abortion were prohibited, then people would see the need for the "cleaner," better-"controlled" form of birth control, which would also ultimately lead to a better human race. Second, both activists appeal to elements of a liberal discourse. Americans have the right to be protected, to monitor their homes, and to maintain their individualism. Neither asks about the rights of those that present the threat, that contribute to an "unclean" America, and that destabilize the house built on sands.

This chapter covers a rather long span of time, from Comstock's polemics beginning in the 1870s to Sanger's activism in the 1920s and 1930s. Still, when their arguments are juxtaposed, similar principles emerge that reveal the limitations of contemporary mainstream abortion politics on both the right and the left. Abortion debates that are rooted in discourses of rights and individual liberties are inherently limited. The discourses of Comstock and Sanger—and the gaps in their discourses— reveal how problematic it is to support abortion using the rhetoric of rights and choice, which can so easily be reversed to argue the opposite.

Brown begins her speculation on the role of rights in American politics by asking, "What is the emancipatory force of rights claims on behalf of politicized identities in late-twentieth-century North American polit-ical life?"[95] As Brown astutely argues, in order to be persuasive, these arguments must provide the illusion that they are granting access based on a naturalized and universalized paradigm. However, it is precisely their ahistoricity that works to curtail their potential emancipatory force because of the power these claims have to foreclose identity and refuse the recognition of those outside its boundaries. Similarly, the mainte-nance of abortion rights through legal provisions that grant either free-dom *from* or freedom *to* always results in a granting of rights that is less than universal. Some populations can always be excluded based on arguments that appeal to a lack of self-will, responsibility, or maturity, in much the same way that Comstock and Sanger attempted to free women from abortion for their own protection.

3 / The Eugenics of Bad Girls: Abortion, Popular Fiction, and Population Control

Were the white world to-day really convinced of the supreme importance
of race-values, how long would it take to stop debasing immigration,
reform social abuses that are killing out the fittest strains, and put an end
to the feuds which have just sent us through hell and threaten to send us
promptly back again?

—LOTHROP STODDARD, *THE RISING TIDE OF COLOR*
AGAINST WHITE WORLD-SUPREMACY

The history of American eugenics is a history of difference. This chapter begins with an outline of an abbreviated history of eugenics to illustrate how the American obsession with race in the early twentieth century was very much focused on building knowledge about how populations differ from each other and how this knowledge about difference could be used to manage lives. As Catherine Mills succinctly argues, "The normalizing forces of racism, which allow for the biological fracturing of population and designating of some races as inferior, are the mechanisms by which a state is able 'to exercise its sovereign power.'"[1] By interpreting sovereignty along more Foucauldian lines as a kind of power that is not solely exercised by the head of state but also replicated and dispersed through family, church, and other institutionalized centers, this chapter examines how antiabortion discourse in popular literature theorizes the connection among power, nationhood, reproduction, and ideals of motherhood. Antiabortion sentiments, I argue, are based in racist ideologies that carve out antagonistic populations wary of the messiness of reproduction and its potential to erase population lines. Thus, any law that worked to control women's reproductive functions was welcomed within the climate of anxiety created by eugenic theories.[2]

I'll be arguing here that antiabortion rhetoric was used as a means to both discipline and ultimately threaten middle-class, white women to behave according to the norms of early twentieth-century womanhood and motherhood and that the ideology of eugenics, which in the early twentieth century gained a foothold in popular culture and scientific thought, shaped American attitudes toward women's reproduction. This argument builds on Dale Bauer's conclusion, where she writes, "Sexualizing relations became a way of marking the middle class off from what once were the 'decadence' and delinquence of the working class and the absolute sanctuary of the leisure class and its unspoken, sometimes unexplained, sexual practices."[3] Eugenics and the abortion rhetoric that emerged from its policies became a means to distinguish a new middle class and construct sexual norms for its members. As chapter 2 already demonstrated, Anthony Comstock and Margaret Sanger also focused on contributing to middle-class mores, which were quickly becoming the object of eugenic ideology. This chapter will continue that argument to show how antiabortion rhetoric was keenly tied to eugenic sentiments as a means of shaping an emerging white middle class.

In 1922 Lothrop Stoddard, an ardent eugenicist and white supremacist, posed the rhetorical question that forms the epigraph at the beginning this chapter. His question does not have an ounce of irony, although a present-day reader might scoff at such a ridiculous attitude. In his time, and for almost his entire career, during which he published several polemical works on the subject of white supremacy, Stoddard was respected and heeded. Presidents Warren G. Harding and Herbert Hoover praised his work,[4] and birth control activist Margaret Sanger asked Stoddard to join the board of the Birth Control League. Stoddard, who received his PhD at Harvard, was viewed as a rational and scientific thinker, and the majority of reviews commenting on his work depict him as such. Part of his appeal was that, unlike his predecessor Madison Grant, who was one of the founders of the American Museum of Natural History in New York and a well-known eugenicist, Stoddard praised all whites as superior to other races without singling out Nordics as Grant did.[5]

The motivation behind Stoddard's work is quite transparent: underlying his writing is a deep anxiety that whites will be soon be outnumbered in the United States. He points out that around the world whites reproduce less than people of other races, which he believed would soon lead to the demise of whiteness, or, in his words, the "fitter race." As he passionately argues, "Everywhere the better types (on which the future of the race depends) were numerically stationary or dwindling, while conversely, the lower types were gaining ground, their birth-rate showing relatively slight diminution."[6] His relentless attack on these "lower types" eventually influenced the US government to pass the Immigration Act of 1924; the act severely curtailed the number of people allowed to enter the country and laid out strict quotas detailing how many people from various countries would be allowed to enter the United States. Every year, with some exceptions, only 2 percent of the number of a national population already residing in the United States would be allowed to immigrate.[7] The National Census of 1890 determined the numbers of immigrants from each country residing in the United States. The act's institution, which continues to influence immigration policy today, would be the most far-reaching accomplishment of both Grant's and Stoddard's racist diatribes.

Grant and Stoddard are part of a longer genealogy of thought that was first named "eugenics" by the British scientist Francis Galton in 1883.[8] Galton, a cousin of Charles Darwin and influenced by his *Origin of Species*, first posited an argument in *Hereditary Genius: An Inquiry into Its Laws and Consequences* (1869), in which he claimed that genius is always inherited and thus runs through certain families and races. Galton wanted to institute an agenda of "positive eugenics," where families from "good stock" would be encouraged to reproduce so as to increase the number of fitter British citizens. In the United States, Charles Davenport was an early adopter of Galton's ideas, but with a stronger emphasis on negative eugenics, which sought to isolate "weak" and "dysgenic" families so that measures might be taken to prevent their reproduction. By the early twentieth century, eugenics, particularly in its "negative" form, was implemented as an American science with researchers publishing case studies and numerous books, such as Henry Goddard's *Kallikak Family*.[9] The sociologists Nicola Beisel and Tamara Kay take a similar approach to examine why abortion became regulated in the late nineteenth century and argue against previous paradigms that have pointed to the American Medical Association's drive to medicalize the practice. As they argue, "Claims that physicians played on fears of independent women miss what was at stake: Anglo-Saxon control of the state and dominance of society."[10] Beisel and Kay continue to explain that shifting demographics in the late nineteenth century caused by a rise of immigration to the United Sates led to anxiety about what constitutes an American citizen and how power would be racially distributed. By passing laws that outlawed abortion, a practice that Beisel and Kay suggest was mostly used by white women,[11] the state could enforce the continued reproduction of whiteness and institute laws that allowed for the control of women's bodies. As women, and particularly white women from middle- and upper-class homes, were told that their national duty was reproduction, abortion became associated with an evasion of that duty and a betrayal of country. For Beisel and Kay the entanglement of abortion with raced policy becomes a demonstration of the intersectionality of race, class, and gender.[12] However, I will argue that the AMA's antiabortion stance was implicated in the demarcation of populations into racial types as a means to stabilize and legitimize racial and class hierarchies and as a way to implicate the medical profession in upholding those hierarchies.

Beisel and Kay focus their essay less on the medical regulation of abortion and more on state policy. Even though present-day physicians would debunk eugenics as pseudoscience, licensed medical doctors from the mid-nineteenth century and into the mid-twentieth century took eugenic ideology seriously in their writings and practice. Since the American Medical Association passed a resolution in 1859 condemning abortion and urging physicians to refuse women who sought the procedure,[13] articles emerged in leading medical journals that connected abortion to what was then called "race suicide." In the 1906 issue of the *Journal of the Missouri State Medical Association*, Dr. T. F. Lockwood writes, "If mothers had full control of conception and gestation, it would be but the expiration of the present generation until the final extinction would come. The civilized portion of the globe would be depopulated by the follies of a people who would willingly sacrifice an entire nation merely for present social enjoyment and selfish motives."[14] A few years later, in the middle of World War I, Dr. Fred Taussig makes the connection between abortion and eugenics even more explicit when he writes in the *Interstate Medical Journal*, "The slaughtering of millions of men in the present war makes it incumbent upon us to take measures at once to replenish as rapidly as possible the waste in human material, or we shall find ourselves seriously hampered on all sides of our development."[15] He continues to argue that if reproduction does not increase among the fit, then the sickly, degenerate, and epileptic will constitute a greater portion of the population because they are not killed by war. In the same year, an article published by Dr. Oswald Beckman in the *California State Journal of Medicine* argues that if abortion continues to be practiced at the same rate, then "it will annihilate the nation, or that portion of it which has been the backbone in times past."[16] These physicians were already consciously employing the language of eugenics—using phrases like "waste in human material," "the civilized portion of the globe," and "the backbone [of the nation]"—to argue that if abortion continued to be practiced among middle-class, white Americans, then Stoddard's prediction of the end of a eugenic Anglo-Saxon America would be realized.

Eugenics is obviously primarily concerned with populations, and its prime concern is making sure they are clearly demarcated, controlled, and regulated. Legislating abortion became one tactic for securing the management of American populations according to a eugenic logic, and by the 1920s popular novels began making eugenic anxiety and its ties to abortion politics apparent. Foucault argued in his lectures on governmentality that government in the liberal state works by deploying tactics rather than by employing laws,[17] and the outlawing of abortion works as a prime example of his argument. The laws that forbade abortion would have done little to deter American women from finding ways to obtain the procedure, and in fact, many women continued to seek abortions even after antiabortion laws were passed. Yet, as Foucault argues, governmentality also works by using the family as an instrument, and thus antiabortion sentiments become part of that instrument by setting up norms that are meant to shape people's behaviors. While Foucault's theories hint at the gendered nature of governmentality, his theories don't explicitly acknowledge how women's roles in the family are specifically targeted. He writes that government is concerned with "men in their relations, their links,"[18] but he doesn't quite explain how this concern expresses itself. In the pages that follow I'll argue that popular literature in the early twentieth century functions as one form of governmentality. It creates relations and links between reader and character but also between readers who shared a work between them. The novels discussed below became one nexus within the circuit of power that used a eugenic discourse to shape a shifting American population. These novels also make explicit how governmentality is always a gendered and racialized form of exercising power, for it works through the threat of dividing populations into segments.

Viña Delmar's 1928 novel, *Bad Girl*, the first work I will examine in this chapter, was published shortly after the institution of the 1924 Immigration Act, when anxiety about whiteness was especially elevated because of the recent waves of immigration to the United States. The novel, with its vague observations about race, when read against its disciplining grain, participates in the widely circulating eugenic fears.[19] I will then turn to Christopher Morley's *Kitty Foyle*, published in 1939, which marks the beginning of World War II, with its very real and wide-scale institution of eugenic policies. *Kitty Foyle* is more complicated in its treatment of race and abortion because, by the late 1930s, Hitler's racist diatribes and eventual actions had changed what eugenics meant both in the United States and in Europe. Finally, I contrast Sinclair Lewis's *Ann*

Vickers with these two novels. Chronologically sandwiched between *Kitty Foyle* and *Bad Girl* with its 1933 publication, it provides a conflicted account of Ann Vickers's decision to abort and her relationships with several men from different ethnic and class backgrounds. Thus I see these three novels as experimenting with abortion and population politics in ways that make apparent the link among race, reproduction, and national identity.[20]

Bad Girls and Class Desire

Bad Girl was extraordinarily popular in the few years following its publication. Delmar's novel, while currently out of print, was a huge best seller when it was first published. It was also made into a play and an Oscar-nominated film in the year of its publication. I've chosen to focus on this text because it nicely demonstrates the way shame and sexuality encompass both the individual and population, but also because it was "the book everybody read, whether he admitted it or not."[21] *Bad Girl* tells a story of individuated bodies and, within this narrative, a story about the regulation of populations.[22] It follows the story of Dot Haley and Eddie Collins's relationship, from their initial encounter on a docked ship where a party for "the masses" is going on, to their marriage, to Dot's subsequent discovery of her pregnancy, to the birth of her son. Both Dot and Eddie come from working-class backgrounds. Dot's father is unemployed, her mother is dead, and her older brother, Jim, supports the family. Eddie recalls accompanying his mother to her job as a housekeeper; he refuses to talk about his father, presumably because of his shameful working-class behavior. The novel is in part the story of Dot and Eddie's slow rise in class position. When Dot realizes she is pregnant, she hesitates to tell Eddie because she worries that he will not want a child; they are not quite financially stable, but more important, it would mean that any disposable income they may have would go toward the child. Eddie in turn senses Dot's hesitancy and feels wary of expressing any enthusiasm. As a result, they both mistake each other's emotions, and Dot feels she should obtain an abortion because it is what Eddie desires. While the novel reads like the simple story of a young couple's misadventures, surrounding them are populations of people reminding them of who they are not.

When they visit Dot's friend Maude in an upscale part of town, Dot notes, "Here one would find no steps full of gossiping uncorseted Jewesses, no squalling, dirty-faced babies. The quietness of Alexander

Avenue demanded quiet, and noisy, ill-bred families who came 'looking for rooms' were always repelled by the aloofness of the old brown houses."[23] This description demonstrates how the novel has already internalized a eugenic ideology to explain difference between populations. "Ill-bred families" shy away from Alexander Avenue not because they know they would not be welcomed, the prices of rooms would be too high, and the landlords would refuse to rent to them, but because a stronger force naturally repels them and distances them from houses where women properly wear corsets, babies are always clean and well behaved, and families can trace their lineage back several generations through Anglo-Saxon ancestors. In the language of the novel, as in eugenic philosophy, the lines between raced populations can never be crossed. Later in the novel, when Dot is placed in a sanatorium for two weeks to heal from the birth of her child, she notes that the clinic is surrounded by homes populated by African Americans. During her labor pains she can hear them laughing and singing outside.[24] From her bed, she watches them through the window of her room; in the evening, she notes, "the house in back was just beginning to show signs of life. The negroes had slept the day away."[25] The people Dot watches are never named; they are a population differentiated from Dot and Eddie by their incapacity to be productive. While Eddie works hard to support his family and Dot recuperates from childbirth, the community of African Americans wiles the day away. Yet Dot and Eddie are part of a population as well, composed of the white Anglo-Saxon middle class (or those striving to be middle class), who determine their individuality through differentiation from African Americans, immigrants, and Jews en masse.

In an earlier scene, Dot and Eddie visit a Chinese restaurant, and for a few paragraphs the novel is focalized through its owner, Herbert Yet Sim Nom, who has consciously constructed the restaurant as a westerner's orientalist fantasy. Yet Sim Nom also organizes his customers by type, but not ones dependent on a raced or classed position. Instead there are those customers who walk in and are awed by the décor and buy into its orientalist mystique, those who are indifferent to the scene around them and blindly consume their food, and those who are disgusted by the atmosphere he has created. Eddie is an example of the second type and that most detested by Yet Sim Nom because his painstaking work of seducing his presumably white clientele goes unnoticed, whereas the naïve Dot is of course the first type, who falls in love with the place and its carefully constructed romantic aura. Yet Sim Nom notices that Dot "wanted to be part of the swaying, squirming mass"[26]—the exact type of customer he wants his business to attract. He finds Eddie stupid and scornful for not sharing Dot's eager excitement. However, Eddie is also the novel's modest hero because he is the mobilizing force in moving Dot into the middle class. In fact, later in the same scene Eddie compares himself to Dot's friend Maude, and for the first time "there was a middle-class oath forming in his brain. 'He'd be God damned if a woman of his would ever tell a filthy story.'"[27] With Eddie's words, the novel presents the white middle class as a break away from "the swaying, squirming mass," which seduces Dot so easily, but which Eddie recognizes as deceptively romantic and cheap. Through Eddie's eyes, Yet Sim Nom and the orientalist mystique he constructs are dangerously destructive because they seduce naïve visitors into an unindividualized, badly behaved mass that disallows the move toward a comfortable middle-class existence. In Eddie's logic—and the novel's—only through achieving middle-class status can he attain the liberal privileges of individuated and autonomous citizenship. However, by constructing this logic, the novel also contributes to a eugenic and orientalist discourse that assumes the middle class as white and the "oriental" as challenging that ideal through its propagation of a dysgenic and dangerous mass.

In a scene that comes close to the novel's end, Dot is lying in a sanatorium, healing from the birth of her son, when she has a conversation with one of the other new mothers in the ward. Her companion tells her about her "Jewess" sister-in-law "who had had eleven abortions," and she informs Dot that when this woman comes to visit, Dot "would know her by the big diamond ring she wore."[28] Dot's position in the sanatorium places her in a liminal space between two classes. Told by her respectable and expensive doctor that giving birth in a sanatorium is the proper thing to do, yet unable to afford a private room, Dot chooses to spend two weeks in the sanatorium in the ward, where four women from potentially different classes and positions might share a room. The story Dot's temporary roommate tells her contradicts the popular narrative told by historians of abortion. Starting in the late nineteenth century, abortion began to be associated with "the poor, the socially desperate, and the unwed."[29] Whether this was actually the case, as chapter 2 demonstrates, Margaret Sanger advanced the connection among impoverished women, eugenics, and abortion in the *Birth Control Review*. Yet *Bad Girl* reveals another layer that links abortion to eugenics when it uses the example of a wealthy Jewish woman to condemn abortion. In this instance, the novel describes abortion not as a practice solely used by naïve working-class girls, but as a reviled choice made by a raced population (here Jewish) that Dot, as a white woman, can distinguish herself from. Bauer reads this scene as associating reproductive control with "the abortive Jews, as well as the bourgeois Jew, who is financially rather than physically reproductive."[30] In this way abortion figures as a means to distinguish populations, paralleling the bind among race, motherhood, and reproduction in literary productions, as theorized by Allison Berg, Laura Doyle, and Alys Eve Weinbaum.[31] Berg, in particular, argues that "the rhetorical and literary uses of motherhood in the early twentieth century reveal the inherent contradictions of maternalist ideology, which served both to articulate a universal womanhood and to reinforce racial hierarchy."[32] In *Bad Girl* abortion figures into this formula as a means to prescribe to white, middle-class women how they must not behave if they are to conform to the ideals of universal womanhood and its contingency on motherhood.

Medical journals from the first half of the twentieth century also suggest that while most physicians denounced abortion, they did acknowledge that it was practiced by women of all classes and races. In the *New York Medical Journal*, Dr. Rabinowitz condemns abortion but admits that "criminal abortions are now being performed in all parts of the city, among all classes of society, and the dire results that frequently follow in its wake are just as gruesome in the palace as in the hovel."[33] Dr. E. M. Buckingham, writing in the *Cincinnati Lancet and Observer*, debunks the myth that single women seek abortion more frequently than married women and goes on to exclaim, "In the first place, and with what convincing force, does the idea come home to every high toned man and woman of desecrating the lofty marriage relation to a mere convenience for the gratification of lust? What a letting down of all the high and holy ideas of man and wife is this!"[34] Dr. P. Michinard also concludes that married women are to blame. He argues in front of an audience attending a symposium on criminal abortion in New Orleans that "it is had recourse to principally by married women, and very rarely seen among the unmarried. And I wish to say right here that the husbands are rarely to blame, showing that the man is not so bad after all."[35] Implicit in all these medical critiques of married women who have abortions is that they are evading their responsibility by refusing to become mothers, and, as Buckingham makes most explicit, they are also desecrating the institution of marriage. As Dot's close friend Edna tells her in *Bad Girl*, having already internalized this ideology, women who have abortions are "dames who'd shoot their fingers off to evade going to war if they were men."[36]

An abortion never actually occurs in *Bad Girl*, but the possibility that it might consumes the plot for twenty-five pages. Both Dot and Eddie misread each other and think that neither wants to have a child. This misunderstanding comprises the plot for almost the rest of the novel because not until its closing page, after the baby is born, do Dot and Eddie finally realize that they both want the child. Yet besides functioning as a device to complicate the plot, the misunderstanding is used as a means to condemn abortion and link it to naïve and irresponsible behavior. Eddie continues to emphasize that the choice to reproduce is Dot's, even as he secretly condemns abortion. When her friend Sue gives her pills that she claims will cause an abortion, but they fail, Eddie asks Dot, "What are you going to do now?"[37] Later, after she visits the abortionist and has a frightening experience, Eddie contemplates her indecision as the narrative focalizes through him:

> Poor kid! Trying to make up her mind. Well, she'd have to come to a decision by herself. A man would have a hell of a nerve to tell her to go ahead and have the baby. It was her job to bear the pain, her job to tend the little thing for years to come. What right had a man to say what she should do? Advice in the opposite direction was an impossibility. It was murder as Eddie saw it, murder to snuff out the little germ of life that flickered so uncertainly, that little germ that grew up to be a kid in overalls with a dirty face who asked for pennies and was proud of his Daddy.[38]

Even as Edna, Dot's friend and mother figure, persuades her not to have the abortion because she risks blood poisoning or death, Eddie still insists that "it's up to her."[39] While Dot never learns about his antiabortion beliefs, readers do and are thus emotionally caught in the tangled miscommunications that would "snuff out the little germ of life" that both Dot and Eddie desire, which they almost abort because they cannot express that desire. Regardless of how contemporary readers might view this scene, the narrative makes clear that abortion would be a disastrously wrong choice for a couple seeking to improve its position.

The novel does even more to emphasize its antiabortion rhetoric. When Dot visits the abortionist's office, one recommended to her by Maude, she intently examines the place from its outward appearance to its shabby interior: "There seemed something dread and ominous in the many drawn shades, something weird and murderous about the cat who innocently took the sun upon the front steps. . . . There was something offensive in the barrenness of the doctor's table. . . . The rug needed sweeping.... Dirty windows, a smeared window.... There was a damp chilliness about the room."[40] Like the uncorseted Jewesses and dirty-faced babies, the room reeks of "ill-breeding" and mismanagement. The decaying space suggests a moral decay, one that is aptly represented by the doctor who lasciviously grabs Dot's breast as she begins to dress and tells her that he likes "to help little girls out. Little single girls."[41] When Dot insists that she is married, the doctor mocks her by sarcastically noting that all girls who come to see him say that as well. He is clearly convinced that anyone seeking an abortion would be an unmarried woman who has had unforgivable, premarital sex. Thus the entire scene constructs abortion as a space of decrepitude, dread, poverty, and illicit behavior. The narrative tension in this moment becomes less about whether Dot will choose to have an abortion and more about what class or population her behavior will interpellate her into. Even if abortion is legal or accessible, its inscription as a despicable practice sought by irresponsible women regulates the very populations that seek it.

"Female Plumbing Is Just One Big Burglar Alarm"

The year 1940 was the year Margaret Sanger's journal, the *Birth Control Review*, came to an end.[42] It was also the year that found most of Europe fully immersed in a second world war, and in which the consequences of Hitler's eugenic policies were becoming more widely known in the United States. While Sanger's journal claimed that it would stop publishing because its funds were being funneled into providing aid for a wide-scaled war, I would also argue that the eugenic views expressed in her journal were becoming less popular as Americans were able to witness the horrors of eugenic ideology put into action in Germany and occupied Europe. Views on abortion and contraception were also beginning to change in the 1940s, as more women were entering the workforce and as the gains of the women's movement from the turn of the century were allowing women more independence and autonomy.[43] Reagan's historical study on abortion pre-1973 argues that beginning in 1940 attacks on abortion clinics and abortionists became more rampant. Before 1940 abortionists were usually only prosecuted if a procedure resulted in death, but in the 1940s and 1950s, state surveillance of suspected providers of abortion was instituted, and even therapeutic abortions became more difficult to obtain.[44] Reagan sees a direct correlation between this new policy of abortion regulation and a nationwide push to encourage women to have more children and embrace domesticity.[45]

If *Bad Girl* was written on the heels of the suffrage movement—it was published only eight years after women received the right to vote in national elections—and first-wave feminism, *Kitty Foyle* is coming from a place where that feminism, or at least women's right to suffrage, is already more entrenched in social consciousness, and the white-collar working woman is already a more accepted part of the workforce. *Kitty Foyle*, at least in its print version, has a more complicated position on the rising status of women in American society. Written by Christopher Morley, known in his time as a popular Philadelphia journalist and essayist, *Kitty Foyle* is narrated in the first person by the eponymous Kitty using flashbacks and foreshadowing. The nonlinear narration always maintains Kitty's quirky voice and her colloquial-isms as she recounts her childhood in a working-class Philadelphia neighborhood, her doomed romantic relationship with Wynnewood Strafford VI from the Main Line (which Kitty calls the aristocracy of Philadelphia),[46] and her more tentative romance with the Jewish Mar-cus (Mark) Eisen. Like *Bad Girl*, *Kitty Foyle* is steeped in a eugenic discourse of population demarcation. In *Bad Girl* those populations are always relegated to the shadows as mostly nameless inhabitants, but *Kitty Foyle* presents a more honest depiction of racial mixing even as it ambivalently writes against the possibility of crossing class and racial boundaries. What interests me most about this spectacularly popular novel of the early twentieth century is how, in the words of Margaret Stetz, its protagonist's "personal history was more than individual."[47]

After Kitty's mother dies, her father hires an African American woman, Myrtle, to come help with the cleaning and cooking. Even as Myrtle becomes intimately connected to the Foyle family, sharing in jokes and opinions about Kitty's dates, she is still presented as vacuum sealed within the confines of her race. As Kitty explains it, "Colored peo-ple don't have to stop and think in order to be wise; they just know about things naturally, it oozes out of them."[48] Although Kitty sketches a posi-tive picture of Myrtle and regularly confides in her, she is still presented as somewhat of a "mammy" figure, one who is foremost classified by belonging to her race. Similarly, Myrtle also feels sympathetic to Kitty's family because she "figured that Irish, like colored people, were sort of on their own, secretly at odds with the rest of the world."[49] Both Kitty and Myrtle view themselves in opposition to other more privileged popula-tions in order to delimit their own identities and affiliations.[50] Foucault argues that the construction of population first arose in its modern con-ception as precisely the means through which to regulate sexuality and ensure the normalizing effects of power. He asks whether the proliferation of discourses about sex are motivated by one concern: "to ensure population, to reproduce labor capacity, to perpetuate the form of social relations: in short, to constitute a sexuality that is economically useful and politically conservative?"[51] In *The History of Sexuality* his answer to that question is ambivalent because he shies away from umbrella statements about what technologies of power ultimately aim to achieve. However, in *Kitty Foyle*, the narrative that Morley constructs is grappling precisely with the question of how a changing attitude toward genetics and reproductive medicine also changes class and racial relations.

Morley's story is not quite as rigid as *Bad Girl*, which makes its theorizing of sexual and class transgression all the more compelling. In one of Kitty's conversations with herself, she explains that she left Wyn because "he was the product of a system. He was at the mercy of that system," and that to stay with him would have made *him* impossibly unhappy. She questions her decision to leave by asking and then answering herself, "Is it not your conviction that there are now no systems? That the whole of society is in flux? Not in—I mean not where Wyn lives."[52] Kitty's conflicted internal conversation exposes the difficult connection between the individual and the population, for what happens if an individual rebels against the population? Does the possibility of this separation undo the construction of population? Foucault stresses that a people and a population are not the same. Populations are constructed through the gathering of statistics, trends, and norms. A people are tied together by a social contract that grants them rights by interpellating them as individuals. The key to this argument is understanding that "the population is pertinent as the objective, and individuals, the series of individuals, are no longer pertinent as the objective, but simply as the instrument, relay, or condition for obtaining something at the level of the population."[53] In other words, the disciplining of individuals works to construct them into populations that see themselves as such. The social contract that forms the series of individuals does so only for the ultimate goal of shaping those bodies into a population that can be demarcated and bound.[54] Morley's *Kitty Foyle* grapples with these tensions as it negotiates interracial relationships, a troubled eugenic ideology, and the role of abortion in white women's lives.

Little critical attention has been given to *Kitty Foyle* since its brief moment of fame in the late 1930s and early 1940s.[55] Today the novel is out of print, and the name *Kitty Foyle* is more likely to be associated with the film that won Ginger Rogers an Oscar. Yet its odd and open embrace of female sexuality and racial discourses positions it as an important text because it reveals a changing view of the relationships among abortion, population management, and racial demarcations. On the one hand, Kitty mourns the loss of her potential child because "if it had been born, [it] would have been almost a gentleman because Wyn came from a cricket club family."[56] Yet she also tells herself that she would "be a better American if I married Mark than if I'd married Wyn. The more we get mixed up, I mean race mixed-up, the better. We got no time here for that kind of prejudice. But I suppose it's all right to wish they wouldn't be so hairy?"[57] Marcus Eisen, the hairy man whom Kitty refers to in the latter quotation, is an upwardly mobile Jewish doctor, who determinedly courts her. While Mark is educated and ambitious—a seemingly ideal suitor—Kitty feels repulsed by him, a reaction she attributes to his "Jewishness." After he admits to using her towel during a visit, she throws all her towels into the laundry because the thought of using the same towel as him disgusts her. Yet later, when she reflects that perhaps she should marry him, she tells herself: "I didn't like to put it in words, but that made me wonder, maybe Mark's being so racial is like Fedor's leg, something that just happened and you've got to put up with."[58] Fedor, a Russian immigrant who courts her friend Molly, lost one of his legs as a young boy. In the same scene, Molly tells Kitty that she is learning to overlook his missing leg and even admire him for how well he manages and never complains. Kitty then begins to wonder whether she should try to overlook Mark's race, implying at the same time that Jewishness is an immutable condition—like a missing limb—that makes one quite literally incomplete.[59] Even though Kitty recognizes that marrying Mark might make her "a better American," a philosophy that runs contrary to popular eugenic thought, her physical aversion to his body still constructs that union as impossible. Whereas her relationship with Wyn was filled with sexual longing and attraction, which eventually led to her pregnancy, it is precisely because she cannot imagine herself in intimate contact with Mark, a condition obviously necessary for reproduction in the early twentieth century, that she resists the idea of marriage. Thus the narrative, while radically opening the possibility of a cross-racial marriage, ultimately forecloses it because reproduction is impossible under its conditions.[60] Kitty cannot imagine producing a child with Mark because physical intimacy with him revolts her, and, more important, the pregnancy that results from her relationship with Wyn has to be aborted because it would sully Wyn's pure line of Anglo-Saxon descent.

In 1939—the year the novel was published—Nazi Germany was already fully implementing eugenic ideologies, many of them borrowed from American eugenicists. In 1933 Germany had passed the Decree for the Granting of Marriage Loans, which gave financial support to non-Jewish couples who were found to be "eugenic." A year later the Law for the Unification of Health Administration passed, specifying that the department's main purpose was to support "heredity and racial care."[61] By December 1935 Germany made its intentions more explicit with the "Reich Decree for the Medical Profession," which deemed doctors' primary responsibility the "stabilization and improvement of health, heredity value, and the race of the German people."[62] While US policies would obviously never become as wide scale and destructive as in Nazi Germany, Stefan Kühl's work has traced how particularly in the 1930s German and American eugenicists closely collaborated and borrowed from each other's work. For example, Otto Wagener, head of the Nazi Party's Economic Policy from 1931 to 1933, in a book about how the American eugenic movement influenced Hitler, claimed that Hitler had carefully studied eugenic laws passed by several states and found them quite influential in his own lawmaking. In a reverse situation, Joseph S. DeJarnette, a member of the Virginia sterilization movement, told *Time* magazine in 1935, "The Germans are beating us at our own game."[63] Therefore, when Kitty finds Mark repulsive because he is Jewish, and when she imagines Mark's "Jewishness" as being an immutable condition that he may not be able to overcome, the novel is gesturing toward a eugenic ideology that was already being shared between the United States and Germany, although the horrific implications of this ideology would not be entirely revealed for a few more years.

The novel also unfolds a narrative that often runs contrary to the nation-building project that eugenicists like Stoddard imagined. After Wyn marries a woman from his class with a similar ancestral genealogy, Kitty speculates whether "a nice girl like Ronnie hasn't slowed up the Strafford family for quite a few generations; just because she's a nice well-bred girl and nothing else. Mark tells me something about the cross-pattern of the genes. It sounds eeny-meeny-miny-mo like counting stitches when you turn the heel of a sock. Still and all, if I was a Family I'd like to knit some genes into it that wants to get somewhere."[64] Kitty's description of Wyn's marriage is both invested in a eugenic understanding of race and at the same time resistant to it. On the one hand, she thinks that although Ronnie is "well-bred," her conservative and old-fashioned beliefs and behaviors will be detrimental to the Strafford

Family. However, she implants the same eugenic logic of inheritance to support her theory that Ronnie's genes are somehow insufficient, and she is wedded to the theory that the Straffords make up a "Family," with a capital "F." Thus Kitty, and also implicitly the narrative voice of the novel, is unable to detach herself from a hierarchical formulation of race and reproduction. While she longs to step out of the system that indicts her relationship with Wyn, she is still interpellated into its constructions of "genetically" differentiated populations. Similarly, when she sees a three-year-old Jewish boy on the street, she simultaneously thinks, "The Jewish hasn't come out on his features yet but you can see it there ready for when it'll be needed," and "That kid's my candidate for the year 2000. If he keeps away from Hitler, that is. . . . He's my secret candidate for the Future. My baby could have been going strong in 2000; at least he wouldn't be 70 yet, and with all those wonderful genes."[65] Kitty, like the novel's narrative, is conflicted: as she imagines a more racially harmonious future and even supports it, she can't quite escape the population markers of her time that have inscribed race through reproduction and genetics.

When faced with the unintended opportunity to reproduce a Strafford, quite literally when she becomes pregnant after her affair with Wyn, Kitty is unable to imagine a situation where that child could be raised within US borders. She briefly fantasizes about having the child with him and living on a Caribbean island together and even goes as far as making a date with him to explain the news. However, as she is waiting for him at a pub, she catches sight of a newspaper announcing the engagement of Wyn to Ronnie. Immediately, she recognizes that her relationship with Wyn is an impossible fantasy and that to tell him about her pregnancy would be to relegate them both to the outskirts of society. Kitty understands that if she chooses to bear her child outside of a socially accepted marriage, then she must either face lifelong reprobation or move outside the juridically confined borders of her state. Given these choices, Kitty quickly decides that the only option for her is an abortion.

Abortion in *Kitty Foyle* is not villainized in the way it is in *Bad Girl*,[66] yet what the abortion scene forecloses is the possibility of cross-class, cross-population reproduction. Kitty's experience with the doctor she visits for the abortion differs from Dot's in a number of important ways. First, she is referred to a more legitimate doctor, one who likely charges fairly high fees and is used to seeing a more middle-class clientele, because her wealthy employer has agreed to help her cover the costs. Kitty even has an amiable conversation with the doctor before the procedure, making her feel comfortable with the process. She describes him as "skilful and decent . . . a good egg,"[67] an experience that is far removed from the foreboding atmosphere that Dot encounters when she visits the abortionist. By the late 1930s medical journals rarely printed articles condemning abortion and abortionists as they did in the earlier part of the century, although Kitty's affectionate assessment of her doctor would still have been anomalous among other public descriptions of abortions and abortionists. Furthermore, after the operation Kitty insists that she "couldn't feel any wrongness. . . . I did what I had to do."[68] Thus, abortion in the novel no longer has the disciplining force that it contains in *Bad Girl*. Kitty is not demoralized or placed on the brink of destitution because of her decision. Little in her life changes because of her decision, and she even has sex with Wyn once more after his marriage. And although the possibility of their marriage is never brought up again after the abortion, this ostensibly occurs because of Wyn's impending marriage. However, the abortion does signify the futility of their relationship. Whereas Dot's ultimate decision to complete her pregnancy represents a rise in class position and a demarcation from other idle, "unfit" populations in *Bad Girl*, Kitty's decision to have an abortion represents the difficulty of undoing constructions of population, even through reproduction.

When Kitty explains her decision to have an abortion, she asserts that it was made because "Wyn wasn't big enough to have a bastard; or the folks he had to live with wouldn't let him be. It would be making people unhappy for the sake of somebody that didn't really exist yet."[69] Thus, like Dot, Kitty makes her decision based on what she thinks others will desire. On some level Kitty recognizes the technologies that ultimately shape our actions. Early in the novel she observes: "I make my living now by trading on women's herd instincts, and I can see how useful it is for them to think they're exercising their own choices when actually they're simply falling in line with what some smart person has doped out for them."[70] Kitty seems to grasp the mechanisms of discipline and to even understand that her choices are not always her own. Given the impossibility of a continued relationship with Wyn and the grueling hardship of single motherhood, which would be socially stigmatized and financially challenging, Kitty decides on an abortion because she has been disciplined as a working-class woman not to expect that Wyn will ever marry her. The relationship with Mark that follows only stresses the rigid markers of population and the powerful controlling discourses of eugenics that normalize reproductive practices. As Kitty describes after a doctor confirms her pregnancy: "It's funny that feeling 'But things like this don't happen to *me*.' I felt like one of those assy letters to the Woman's Page."[71] When Kitty becomes pregnant, she recognizes herself, perhaps for the first time, as part of a population of working-class women whose illicit pregnancies function to keep them within the confines of their class, race, and social status. She's no longer just idiosyncratic Kitty, but part of a population of "assy" letter writers whose bodies are shaped through a biopolitics that works to simultaneously maintain racial demarcations and hegemonic norms.

Ann Vickers: A Counterargument

In 1930 Sinclair Lewis became the first American to win the Nobel Prize in Literature. The first novel he published after the award, *Ann Vickers*, in 1933, now receives little attention compared to *Babbitt*, *Main Street*, or even *Elmer Gantry*. Yet in 1933 Americans were watching Lewis because of his recent international recognition, and *Ann Vickers* became a best seller, was translated into thirteen languages upon its publication, and was soon made into a Hollywood film. Wedged between *Bad Girl* and *Kitty Foyle*, the novel is more complicated and nuanced in its presentation of abortion. Initially the narrative produces a strong argument in favor of legal abortion, and Ann Vickers successfully has an abortion and seeks one for one of her charges in the settlement house that employs her as a social worker. Yet soon after her abortion, she is filled with regret, and while she continues her feminist, career-oriented pursuits, as the novel progresses, she becomes more obsessed with having a child and finding a romantic partner.

Ann Vickers was greeted with mixed responses. The *New York Times* reviewed it favorably, describing Ann as having a life independent of her author, and (wrongly) predicted that the novel "will surely take its place with the major creations of Sinclair Lewis."[72] Yet a review in the *Journal of Criminal Law and Criminology* critically ended on this note: "Another question that must be asked is whether Ann Vickers is representative of the average woman. Ann, the flighty and unconventional woman, who reaches for freedom and outlet, engages in free love, practices abortion and adultery, plays the role of reformer, and then relapses to the unconventional—to concede that she is typical of the average woman is to blast our faith in womanhood."[73] Reading this review, one wonders whether the *Times* describes Ann Vickers as not pleasing "uncompromising feminists" because by the end of the novel, "more than anything else, she realized, she wanted to be loved and she wanted a child." At the same time the Catholic Church in the United States condemned the novel, calling it obscene and labeling it "smut" that tries to "perfume sin and garb it in rainbows."[74] This mixed response to the novel is unsurprising; *Ann Vickers*, unlike *Bad Girl* and *Kitty Foyle*, is slippery. At times it appears in favor of feminism and reproductive freedom, and then at other times, it seems to retreat its radical argument to turn Ann into a conventional woman, who believes that without love and a child she will never find fulfillment.[75]

The novel doesn't shy away from calling Ann a feminist. When she was still a child living in the small midwestern town of Waubanakee, she shocked her Sunday school teacher by declaring, "Why shouldn't Mrs. Lot look back at her own hometown? She had all her neighbors there, and maybe she'd had some lovely times with them. She just wanted to say good-bye to Sodom!" The narrative describes this as the moment when "she first exploded as a feminist."[76] As a college student in the small women's college Point Royal in Connecticut, Ann formed the Socialist Club, which had about six members. Mostly its members discussed suffrage, but

> once Tess Morrissey, a stern young woman, said they ought to study birth-control, and they gasped and talked with nervous lowered voices. "Yes, women should be able to govern their own destinies," Ann whispered. But when Tess, from her work in biology, murmured of actual methods of control, they looked uncomfortable and began to discuss the beauties of woman suffrage, which was to end all crime and graft.[77]

Later Ann might have wished she had listened more carefully to Tess, for when she begins her first affair, with Lafayette (Lafe) Resnick, a Jewish captain who is about to be drafted to fight in the war, the issue of birth control comes up again. Lafe warns Ann that their unprotected sex might result in pregnancy, but Ann responds lightly, "Things like that don't happen to a social worker. No, really; don't laugh. They just don't, somehow. Besides, I could do something. . . . I talk so authoritatively to the girls at Corlears House about sex, but I don't really know much about the technique of not having babies. But I can find out."[78]

In contrast to *Kitty Foyle* little is made of Lafe's identity as Jewish. He is clearly assimilated into American culture and even makes fun of his identity. When they first meet at a party at the settlement house where Ann works as a social worker, he flirts with her and then says, "Let's get out of this—this damn military-plus-Yiddish atmosphere. Little too kosher—." At first Ann is shocked and begins to think she mistakenly took him to be Jewish, but he confirms and mockingly says, "Of course I am, idiot! Grandfather a rabbi (or so my dad claims; but I think he ran a butcher shop on the side)."[79] Whereas Mark's Jewishness repulses Kitty, Ann finds it romantic and attractive: "He seemed to her—just then— so gay, so needle-fine, so honest about his fear, while the other recruits pretended to bland blond heroism."[80] Her affair with Lafe is her first romance after an adult life that has been admirably committed to her career: after she earns her BA, she works as a suffragist, a social worker, and a prison reformer. She dismisses advances from various men, including her handsome college professor, and insists that as a feminist and socialist her life will be dedicated to a higher cause. Yet Lafe disappoints her. After their short affair, he moves to a military base in Pennsylvania, where he soon meets a Jewish family with two marriageable daughters. By the time Ann finds out she is pregnant, his relationship with one of them has clearly begun.

Ann Vickers presents a moving case for why abortion should be legal, while also portraying Ann facing deep regret for her decision. Unlike *Bad Girl*, and even *Kitty Foyle*, it realistically portrays how both working-class and educated women sought abortions, yet it differentiates Ann from the naïve and Jewish Tessie Katz, who like Ann finds herself pregnant after her lover is transferred to his base and stops writing her letters. Tessie is described as "young, vibrant, hook-nosed, handsome, a fur worker who sat about the Corlears Hook Settlement and often brought her troubles (mostly amorous) to Ann."[81] When both women discover they have lovers who are separated from them because of war, they are brought closer, despite Ann's superior position as a social worker in Tessie's settlement. The novel consciously describes this as an erasure of racial difference: "One afternoon she invited Tessie Katz to have coffee with her out of the majolica cups, and the two girls, the volatile city Jewess and the small-town Mid-Western Nordic, forgot all differences as they contested for chances to talk about Morris and Captain Resnick."[82] As time passes both women hear less frequently from their lovers, and after ten weeks Ann begins suspecting that the nice Jewish family that often invites Lafe for dinner has a daughter who interests him for marriage. At the same time, Tess comes crying because Morris, her lover, hasn't written in weeks, and she suspects that she is pregnant. She tells Ann:

That *Mamzer!* Oh, I wouldn't mind. But I guess he's got a new girl and he'll tell me—oh gee, you don't know how violent that guy gets—he'll tell me to go jump in the lake! If I only had a fellow like yours! But it's my Pop. We're orthodox, and Morris, he ain't hardly better than a Goy. Honest, if I were to marry him, Pop would come after us both with a shotgun. And if I was to have a kid without marrying, he'd come after me with a couple of guns![83]

While Ann doesn't admit to Tessie the similarity of her own position, back in her room she recognizes the irony: "Wish I was like you, Miss Vickers!" she groans, in bitter caricature of Tessie Katz; then, "I've got to face it. Ten weeks. There's no doubt. But—*me*—Ann Vickers! And I can't even write to Lafe that I'm going to have a baby, unless he shows me some sign that he wants me. I don't know what to do!"[84] Almost mockingly—for Ann earlier confidently bragged to Lafe that girls like her, educated social workers, just don't become pregnant out of wedlock with a deserted lover—the novel reminds readers that the consequences of sex do not discriminate between women of all classes and races.

Tessie immediately decides that she needs to have an abortion, and she explains to Ann how she unsuccessfully tried to force miscarriage. She then pleads with Ann to help her find a reliable abortionist, and in the most proabortion moment of the novel—and perhaps in early twentieth-century American literature—Ann favorably considers her request:

> Instantly, in ten seconds, Ann skimmed through the whole subject of abortion and came out convinced. . . . Life demanded that normal women bear children, without the slightest consideration of the laws passed by preachers, or by small-town lawyers in legislatures. But these laws still remained. And society punished by a lifetime imprisonment in the cells of contempt any girl who was false to them and still true to the life within her that was the only law she knew. Then it was as righteous for a girl thus threatened to flee from her neighbors' spitefulness as it was for a revolutionist to flee from the state's secret police.[85]

And so Ann responds: "Yes, I'll find someone. Got any money?" And when Tessie answers negatively, she agrees to pay for the procedure too. In deciding to break the law to help Tessie, Ann concludes that unjust laws can be broken if they unfairly discriminate against their subjects. Interestingly, in the passage quoted above, the phrase "the life within her" doesn't reference fetal life but the inner life of the woman and her ambitions. At this moment Ann appears quite forward thinking in privileging the life of the woman over the life of the fetus, a position that was becoming increasingly uncommon in early twentieth-century America.

In fact, in 1916 Dr. Fred Taussig, in an article condemning abortion, addressed exactly the type of woman that Ann was becoming: "One group of socialist women claim that they have an absolute right to do as they choose with the products of their body and brook no interference by the state. If they do not care to shelter the child growing in their womb, it is for them to decide upon its expulsion. This extreme doctrine runs counter to all our ideals of humanity."[86] Taussig's description of "socialist women" is now the familiar argument in favor of legal abortion: that women do have a right to control their own body. Yet in the decades before *Roe v. Wade* this argument was still marginalized among more left-leaning groups. Therefore, it is even more surprising that the novel's narrative seems to concur with its heroine's proabortion conclusion as it describes Ann's predicament in ironic terms, "A physician who keeps a rich woman abed and nervous is a great and good man; a physician who saves a girl from disgrace is an intruder who, having stolen from society the pleasure of viciousness, is rightly sent to prison."[87]

Ann does find an abortionist for Tessie, described as "a youngish Italian doctor on East Broadway," who "was a kindly person, who was supporting three relatives in America and five in Italy. He played the clarinet and was a champion swimmer." Despite this rather positive description, he also caresses her shoulder and calls Ann "little girl." He does not believe her when she tells him that it's not her who is pregnant. She says, "I tell you, it's *not* myself! How could you! Ridiculous! I tell you, it's a Jewish girl who's one of my charges." For all of Ann's commitment to equality, reproductive freedom, and class struggle, when the doctor (rightly) assumes that she needs an illegal abortion, she cannot stand being mistaken for Tessie. The doctor, recognizing his mistake, reassures Ann that he hasn't upset her class hierarchy by reaffirming what she would like to believe: "You're a fine educated young lady—I could tell, the minute you come in—I was just joking about thinking it was you and not the Yid."[88] Educated, Anglo-Saxon women do not have abortions.

Ann is aware of her hypocrisy. She finally turns to her good friend Dr. Malvina Wormser for help. In explaining her situation and how she found an abortionist for Tessie that she couldn't submit to because it "would be intolerable to her dignity as a social worker," she also explains to Dr. Wormser: "We're all so democratic, we 'socially minded people,' till it comes to the marriages of our sisters and daughters, or to an operation. Then, phut!" And so, Dr. Wormser agrees to give her an abortion.

Malvina tells Ann that she has only performed five abortions in her career, and each time it was because "the patient was more valuable to the world than what I'm pleased to call my honor as a physician and citizen." After all, Dr. Wormser would likely belong to the American Medical Association, whose members were bound to its resolution to never perform abortion or assist women seeking abortion. Therefore, while agreeing to help her friend, Dr. Wormser also warns Ann that "abortion is a crime," that she "may never be able to bear a second child," that "it is abnormal and dangerous"; yet she explains that as long as patriarchy has "made our one peculiar function, child-bearing, somehow indecent and exceptional, we have to fight back and be realistic about it, and lie and conceal as much as they do."[89] With those words, Ann has her abortion. She comes out feeling not "ruined" or indignant but filled with regret.[90]

With Ann's abortion the novel also turns on its strong stance for women's reproductive freedom. As the *New York Times* review celebrates, Ann morphs into a more traditional woman; she wants to be a mother, and she begins to value this desire over her career, her education, and her ambition:

> In her earlier apprehension of being disgraced, Ann thought solely of her own dilemma. Neither she nor the realistic Tessie Katz had been so imaginative as to give much heed to the rights of the coming babies. Now, unreasoningly, her baby became a reality to her, and she longed for it, wistfully, then savagely, accusing herself of its murder. It became an individual; she missed it as though she had actually nursed it and felt its warmth. She began to want it more than she wanted any career, or the triumph of any beautiful principle.[91]

She imagines that her pregnancy would have resulted in a baby girl, and she names her Pride. Years later, when she works in a jail, she meets a woman imprisoned for infanticide. Miserable in her new position, yet insistent that she must continue, she thinks, "That's why I'm here. That's why I must stay here. I killed my baby, too."[92] *Ann Vickers* is more ambivalent, more nuanced, more conflicted. Like *Bad Girl* and *Kitty Foyle* it portrays a society still influenced by eugenics and divided by racial lines, even as Ann does not think twice when she begins an affair with a Jewish man. It also portrays the current American struggle with how much freedom women can have over their reproductive lives, yet it cannot have Ann let go of dreams to become a mother. It wants to privilege maternal life over fetal life, yet at the end Ann gives her fetus an individuality, a name, and even an imagined future that can never be realized. It does not allow her to let go of her remorse, for when she does finally have a child at the age of forty, she bears a boy who can then never replace the daughter she believes she lost.

When Bad Girls Go to Movies

Bad Girl, Ann Vickers, and *Kitty Foyle* were all made into films in the years following their publications.[93] Unsurprisingly, all three films had to be heavily censored to meet the requirements of the Motion Picture Production Code, colloquially called the Hays Code, the 1930 film guidelines that banned any reference to sex or other topics that were deemed morally unacceptable, including abortion, although the code makes no explicit reference to it. Importantly for the adaptation of *Kitty Foyle, Ann Vickers*, and *Bad Girl*, laws, both civil and "natural," could not be mocked, nor could there be any sympathetic representations of people breaking those laws.[94]

Because of the Hays Code, and because production studios knew they would have to heavily censor Delmar's novel before it was "picturized," it took three years from the publication of *Bad Girl* to turn it into a film. Two studios approached Jason S. Joy, head of the Studio Relations Committee, which was responsible for ensuring films met code guidelines, before Fox Film Corporation agreed to take on the project and meet censorship guidelines. In fact, Joy had read the novel the year it was published and wrote to Hays's executive assistant that he thought the novel "was spicy and well written," but that it did not represent "picture possibilities" because there was "an illegitimate child, several illegal operations, and a sordid, painful sequence of obstetrics."[95] Fox, however, readily agreed to comply with the code with little debate—to Joy's relief—and excised the scene depicting Eddie and Dot's premarital sex and any reference to abortion.[96] Histories of film censorship all depict Joy's chairmanship of the Studio Relations Committee as mostly ineffectual. Joy could recommend that a studio cut an "inappropriate" scene, yet he could do little to enforce it. In an attempt to strengthen the code, Hays briefly replaced Joy with James C. Wingate and then by 1934 renamed the committee the Production Code Administration (PCA) and appointed Joseph I. Breen, a staunch Catholic and believer in the code, who began strictly enforcing the code's rules. *Ann Vickers* became one of the first films in this new testing ground.

In 1933 RKO Pictures bought the expensive rights to *Ann Vickers*, which was guaranteed to be a best seller because of Lewis's recent Nobel

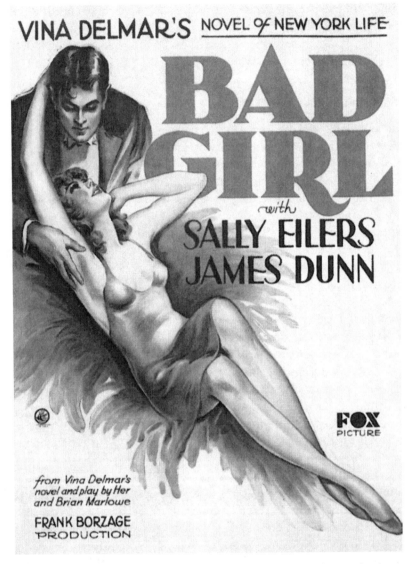

FIGURE 4. The movie poster for *Bad Girl* presents a somewhat misleading version of the film, as it depicts Dot in a sensationalized and risqué position, a stance that would have likely scandalized the "picturized" version of Dot. (Image courtesy of Photofest)

Prize. By code regulation the script was sent to the PCA, where Breen reviewed it and wrote to James C. Wingate, his superior at the time, that "not in years have I read anything quite so vulgarily offensive. The whole thing is so definitely out of line that I respectfully suggest that you lose no time in letting the R.K.O. people know that this script *will not do* and must be radically changed if its production is to be carried through. I see great trouble, both for the industry and the company, if this script, based upon a current best seller *which is known to be vile and offensive* is not checked at once."[97] In a letter to the film's producer, Wingate faithfully repeated this message, only to receive an angry and incompliant response from the producer that he was "in thorough disagreement" with Wingate's reading of the film. The tension between the men escalated; telegraphs and letters were furiously exchanged among Hays, Breen, and Wingate; and eventually Hays decided to communicate directly with RKO's president to settle the matter. At the end, RKO produced a film that somewhat censors the story, although it still depicts Ann's adultery and illegitimate child, but in the film she is also expelled from her position as head of the women's prison for her actions, so that viewers could see that her actions were punished. Her abortion is also turned into a stillbirth. Wingate settled for this revised version, although he felt that the heroine still did not show enough remorse for her actions. Several years later, in 1937, when Breen was firmly established as head of the now-stringent PCA, he reversed Wingate's concessions and asked RKO to withdraw their certification for *Ann Vickers*.

Ann Vickers was one of the last films that was allowed some leniency in complying with the Hays Code. With Breen heading the PCA beginning in 1934, there was no question that *Kitty Foyle* would be censored as it was adapted to film. While the film *Kitty Foyle* also omits any direct reference to Kitty's abortion, there are more obvious allusions to its occurrence. In order to portray Kitty's sexual relationship with Wyn, which is a central component of the novel's plot, the film version has the couple marry, then consummate the relationship, only to annul the marriage shortly after. It is during their brief marriage that Kitty presumably becomes pregnant, but by the time she discovers her condition, her marriage to Wyn is over. Rather than willingly terminate her pregnancy, the film suggests that she carries it to term, only to give birth to a stillborn boy, whom she never sees. The infant's premature death ultimately serves the same purpose as the abortion in the novel as it demonstrates, quite literally, the dead end of Kitty and Wyn's relationship because it is reproductively unfeasible. Even as the Hays Code makes the explicit depiction

FIGURE 5. A scene from the film *Ann Vickers*. Here Ann is recovering after the birth of her stillborn son. In the novel a similar scene takes place after Ann's abortion. (Image courtesy of Photofest)

of abortion taboo because, in the logic of the code, depicting an abortion would condone the practice, it implicitly disciplines viewers (and especially those who previously read the novel) to regard abortion as illicit and transgressive. Thus, while the novel refuses to condemn abortion, the film regressively inscribes an antiabortion ethic.

Another striking difference between the film and the novel is that Mark is never portrayed as Jewish or ethnicized in any way. Rather, the film presents him as a hard-working doctor with long hours, who primarily helps working-class families. In an early scene, Kitty helps him deliver an infant in a tenement apartment. Few preparations were made for the child's arrival, and Kitty has to construct a makeshift cradle for him out of a cardboard box and a tablecloth. Kitty enthusiastically greets the baby, but Mark scornfully replies that the child would have been better off if it had never been born. Because the film presents Mark as ethnically white, it frames his relationship with Kitty as the most desirable option for her. In the last scene of the movie, Kitty has to choose between Mark and Wyn, and she unequivocally chooses marrying Mark.

Perhaps the film's most important diversion from the novel is in its opening framing scenes, which depict an anonymous woman dressed in nineteenth-century clothing and traditionally pursued by a young man, which ends in a happy and serene marriage. In a second scene, suffragettes rally for the vote, while the same woman is dressed in a more modern early twentieth-century style, and as she boards a trolley, several men jostle her, refusing to acknowledge her or give up a seat. The film then jumps to introduce Kitty. Implicit in this opening is a critique of the modern woman, who in order to gain independence has given up the easy choices of marriage and men's respect. These opening scenes thus emphasize what the novel only hints at: that this new system—what Kitty, in both the novel and the play discussed below, calls a "system in flux"—has ultimately destabilized an order that once functioned smoothly and easily, but that with the unsettling of population markers has now wreaked chaos particularly on women's own bodies. Yet the play, which provides the tamest version of the story, also finally makes feasible Kitty's marriage to Wyn.

In 1942 *Kitty Foyle* was scripted into a play, first performed that August at the Michiana Shores Theatre. While the characters in this version remain the same, the overall arc of the story has dramatically changed, especially as the performance closes with the presumed marriage of Wyn and Kitty. Mark Eisen is mentioned only in name and only in passing as Kitty's boyfriend in New York; as in the film, there's no reference to his ethnicity or to Kitty's ambivalent relationship with his Jewishness. A refrain throughout the play is Kitty's insistence that "today the social system is in a state of flux."[98] While her Irish father and the African American maid, Myrtle, seem skeptical of this change, only in this scripted version of the story does Kitty prove them wrong. Interestingly, the play emphasizes that Kitty is only one-fourth Irish—a point that's also made in the film but never appears in the novel. And Wyn's family, particularly his mother, feels persuaded by the union because she acknowledges, "The Straffords need new blood."[99] However, she attempts to convince Kitty to go to finishing school for a few years so that she can learn to be a society lady, terms that Kitty refuses to accept. Ultimately, Wyn agrees to follow her to New York against his family's wishes, and the play closes with Wyn and Kitty fantasizing about their yet unborn—and presumably unconceived—son. As Wyn announces, "Wynnewood Strafford the seventh should be quite a boy," Kitty corrects him to trace a

Figure 6. The movie poster for *Kitty Foyle*. (Image courtesy of Photofest)

different genealogy: "Oh, Wyn—he's not going to be Wynnewood Strafford the seventh. We'll call him Thomas—after my father!" and the stage
direction notes that the curtain closes.[100] Thus the play, while offering
a tempered version of the novel, actually revises its eugenic slant as it
insists that Kitty's marriage to Wyn is possible and that their reproductive possibilities do not have to be aborted. Yet at the same time their
progeny must follow her genealogy since Wyn, by marrying Kitty, must
reject his.

I end this chapter with a discussion of the performed versions of *Bad
Girl*, *Ann Vickers*, and *Kitty Foyle* because they reveal the seemingly
secretive nature of abortion politics in the middle of the twentieth century. Only the staged adaptation of *Bad Girl* attempted to keep the abortion plot in its narrative, and that was quickly thwarted. The fact that even
as abortion started to appear more prominently in the plots of novels in
the early twentieth century, its depiction in plays and films, which would
have always been publicly viewed, was still forbidden suggests what Reagan describes as the "open secret" culture of abortion during the years
it was outlawed. Novel reading was done privately, and therefore more
taboo subject matter that would have been off-limits on the screen or
stage was less often censored. Women of all classes and races commonly
sought abortions in the 1920s and 1930s—the plots of *Ann Vickers*, *Kitty
Foyle*, and *Bad Girl* would not have been shocking to most of their readers had these stories been told through word of mouth. More surprising
about these novels is their frank and detailed discussion of abortion and
female sexuality, which only appears in earlier novels in more disguised
language. For example, Edith Wharton's *Summer*, published ten years
before *Bad Girl*, presents abortion in more abstract terms. In *Summer*,
Charity also visits an abortionist, but her body is not sexualized during
the visit, and the abortion ultimately never occurs. In *Bad Girl* and *Kitty
Foyle* readers could recognize themselves in Kitty and Dot because they
are not just individuals but segments of a demarcated population. It was
precisely because these novels work on the level of population—a population that today no longer exists because of the shifting forces of control
and regulation—that these novels can tell us as much about abortion in
the early twentieth century and its ties to racialized hierarchies and the
forces of eugenics.

4 /   Economies of Abortion: Money, Markets, and the Scene of Exchange

> *According to the materialist conception, the determining factor in history is, in the final instance, the production and reproduction of immediate life. This, again, is of a twofold character: on the one side, the production of the means of existence, of food, clothing, and shelter and the tools necessary for that production; on the other hand, the production of human beings themselves, the propagation of the species.*
>
> —FREDERICK ENGELS, *THE ORIGINS OF THE FAMILY*

"How much will it cost?" is the first question the protagonist of Agnes Smedley's *Daughter of Earth* asks the doctor who provides her with advice about procuring an abortion. Smedley's autobiographical novel, first published in 1929, traces her own development through radical leftist politics and openly admits that access to abortion—indeed, the politics of abortion—is always tied to money. Marie, the novel's protagonist, has two abortions, and both times she reasons with herself that an abortion "would be cheaper"[1] than carrying a pregnancy to term and raising a child. *Daughter of Earth* is perhaps not a typical example of "the scene of exchange"—the moment in many novels from the early twentieth century that depicts abortion as part of a monetary transaction—because its heroine is already attuned to Marxist readings of her world.

Yet, if a common trope were to be traced through early twentieth-century novels that discuss abortion, it would be this scene that ties abortion to economy. Usually the protagonist, or whoever in the novel is seeking an abortion, finds a doctor, midwife, or professional abortionist to perform the procedure only to discover that the cost of the abortion exceeds her expectations. In some versions the character visits the clinic or pharmacy to be told that her money will not buy her what she seeks. In Edith Wharton's *Summer*, Charity visits an abortionist only to ascertain she is pregnant (or so she convinces herself) and still owes the abortionist five dollars, which she can't afford to pay, so she leaves a precious brooch from her former lover as a down payment. This exchange haunts her until the closing scene of the novel, when she uses the money given to her by her new husband for a wardrobe to buy back her brooch, which in turn pays for the abortion she almost had. In this scene of exchange, as in several other novels that verge on condemning abortion—or more commonly abortionists—the payment demanded by the doctor is depicted as a transaction of deception, theft, and in some cases molestation. The characters never have enough money, yet they are forced to pay for a service because it was given consideration. Charity must pay the abortionist for examining her; Dot in Viña Delmar's *Bad Girl* similarly has to hand over the little money she has to the abortionist who examines her and molests her, even though she too decides not to have the procedure; and under different circumstances, Dewey Dell in William Faulkner's *As I Lay Dying* is forced to give her ten dollars to her father because she can't admit that she received the money from her lover to pay for an abortion. In all these novels, abortion is clearly portrayed as part of a market economy, yet an illicit one where transactions always involve deceit, abuse, and the disempowerment of women.[2] The merchants in this economy, by refusing to allow abortion to enter into a public and open marketplace, use the "open secret" nature of abortion to propagate a shadow economy.

Scene of Exchange I: *As I Lay Dying*

William Faulkner's modernist novel *As I Lay Dying*—a well-known work that traces the Bundrens' trek across the South during a humid, hot summer month to fulfill their wife and mother's wish to be buried in her hometown—has already been recognized as a narrative about economy and commodification. John Matthews writes that the novel draws attention to the ways in which "the language of the market" has "saturated the most private formulations of personal identity."[3] Darl, for example, a middle child in the Bundren family, in trying to capture his selfhood becomes a self that is "severally possessed"[4] because of his family's poverty, ill luck, and dependence on others in their poorly timed and badly executed expedition. Yet, if Darl struggles to gain self-possession without being shaped by market forces, then his pregnant sister, Dewey Dell, has already recognized that her individuality—her aloneness, as she calls it—is lost. When she realizes she is pregnant, she narrates, "I feel my body, my bones and flesh beginning to part and open upon the alone, and the process of coming unalone is terrible."[5] The rest of Dewey Dell's experiences in the novel are also terrible, as her body is constantly exposed and subjected to a market that she doesn't understand but in which she hopes to be able to obtain an abortion. In a novel, as Matthews points out, that is so much about economy, commodification, and commercial transactions, the appearance of abortion—of biological reproduction—as a crucial plot element has important theoretical implications about the ties between reproduction and market forces.

Dewey Dell's lover, Lafe, gives her ten dollars and tells her that with this money she can buy abortifacients from a pharmacist. While the American Medical Association's crackdown on abortionists and abortion-inducing herbs was in full effect by the early twentieth century—thereby slowing the market that in the mid-nineteenth century would make Madame Restell a rich woman—druggists could still be found who would offer women illicit remedies for unwanted pregnancies.[6] Leslie Reagan notes that by the early twentieth century ailing patients, including women looking to terminate their pregnancies, often consulted pharmacists before turning to doctors. Reagan cites one advertisement for an abortive pill that circulated during the 1922 Pageant of Progress in Chicago and promised "Curing Ladies Stomach Sick and No Menses Every Month Medicine . . . 1 ounce for $25.00."[7] The price of this abortifacient suggests that even if Lafe weren't sending Dewey Dell on a wild goose chase to find abortive pills, the ten dollars he supplied her with would not be sufficient to pay for the drugs she managed to find. However, Reagan also notes that these drugs did not always result in the desired effects. This point echoes Margaret Sanger, who complained to a friend and colleague, "We have records that 43 percent of the contraceptive chemicals on the market are absolutely useless. A woman doesn't know where else to go. She will go to the druggist and ask what to do, or her husband will ask, and the druggist will give them whatever a high-powered salesman has loaded him up with."[8] Sanger's point is a valid one; beginning in 1917 the American Medical Association began investigating the claims of various drugs on the market under a campaign titled "The Propaganda for Reform in Proprietary Medicines." As a result, the AMA discovered that many drugs were being sold with false claims that promised wide-encompassing cures without any evidence that the chemical compounds could give patients those results.[9]

Likely hearing somewhere that pharmacists could provide women with pills to restore their menses, Lafe sends Dewey Dell on a chase to find a pharmacist who will sell her these magic pills as she follows her family on a roundabout route to bury her mother. The only thing empowering Dewey Dell is that she believes she has the money to pay for what she seeks. In the first pharmacy she visits, she encounters the moralizing

Moseley, who tells her that he is a "respectable druggist" and "a thousand dollars wouldn't be enough in my store and ten cents wouldn't be enough." Yet, at first, Moseley's argument doesn't faze Dewey Dell. She begins with insisting, "I got the money to pay you." Even after Moseley explains his own moral opposition to her quest, she repeats, "He told me I could get something at the drug store. He said they might not want to sell it to me, but if I had ten dollars and told them I wouldn't never tell nobody. . . ."[10] Dewey Dell believes in the power of money—the power of exchange. Her repeated insistence that she does indeed have the money to pay for her abortion underlies her belief that with money she can get what she seeks despite people's moral objections.

Early in their conversation, after Moseley comes to understand Dewey Dell's presence in his shop, he asks her, "Is it your own, or did he act enough of a man to give you the money?" And Dewey Dell responds, "He give it to me. Ten dollars. He said that would be enough."[11] Dewey Dell believes that because she has a desire to consume a product, that product should therefore exist. Her belief resonates with Karl Marx's argument in the *Grundisse*: "Production, then, is also immediately consumption, consumption is also immediately production."[12] This argument, while seemingly very simple, actually invokes a complex understanding of subject formation. Marx argues that consumption becomes production in a double way. The first is most obvious: a product can only become a *real* product by being consumed, used. Thus consumption is the finishing touch of production. It is, he writes, "the object for the active subject." The second argument Marx makes is that consumption drives the need for production; it impels the process and the ideal. In other words, "Production creates the consumer. . . . Production not only creates an object for the subject, but also a subject for the object."[13] Implicit here is the process of subject formation. Marx is suggesting that the subject, and perhaps subjectivity, is formed by production through the act or force of consumption. However, for Dewey Dell it doesn't work this way.

Like most women seeking abortions in early twentieth-century novels, she is never allowed to enter into the contract of consumer/producer/distributor, either as a consumer or purchaser. Her only productive power is reproductive power, and if she has access to cash, then it is money that was given to her by a man. In *Summer,* in order to pay the abortionist she visits, Charity must exchange a brooch given to her by a lover; then later, to obtain the brooch, she hands over all the cash she received from her new husband. Dot in *Bad Girl* must pay for her visit with the abortionist with her husband's money since she doesn't work. Roberta in *An*

American Tragedy, which will be discussed in the next section, has to financially rely on Clyde to fund her abortion, which they are also never able to obtain. Dewey Dell's dead mother, Addie, when given the chance to narrate her own story in *As I Lay Dying,* understands that her own economic power can only be a reproductive one. When reflecting on her childbearing years, she notes, "I gave Anse Dewey Dell to negative Jewel. Then I gave him Vardaman to replace the child I had robbed him of. And now he has three children that are his and not mine."[14] Addie's equation is the result of an adulterous love affair that led to the conception of Jewel. Perhaps stubbornly, perhaps as a way to maintain autonomy and a sense of self-responsibility, Addie sees her sexual and marital relationships in economic terms. Children are property born out of negotiation and production and therefore must be properly distributed. When she married Anse, she made him an economic promise that she saw fit to keep. Addie views her marriage within the tenets of a liberal contract. As Pamela Haag argues, "one of the most basic legacies of classic liberalism—particularly evident in the postbellum context—is that it defines normative social relations as forged between theoretically equal and free agents, and transacted through *property* of a figurative or literal sort."[15] By viewing her children as parcels of property in an economic transaction with her husband—they are, she tells us, *his* and not *hers*—Addie attempts to construct herself as an equal and free liberal individual engaging with another liberal individual, who has already been given these rights because he is male. Once her transaction is complete and she has attained this freedom, she tells us, "and then I could get ready to die."[16] Unlike her mother's, Dewey Dell's attempts to engage in economic transactions are futile; her aloneness, her individuality, has slipped away almost from the opening pages of the novel. Because she cannot take part in an economic exchange—enter into a capitalist economy—the narrative suggests that the market does not recognize her as a liberal citizen.

While Moseley refuses Dewey Dell access to abortifacients, her next encounter in a pharmacy proves to be even more traumatic. This time she enters looking for a doctor, and because MacGowan, the man who happens to be behind the counter, finds her attractive, he pretends to be a physician. Again, Dewey Dell repeats three times, "I got the money," as though the sheer incantation of these words will make the desired pills appear. Since MacGowan actually has no idea how to help and is just playing at being a doctor and a pharmacist, he uses the power of his created position for his own sexual pleasure. Letting Dewey Dell know that her money will not buy anything, he explains, "You see I cant put no price on my knowledge and skill. Certainly not for no little paltry sawbuck." Dewey Dell quickly understands his meaning, and she agrees to return later for a sexual encounter if he will only give her medicine that will cause an abortion. MacGowan grabs an unlabeled bottle with a clear liquid that smells like turpentine, only hoping that he's not about to poison her because "a man that would keep poison around in an unla-belled bottle ought to be in jail, anyway."[17] Then later Dewey Dell returns at their agreed time for what the narrative implies is a sexual transaction, one that Dewey Dell only agrees to because she hopes the desired abor-tifacient might appear as a result. Money in the hands of Dewey Dell, the novel tells us, gives her no access as a consumer and a member of an economy. If anything, her attempts to enter the marketplace almost kill her. Agreeing to have sex with MacGowan is Dewey Dell's submission that money will not open the doors Lafe promised, and so, like many women before her, she hopes sex will.

Dewey Dell doesn't die. Presumably the turpentine-smelling sub-stance also doesn't produce an abortion. In her last scene in the novel, only pages before it closes with her brother's parting words, her father discovers the ten dollars hidden in her handkerchief. Excited about learning of this spare cash, Anse tells her he'll just borrow the money from her, and Dewey Dell in desperation reassures him that if she could give it to him, she would. Suspecting that the money was obtained illic-itly, he pressures Dewey Dell to tell him why she has it. However, she refuses him the knowledge. She begs him not to take it with the plea that she desperately needs it. Haag explains that "the proprietary claims of the master over his servant's labor and body made consent—and the daughter's distinct will—immaterial."[18] Similarly, Dewey Dell's need to keep her money is immaterial to Anse. Like the "beautiful victims" Haag describes in nineteenth-century seduction trials, Dewey Dell is not and is not seen by her father as a "homo economicus."[19] Anse "took the money and went out."[20] Dewey Dell is left robbed of her money and still pregnant. Whatever economic power, individuality, and autonomy she might have sought with the ten dollars and with an abortion are now stripped away. She cannot be a consumer, a player in the marketplace, and a participant in a liberal marketplace. She is not a liberal individual, the novel tells us, because she is young, poor, and pregnant. Indeed, the tenets of liberalism in early twentieth-century America work precisely to exclude single, pregnant women from the privileges of a free market, and the outlawing of abortion becomes one piece in ensuring that exclusion. For Dewey Dell, there is no new hope.

Scene of Exchange II: *An American Tragedy*

In early twentieth-century American fiction, perhaps it might be a truism to say that more than any other novelist Theodore Dreiser was concerned with American consumerism and capitalism. In a scene that Walter Benn Michaels memorializes in his reading of *Sister Carrie*, Dreiser explains to readers that money "stands for . . . stored energy" and should therefore be "paid out . . . honestly" and "not as a usurped privilege."[21] Benn Michaels explains that Dreiser is critical of Carrie because she "completely fails to grasp the relation between either value or production or value and exchange."[22] For Carrie, Benn Michaels writes, money has intrinsic not symbolic power. In presenting Carrie's desire to obtain money because she equates it with power, Benn Michaels believes that *Sister Carrie* ultimately doesn't critique the free-market forces of capitalism but is an "unabashed and extraordinarily literal acceptance of the economy that produced those conditions."[23] Benn Michaels's reading of *Sister Carrie* as representing capitalism as "an economy of desire"[24] is quite powerfully convincing; yet, when applied to *An American Tragedy*, a novel Dreiser published twenty-five years after *Sister Carrie*, cracks emerge in Benn Michaels's argument that are important for seeing the links among reproductive politics, abortion, and economy.

Dale Bauer sees Dreiser's erotic economy as "based on the fulfillment of desire, where even shoes have expression and speak to potential buyers."[25] Like Benn Michaels, Bauer uses sexual metaphors to describe the forces of capitalism. However, in *An American Tragedy* the metaphor can be flipped again so that sexual desire is described through the metaphor of capitalist desire. Clyde, the at times unsympathetic protagonist of Dreiser's 1925 epic novel, is filled with desire from the opening pages of the novel. He desires money, but almost as equally, he desires sex. In fact, his desires for both wealth and female attention are so strong that they often become entangled, and it becomes difficult to judge which force is more powerful. For example, his first love affair, with the materially obsessed Hortense, becomes as much about gaining her attention as it is about purchasing things for her—in particular an expensive coat—and demonstrating that he has access to this money. Clyde is convinced that with money he can attain significance and attention. Like Carrie, who believes that money is everything and with money everything is obtainable, Clyde too is obsessed with the notion that if he only had enough money, then everything would be within his reach. To a certain extent the narrative justifies his obsession, for Hortense begins returning Clyde's affection because he "seemed to have real money and to be willing to spend it on her freely."[26] At the same time, Hortense's attention is clearly fleeting. She'll desire Clyde only for as long as he has something to offer. In this way, sexual desire is understood through a materially based capitalist desire.

Hortense is not alone in wanting people because she wants to accumulate things. Dreiser doesn't depict Roberta, Clyde's second major love interest and the woman who contributes to his downfall, as innocent. Even though Roberta is a poor country girl, who seems to genuinely love Clyde, Dreiser explains that one of the first things Roberta wants to know about Clyde when she meets him at his uncle's factory is whether he is rich.[27] Her own motives for moving to the industrial town of Lycurgus to work in a factory centered on hopes of finding a husband who would help her rise in class position. Roberta is initially attracted to Clyde because he shares his last name, Griffiths, with the factory owner, and Roberta sees him as a route to a more affluent future. Clyde's love for Roberta has an authenticity during their brief romance, but the courtship is also tinged with his loneliness and desire for company. His uncle and cousins virtually ignore him during his first few months in Lycurgus because he is the poor relation, and finding himself friendless, his romance with the pretty and sweet Roberta becomes an antidote to his isolation. Yet at no time during the high moments of his affair with Roberta does Clyde indicate to her that marriage is in their future. Therefore, the moment Sondra Finchley, the only daughter of the Wimblinger Finchley Electric Sweeper Company's owner, shows interest in Clyde, he loses interest in Roberta. After all, Clyde recognizes Sondra as connected to "one of the largest manufacturing concerns here,"[28] and it is this connection that seduces him to forget about Roberta in exchange for Sondra. Love, for Clyde, is ultimately about economics and exchange. When Sondra begins expressing interest in him, he reflects on his position in relation to the two women: "As contrasted with one of Sondra's position and beauty, what had Roberta really to offer him? And would it be fair of one in her station and considering the connections and the possibilities that Sondra offered, for her to demand or assume that he should continue a deep and undivided interest in her as opposed to this other? That would not really be fair, would it?"[29] Clyde sees no shame in viewing his relationship with each woman through capitalist terms. Since Sondra can be exchanged for more, since she clearly has more value, his decision to drop Roberta for Sondra is the obvious choice.

Benn Michaels is aware that he uses metaphors of female sexuality to describe the work of capitalist desire in *Sister Carrie*. "Feminine sexuality," he argues, "thus turns out to be a kind of biological equivalent to capitalism or, rather, in the slipperiness of its own biology, a figure for capitalism's ability to imagine ways out of what appear to be biologically immutable limits."[30] Still, this metaphor has limits. What is curious about Carrie's sexual practices in the novel is that while she ostensibly has sex with several men, unintentional reproduction never arises as a possible issue. Perhaps the men she sleeps with use condoms; perhaps the "pull out" method, advertised in manuals for women, actually works for Carrie; perhaps Dreiser in creating this fictional narrative decided he didn't want to bother with writing about pregnancy. Most likely, however, is that Dreiser's portrait of Carrie as wielding her sexuality and sex to achieve upward mobility required him to ignore the biological repercussions of heterosexual sex. Carrie could never have attained her fame and fortune if she had to confront a pregnancy that could not be aborted. Fortunately for the fictional Carrie, her plans are never interrupted by any unintended consequences of sex, and there the realism of Dreiser's novel ends.[31] In *An American Tragedy* this blissfulness is no longer the case. Nearly concomitant with Sondra's sudden interest in Clyde, Roberta tells him she is pregnant. And in turn, Clyde discovers that capital has limits, that in fact there are "biologically immutable limits" that he cannot imagine his way out of.

Roberta's pregnancy—and more accurately Clyde's desire to find a means of abortion—marks the limit of what his money can buy. Indeed, the novel presents Clyde's quest for first abortifacients and then an abortionist almost entirely in monetary terms. When hearing about their predicament, his first thought is to visit "some local or near-by druggist who might, for a price, provide him with some worth-while prescription or information. But for how much?"[32] When he finally finds the courage to enter a pharmacy, and then finds a pharmacist willing to help him, the narrative documents the exchange as follows: "Did he wish a box? That (because Clyde asked the price) would be six dollars—a staggering sum to the salaried inquirer. However, since the expenditure seemed unescapable—to find anything at all a great relief—he at once announced that he would take it, and the clerk, bringing him something which he hinted would prove 'effectual' and wrapping it up, he paid and went out."[33] For Clyde finding an abortion is inextricably linked to his cash flow. To put the cost of the abortifacients in perspective, later during Clyde's trial for the murder of Roberta, he tells the jury that his room cost him seven dollars a week and his board cost between five and six dollars a week. By working at his uncle's factory he earned twenty-five dollars a week.[34]

Therefore, six dollars for pills equaled as much as he might spend for food in a given week; yet at the same time the six dollars were affordable and within the limits of his budget. A surgical abortion performed by a doctor, midwife, or abortionist would be far more costly.

In "A Study of Pregnancy Wastage," published in 1935 in the *Milbank Fund Quarterly*, Regine K. Stix, a medical doctor, interviewed twenty women about the cost of their abortion. She found that

> the highest price was $200, and the lowest $2.00, with about $60 as the average. In three cases the charges were by midwives and were, respectively, $35, $40, and $60. The two-dollar abortions were done by a man described by the patient as a doctor. She assured the author that his patients were given slips of paper with numbers on them and waited in line. She also said she thought his instruments were rusty. The patient had returned to this "doctor" a number of times, in spite of having had one abortion followed by severe septicaemia and two by serious hemorrhage.[35]

In a 1931 study printed in *American Medicine*, John J. A. O'Reilly, also a medical doctor, estimated that abortion yielded an average of $100 million per year and that a typical abortion cost $84.21.[36] Both studies, while giving different figures, suggest that abortion was part of a vibrant—if shadow—economy. After Clyde gives Roberta her six-dollar package of pills, which don't produce the intended results, he returns to the pharmacist for another package and more explicit instructions. However, at this point he recognizes that his twelve-dollar expenditure is probably useless. He reflects that the "troublesome thing in connection with all this was the thought that he knew nothing that would really avail in such a case, other than a doctor. Also that that probably meant money, time, danger—just what did it mean."[37] Later he also thinks that other than buying her another package of pills, he might find "some low-priced shady doctor somewhere, who, for a small fee, or a promise of payments on time, would help in this case."[38] However, Clyde genuinely has no idea how much money an abortion might cost, and had he been able to contact an abortionist and learn that he would need close to one hundred dollars to procure one, he might have gaped at that prospect.

Through an acquaintance Clyde manages to find the name of a doctor who supposedly performed abortions in the past. Hopeful that the problem of Roberta's pregnancy might be finally solved, he still worries about how much the procedure might cost him. Finally he manages to convince Roberta that she should approach the doctor without him. He reasons, "And again, as it now came to him, would she not be able to get it done cheaper? For looking as she did now, so distrait—If he could get her to say that she had been deserted by some man, whose name she would refuse to divulge, of course, well, what physician seeing a girl like her alone and in such a state—no one to look after her—would refuse her? It might even be that he would help her out for nothing. Who could tell? And that would leave him clear of it all."[39] Thus even though Clyde believes that more than anything he must rid himself of any obligation to Roberta, he still can't disentangle himself from worrying about how much that might cost him. Through this process, Roberta's life literally becomes meaningless as his concern with finding her a cheap abortion—even if it causes her death—becomes his priority.

However, Clyde has it all wrong. The doctor refuses Roberta precisely because she is socially insignificant and distraught. The narrative explains that "although in several cases in the past ten years where family and other neighborhood and religious considerations had made it seem quite advisable, he had assisted in extricating from the consequences of their folly several young girls of good family who had fallen from grace and could not otherwise be rescued, still he was opposed to aiding, either by his own countenance and skill, any lapses or tangles not heavily sponsored by others."[40] Money seems to gain access to everything, except abortion. At this moment, the novel seems to question whether free-market economies that allow people to quickly rise in class position really are all that free. As Clyde consistently seems to hint, if he had more access to cash and resources, would his problem be more easily solved?

Abortion becomes a question of access and reveals how economy works on a number of levels, not all of them as laissez faire as early twentieth-century capitalism publicly presents. Clyde goes to get his hair cut and receives advice: "'Well, that's not so easy as you may think, particularly around here,' elucidated the wiseacre who was trimming his hair. 'In the first place it's agin' the law. And next it takes lotta money. An' in case you ain't got it, well, money makes the mare go, you know.' He snip-snipped with his scissors while Clyde, confronted by his own problem, meditated on how true it was. If he had a lot of money—even a few hundred dollars—he might take it now and possibly persuade her—who could tell—to go somewhere by herself and have an operation performed."[41] While obviously more connected than Dewey Dell—for Clyde can procure pills if not a doctor—his lack of cash flow ultimately forestalls his rise in class position. Without money he cannot access a doctor willing to give Roberta an abortion, and without obtaining an abortion for Roberta, he cannot continue his pursuit of the wealthy and socially significant Sondra.[42] In Michael Trask's words, "The logic of equivalence that underwrites the world of hotels, trains, and department stores—where each consumer is substitutable for any other—has the effect not of generating social equilibrium but of voiding it."[43] Similarly, Clyde has access to new technologies and transportations; he takes the train to find abortifacients and has the luxury of visiting several pharmacists, yet his lack of monetary power and social connection means that he will never be able to find the abortion he seeks. In the eyes of the pharmacists and the doctor who refuses to perform an abortion, he is just another consumer who does not have access to enough cash to buy himself social mobility.

Therefore, finding that he does not have the means to find Roberta an abortion, Clyde in stupid desperation instead plots to murder her. Midway through the novel Roberta is found dead at the bottom of a lake. Whether Clyde is indeed her murderer or just a bystander who refused to help her while she accidentally drowns creates the next moment of narrative tension. Joseph Karaganis argues that "Dreiser leaves open the question of whether the crime is a consequence of American values or a transgression of them—an ambiguity that, far from hurting the novel, allowed readers across the ideological spectrum to find in it the critique or affirmation of American society that they preferred."[44] The same thing could be said about the way abortion functions in the novel. Is the novel condemning the inaccessibility of abortion, which is what ultimately causes Clyde to lead Roberta to her death? Or is it condemning the sheer fact that both Clyde and Roberta turn to abortion once they discover that sex often leads to undesired circumstances? Regardless of the answer, the novel makes an argument for considering the gendered ties among economy, reproduction, and abortion. If we accept Benn Michaels's reading of *Sister Carrie* as a novel that upholds the free-market forces of capitalism, we still have to admit that because Dreiser allowed reproduction to ensue in *An American Tragedy*, the free market is no longer in full force. Clyde and Roberta discover a limit to the American dream: they can't control their reproduction. It is ultimately that limit that leads them to fail in their identical quests: to rise in class position and rank, to marry upward, and to join the middle class.

Scene of Exchange III: The Economies of Madame Restell

Both Roberta's and Clyde's dreams lead to their deaths, but Clyde's end is more gruesome and drawn out. The last third of the novel plays out Clyde's trials for Roberta's murder and is notoriously based on the true-life case of Chester Gillette, which Dreiser followed through collecting newspaper clippings about the trial. Like Clyde, the real-life Chester was found guilty and sentenced to death, and his case subsequently became larger than life, inspiring several books—both nonfiction and fiction—plays, and films.[45] Even though it may initially appear as a non sequitur, I'd like to turn to an earlier infamous case that also ended up in court and pivoted around the issue of a potential abortion. Like Dreiser's novel, Madame Restell's career and 1858 court trial make transparent the ties among abortion, economy, and exchange. Examining Madame Restell's life and its popular representation in the media through this lens also provides important historical context for how the outlawing of abortion was linked to economy from the beginning of the conversation about whether abortion should be legal in the United States. While this section shifts from discussing the representation of abortion in fiction to the rhetoric of abortion politics in a historical case, I see both as illustrations of a circulating discourse that emerged in the mid-nineteenth century and became entrenched in American cultural rhetoric about reproduction by the early twentieth century. A. Cheree Carlson argues that too much emphasis is placed on whether historical novels represent "real life" and not enough on how they participate in a reality. Similarly, I argue here—and throughout the book—that novels, along with films, periodicals, and other popular representations, participate in producing a history, a rhetoric, and a reality rather than working to simply represent that reality. In turning to Madame Restell's case, I hope to demonstrate how the popular press produced a particular narrative about abortion, economy, and women's reproductive power that would contribute to the conversation both Faulkner and Dreiser present in their novels.[46]

In 1858 Madame Restell, a well-known New York City abortionist whose given name was Ann Lohman,[47] was tried in court for giving Maria Bodine an abortion after quickening had already occurred. It was not the first time that Restell had been arrested, but because of changes to New York state law regarding criminal abortion, it was the first time that Restell faced the actual possibility of serious persecution and a lengthy incarceration. In her chapter on Madame Restell's trial, Carlson notes, "Although she was repeatedly arrested and tried, she never once admitted that what she was doing was a crime. She was a businesswoman, she protested, supplying a much-needed service."[48] In other words, Restell saw her service in economic terms: the market demonstrated a need for abortions, and as a result, Restell opened a business to supply that demand. Unsurprisingly, the popular press did not view her services in similar terms.

In 1872 James McCabe Jr., a popular writer and journalist, published an exposé of New York City that was meant to reveal to both respectable inhabitants of the city and to those who would not dare visit the terrible crimes perpetuated within its borders.[49] Included in these terrible crimes is a chapter on abortion entitled "Child Murder," which almost exclusively focuses on Madame Restell.[50] Quoting an unnamed recent writer more familiar with the practices of abortionists, the chapter decries the number of women performing abortions "who are literally rolling in wealth, the result of their illegal and unnatural pursuits."[51] While both McCabe and the unnamed writer emphasize that their opposition to abortion lies in "the fact that to expel the foetus at any period of pregnancy is to take life,"[52] the majority of the chapter focuses on the profit Madame Restell has made because of her business. McCabe emphasizes that "most of the better and most successful of her kind are in the habit of receiving no less than one hundred or one hundred and fifty dollars for each case, and often as much as five hundred or one thousand dollars," and then continues to explain that this profit is the abortionist's only motive for they "have no interest in their 'patients,' either scientific or humane."[53] Describing abortion as a means "to extort money" from victims, McCabe's anonymous writer then turns to what Madame Restell has done with her wealth. Her home is described as "furnished like a palace," with "fifty-two windows, hung with satin and French lace curtains." The writer lists all the expensive and magnificent pieces that could be found in her home, including a "grand hall of tessellated marble, lined with mirrors," a "butler's pantry, lined with solid silver services," a "dining room with all imported furniture," and a fifth floor with a "billiard room" and a "dancing hall with pictures, piano, etc., . . . [which] commands a fine view of fifth avenue."[54] While McCabe begins his chapter with a mourning of the loss of "infant life," the chapter actually focuses on his horror that Madame Restell has been able to profit so successfully from her enterprise.

The chapter in McCabe's exposé is not unusual in its description of Madame Restell or even in its condemnation of abortionists—particularly female ones. The *Police Gazette*, the *New York Times*, and countless other publications demonized Madame Restell and portrayed her as an uncaring, unfeminine monster for performing abortions. For example, an earlier work, published in 1847 by an anonymous physician—or so he describes himself—similarly denounces Madame Restell for her wealth and success. Entitled *Madame Restell: Her Life and Horrible Practices*, the book was published by the author through the penny press as a means to establish a wide audience.[55] Like McCabe's later book, the author of this text found Restell particularly despicable because of her businesslike sensibility, although he also wondered whether the success of her enterprise was because of her husband's intelligence and not her own. Madame Restell's wealth, the physician argued, was due to the fact that she saw "that people will pay liberally for the gratification of their passions and propensities, however close they may be in the common concerns of life." And in understanding the needs of the market, "this woman, if we give her credit for the plan, had also the talent and courage, or audacity, to turn then to practical account."[56] Like McCabe, the physician accuses Restell of "purely mercenary motives" for "those who would not control their appetites."[57] For the author-physician, Madame Restell embodies the evil accumulation of wealth through immoral means. Drawing on the term that had already been circulating in New York—restellism, which had come to be synonymous with abortion—the physician declares: "This is Restellism—a catering to the weakness and wickedness of human nature, which enables Madame to live in luxury, to dress with splendor; to take her daughter to France, to complete her education, as it was very proper she should— to drive her carriage with four superb horses, and servants in livery, to indemnify bail of ten thousand dollars, and pay lawyers' fees of a thousand; which may have enabled her, with all her expenses, to have accumulated, even now, an enormous fortune."[58] Historians Eric Homberger and Helen Lefkowitz Horowitz both argue that Madame Restell's success was in part due to the business sense she and her husband, Charles Lohman, shared. Homberger writes that Lohman understood that in order to advance his wife's business, they needed a "modern marketing campaign" and that this foresight placed them at "the vanguard of business thought in the 1840s."[59] Lohman's business plan consisted of the advertisements he wrote and had published in the numerous newspapers that circulated in New York City and its surrounding area. Similarly, Horowitz writes that Madame Restell's advertisements in the penny press—beginning in 1838—stood out because "they did not use the guarded language of their predecessors but were open and direct."[60] For example, an early advertisement in the *Sun* resonates with the language Margaret Sanger would use almost a hundred years later:

> Is it not but too well known that the families of the married often increase beyond the happiness of those who give them birth would

dictate? In how many instances does the hard-working father, and more especially the mother, of a poor family, remain slaves throughout their lives, tugging at the oar of incessant labor, toiling to live, and living but to toil; when they might have enjoyed comfort and comparative affluence; and if care and toil have weighed down the spirit, and at last broken the health of the father, how often is the widow left, unable, with the most virtuous intentions, to save her fatherless offspring from becoming degraded objects of charity or profligate votaries of vice? Is it desirable, then, is it moral for parents to increase their families, regardless of consequence to themselves, on the well being of their offspring, when a simple, healthy and CERTAIN remedy is within our control?[61]

In contradiction to McCabe's presentation of Madame Restell as only seeking to drain her patients of their money, Restell's advertisement honestly depicts the necessity of abortion in financial terms. Foreshadowing Margaret Sanger's message in the early twentieth century about the financial costs of bearing too many children, Restell similarly appeals to women (and men) who might feel trapped by their inability to control their reproduction. Her clinic is thus giving them a way out of the cycle of toil.[62]

Additionally, rather than viewing her wealth as resulting from the theft of innocent victims, Homberger explains that she viewed her financial success and material goods as "proof of her high-minded devotion to the allaying of female fears, the removal of agonies, the concealment of sorrows and misfortunes of those abandoned to their fate by the harsh social order. . . . The lesson imparted was that she saw herself as a successful business woman and something of a public benefactress, not as a miserable and wretched sinner."[63] Restell thus placed an exchange value on her labor by valuing women's labor and women's desires. She saw a need in the market that could both help women and help her rise from her immigrant and rather indigent beginning in New York. Rather than a deceitful enterprise, her business was a resourceful response to the needs of the market. She was also able to respond to women's needs through immaterial labor—to use Michael Hardt's term; her labor, rather than producing a tangible product, was similar to centuries of women's work. As her advertisement points out, abortion contributes to a domestic economy, one that is often made invisible in the public marketplace. Yet Madame Restell made it visible both because she advertised and because she made so much money.

In 1845 the New York State legislature passed a law that made the death of a woman or fetus by abortion after quickening a felony—manslaughter in the second degree. This law had an immediate impact on Madame Restell's business. In response to the law she published a letter in the *New York Tribune* that is worth presenting in its entirety because it reveals the ways in which Restell perceived her practice.

> It would appear that the well-established maxim that every person shall be deemed innocent until proven guilty is to be superseded by one which shall deem every one guilty until proven innocent.
>
> I would ask, farther, whether there are any individual rights guaranteed to us? How far we are at liberty to indulge our individual tastes in our expenditures?—Whether we can use two horses or four (if an emergency occurs of long distance and heavy, bad roads) without being subjected to spiteful and malicious animadversions from every "sour grapes" through the medium of respectable papers? And how is one "defying public opinion," "scorning laws," and doing a variety of atrocious deeds by using more than two or "three bays" (one, by-the-by, is a chestnut) and a gray?
>
> Surely it is not within the province of "public opinion" to say whether a person shall have a coat of blue, brown, or green. It is alleged, and with some force, that individual independence is already crushed by the many-headed monster "public opinion" and would be completely tyrannized over if some people had their way. . . . In conclusion, Sir, I would leave it to every impartial, liberal, high-minded person, whether these uncalled for attacks partake not of the fell spirit of persecution, even if not of worse motives.[64]

In her letter to the *Tribune* Restell directly questions why the public is so obsessed with her wealth. While Restell was indeed wealthy, Homberger estimates that at the time of her death (via suicide) she had approximately $100,000.[65] Most sources list her annual income to have been $30,000 in 1869, and her total wealth nine years later was said to be between $850,000 and $1,000,000. In her letter Madame Restell acknowledges this wealth, but she wonders why it matters to the public, and she invokes her individual rights by declaring that as a liberal citizen she should be left alone when deciding how her fairly made money should be put to use. Yet Restell does not address the fact—and perhaps would not realize it until forced to end her life because of Anthony Comstock's persecution—that as a successful businesswoman she is a threat and needs to be stripped of the freedom she achieved in the marketplace.

Horowitz chronicles the persecution of Madame Restell, which she traces to George Washington Dixon's 1841 antiabortion campaign with Restell as his target. Dixon's attacks would be just the beginning and, as I described above, would be followed by tirades against her in the *New York Times*, the *Sunday Flash*, the *Whip*, and especially the *Police Gazette*, which sought to banish her from New York City. Horowitz explains the persecution of Restell in the popular press as "part of the commercialization of male vernacular culture. Underlying this new breed of publication was an acceptance of male sexuality on the old terms: boys will be boys. . . . That women had a meaningful life apart from male knowledge and control was unthinkable to the sporting press." In contrast, Horowitz describes Madame Restell as working to bring women's cultures and desires into the popular press by commercializing what had once been private and spoken about only in secret.[66] In other words, Restell brought sexual culture and practice into the market, and as a result, Madame Restell, and those who followed her, profited. In her assessment of Restell's persecution, Carlson argues that Restell was "targeted because of her symbolic stature" rather than because her acts were seen as particularly pernicious.[67] Similarly, Horowitz views the attack against Madame Restell and on abortion as a "fight against female agency."[68] I would add to that female economic agency and, more specifically, a woman who declared herself to be financially independent and successful and who could also compete in the world of autonomous, self-reliant men: the men embodying America's liberal ideals. Most symbolic about Madame Restell is that she attempted to carve out an economic space where women could both thrive as entrepreneurs and free themselves from the economic constraints of unrestrained reproduction. It was this quest that made her so threatening and gave her the title of the "wickedest woman in New York." In 1878, after it became clear that she would lose her court case to Anthony Comstock and be sent back to prison, she killed herself by slicing her throat. In a report about her death, the *New York Times* wrote, "The death of 'Mme. Restell' by her own hand is a fitting ending to an odious career. The fact that such a woman should have amassed property to the value of three-quarters of the millions of dollars is a sufficiently conclusive proof of the magnitude of the ghastly trade of which she was the most notorious agent. . . . The woman made a fortune out of child murder."[69] Even after her death the press could not help but obsess over her wealth and entrepreneurial skill. True, she had made a fortune, but like every good business-minded person, she simply gave the market what it wanted.

Scene of Exchange IV: Feminist Economies

Although Madame Restell's life precedes the novels discussed in this chapter by as much as one hundred years—from the time she began publicly advertising her practice—her case demonstrates the economic anxieties many early twentieth-century novels representing abortion respond to. Madame Restell may have died fifty years before the fictional Dewey Dell or Roberta was imagined, but she displayed an economic agency that was not available to either of them, partly because of the strict antiabortion laws that arose shortly after Restell's death. In many ways Madame Restell lived through a transitional era; she saw the opening of economic opportunities for women through the help of advertising in the popular press, but in the few decades before her death she saw a foreclosing of open attitudes toward women's reproduction. Ironically, when Madame Restell began her practice, the control of women's sexuality was seen as private and purely in the female sphere. As moral reformers like Anthony Comstock denounced advertisements for contraceptives and abortion, and in turn demanded that they should be inaccessible to women, they finished the process of bringing women's reproductive issues into a public sphere that now saw reproduction as something that should be legislated by a government and its representative agencies.

While it is unlikely that Madame Restell would have viewed her practice as feminist—and in fact the feminists of the era would have mostly condemned her—she has become a feminist icon for both her persistence in providing women with reproductive options and her business sensibility.[70] However, in the 1920s, when the feminist and socialist Agnes Smedley, who was known for her close connection to Margaret Sanger and her support for Sanger's birth control movement, needed an abortion, a Madame Restell was difficult to find. As a response to the oppressive conditions she experienced, Smedley wrote *Daughter of Earth*, a novel that presents a position on reproductive politics that is more radical than almost anything else published in Smedley's lifetime.[71] Perhaps since the death of Madame Restell no woman in the twentieth century so clearly articulated the relationship between abortion and economy. Marie Rogers, the novel's protagonist, is a working-class woman born into harsh conditions and almost destined to follow her mother's footsteps by marrying young, bearing several children, suffering abuse and poverty, and then dying young. Marie, however, radicalized at a young age, decides to resist this path and struggles to find a way to educate herself and escape poverty. The novel traces her many adventures through numerous jobs, near starvation, attempts to complete various stages of education, and several failed relationships. Halfway through the novel Marie meets Knut and Karin Larsen, siblings from Denmark, who introduce her more fully to socialism and political movement. Marie soon marries Knut in the hope that they can have an equal, feminist marriage, one that she insists be premised on not having children. Marie tells Knut that aside from wishing to remain childless, she also doesn't want a home: "no cooking, washing, scrubbing. I want to earn my own living, and you earn yours."[72] For Marie, this also includes abstaining from sex, because without a reliable method of birth control, it would surely only lead to reproduction. However, soon her commitment to abstinence wavers, and she becomes pregnant.

In the weeks before Marie discovers her pregnancy, she begins working as a journalist with the intent to save money so that she and Knut can continue their university educations. "Work, money, school"[73] becomes her mantra, and she imagines her future opening. The news of her pregnancy fills her with rage and despair, as she threatens to kill herself if she is forced to have a baby. She finds a doctor who only tells her that he can do nothing to help her, unless she obtains abortifacients at a drugstore, and then he can help her finish the process after she poisons herself. This is when she asks him about his cost. "I'll make a special price for you of one hundred dollars," is what he tells her. Still, Marie is unable to obtain the pills—or at least figure out how her reproductive system works so that she can abort herself. Instead, Knut goes to plead with the doctor and tells him that his wife will commit suicide if she does not have an abortion. After hearing Knut's plea, the doctor agrees to perform the procedure.

To this point in the narrative, Marie's experience mirrors that of others told in fiction and fact. The next decision she makes is striking: she refuses to let Knut help her pay for the abortion. She uses her savings to pay for the procedure and then notes, "I would not let him pay for the operation. . . . It was my body and I would let no man pay for it, I said. He had become very pale at that."[74] Whereas *An American Tragedy* and *As I Lay Dying* make a point of noting that the men responsible for the unintended pregnancies will be held financially accountable, in *Daughter of Earth* Marie intends to counter this narrative by insisting that she will pay for her abortion as a means to assert her own liberal individuality. "It was my body," she insists, thereby inserting herself and her abortion into an economy that is closed off to both Dewey Dell and Roberta. Even as Marie wishes to overthrow a political system that privileges individuality over all else, she also recognizes that while living in that system she needs to attain autonomy and self-reliance—characteristics that are valued in a capitalist, liberal state—because in this system only women freed from sexual reproduction and the care of children can become liberal individuals who can claim a right to their own bodies.

Marie's experience with abortion does not end there. She becomes pregnant once more in her relationship with Knut, and once more she insists on an abortion. Feeling panicked about the possibility of having a child again, and now in San Francisco, far from the abortionist who first illegally performed the procedure, Marie and Knut once again search for an abortionist. This time they find a doctor "whose trade was secret operations,"[75] and they make an appointment. In describing her experience Marie pays close attention to the economic conditions of the women around her: "The house stood on a broad, respectable street in San Francisco where such men ply their practice and make fortunes. We waited for two hours in a reception room filled with other women,—respectable women, young and middle-aged, wives and mothers. Well-dressed women—only women with money could afford such an operation."[76] Shortly after, Marie asks Knut for a divorce, and against his will—to make her happy—he complies. Marie views her reproductive potential as a trap; because she cannot control her reproduction, her choices are either to enter motherhood—an oppressive choice based on what she saw happening to her own mother—or continue to have abortions—which also places her within a privileged sphere of women who can afford the practice. Since she wants to escape both spheres, abstaining from sex and therefore divorce become her solution to escape entrapment.

Beth Widmaier Capo calls the body of Smedley's Marie Rogers a site "for cultural critique of economic and reproductive policy." She writes, "birth control has the potential to disrupt a sexual economy that values the female body for its reproductive capacity."[77] Although Margaret Sanger fought to separate birth control from abortion (see chapter 2), I argue that abortion disrupts sexual economies even more powerfully than birth control. To take that argument even further, the power of abortion is that it allows women to enter into a sexual economy and completely control—as individuals engaged in a marketplace—when they will become reproducers, consumers, and distributors. Even more powerfully, once abortion is removed from an open marketplace, as it is in all four scenes I discuss in this chapter, it also functions as a means to remove women—and particularly women with unintended pregnancies—as liberal agents who can participate in a market. Since the 1970s feminists have understood that sexuality is deeply embedded in economy, even if it does not directly deal with issues of paid labor.[78] Dewey Dell's ten dollars become meaningless to her as they won't buy her abortifacients, and she is forced to exchange sex in hope of attaining the product she wants. Roberta is completely reliant on Clyde's money and resources, and when he fails her she loses her life. Charity in *Summer* marries her adoptive father because she needs his financial protection. It is no wonder then that Marie Rogers insists on paying for her own abortion. She becomes human then. Perhaps Marie wishes she lived in a world where subjectivity does not depend on being able to purchase things, but unfortunately, she doesn't.

5 / Making a Living: Labor, Life, and Abortion Rhetoric

From the standpoint of "making a living," every activity unconnected with labor becomes a "hobby."
—HANNAH ARENDT, THE HUMAN CONDITION

Human life has value. In contemporary American society this belief is held as a truism, one that is so essential to understanding contemporary politics that even to question it publicly would be disquieting. As I discussed briefly in chapters 1 and 2, the emphasis on valorizing individual human life is key to the theories of liberalism and the foundations of the American state. Yet, while the importance of life might seem like a fundamental axiom, taken for granted in human rights treatises and the constitutions of liberal governments, the valuing of life has its own genealogy. The rise of Judeo-Christian religions and what we now consider the modern western state had a profound impact on the way life is valued.[1] In Hannah Arendt's words, life has "overruled all other considerations."[2] However, it is the particularized form of individual life that was given such importance. The emphasis on individual life also translates into an emphasis on family and property, or the confines that encapsulate what one can individually own and control. The transition that Arendt observes also touches on so-called pro-life abortion politics,[3] which draws its suppositions from this same valorization of individual human life. In the words of an antiabortion demonstrator, being pro-life is "really about understanding the value of each individual life as having intrinsic worth."[4] The reproduction of human life—itself a kind of laboring—is reified, while the life of the body politic dwindles to insignificance.

This chapter demonstrates how liberalism and economics, both of which undergird the rhetoric of choice, also configure how life is demarcated. I suggest that definitions of life, particularly in pro-life abortion politics, are rooted in a capitalist valuation of reproduction for the sake of reproduction. Extending from my analysis in previous chapters, I conclude that constructions of life are ultimately politically bound and invested in reifying individualist and reproductive living. This chapter thus explores a theoretical alternative to life discourse in abortion rhetoric through William Faulkner's *The Wild Palms*, which narrates the story of both an illicit and botched abortion and the 1927 Mississippi Flood.

The first half of this chapter examines what Hannah Arendt calls the human condition and her idea that the modern world ushered in a desire for the ultimate conquest of nature and a quest for the human to see himself outside of this "nature." In other words, Arendt argues that the rise of technologies that allow us to leave earth or to see ourselves as controlling the earth without being part of it has opened an aporia between the human and nature. She further suggests that what has caused this alienation is the elision of the public sphere, where collective human action—and not labor—is valued. In other words, a capitalist ethic privileges the making of things only so that more things can be produced. Therefore, she concludes that the endless cycles of labor, which consist only in consumption and production, have valorized the individual and the individual family unit in the private sphere. Arendt's theories have influenced several generations of feminist scholars, yet her theories about labor have usually been applied quite literally. In the following discussion I offer a feminist reading of Arendt through William Faulkner's *The Wild Palms* that provides a new way to think about the rhetoric of life in abortion discourse.

Faulkner's novel consists of two narratives, titled "Wild Palms" and "The Old Man," which seemingly have no connection. There are no overlapping characters, the stories take place ten years apart, and in one an abortion constitutes the pivotal scene, while in the other the birth of a infant plays a crucial role. The first part of this chapter will focus on "Wild Palms" and Harry and Charlotte's attempt to escape the laboring cycles of their society. Importantly, I ask how the novel configures a different understanding of life, particularly a life that is not grounded in individuality and set against nature. Ultimately, through this conversation, this section theorizes how Faulkner's configuration of life challenges the terms of life discourse in abortion politics and how Charlotte's abortion in the novel presents a new way to think about fertility, work, and human action.

The following section of this chapter takes up the secondary narrative of *The Wild Palms*, "The Old Man." In the backdrop of this narrative is the 1927 Mississippi Flood and the thousands of displaced people who were pressed into refugee camps and, in some cases, forced labor as a result of the disaster. This section focuses on Giorgio Agamben's theorization of the state of exception,[5] a concept that aptly describes a crisis like the 1927 flood. The state of exception exists when the state is confronted with an emergency that demands that the law be suspended. War is the most common example of a crisis that brings about the exception; however, natural disasters also often demand that the law be pushed aside so that sovereign decisions can be made to deal with the emergency. "The Old Man" is about a nameless convict, who is separated from his prison group after they are brought to work on the levees. Throughout this section of the novel, the convict desperately attempts to return to prison, but the flooded landscape makes his quest difficult. Additionally, he has responsibility for a pregnant woman, who eventually gives birth under his care. As the convict and the woman try to find a way back home, they witness the conditions of bare life brought about by the horrible state of the refugee camps set up for homeless survivors of the flood. Everywhere the basic necessities for living are missing—food, shelter, solid ground, and sanitary conditions.

Life, Labor, and Fertility

A key trait of a society that privileges individuated life is its entrapment in a labor philosophy that mirrors what Arendt calls the cycle of fertility. Because individual life has such worth, it must be reproduced and preserved, again and again. In pro-life rhetoric this translates into the sacredness of the human embryo, which represents the call to reproduce human life endlessly.[6] As Arendt writes, "the productivity of labor power produces objects only incidentally and is primarily concerned with the means of its own reproduction; since its power is not exhausted when its own reproduction has been secured, it can be used for the reproduction of more than one life process, but it never 'produces' anything but life."[7] Placed in the context of antiabortion sentiment, Arendt's argument reveals that pro-life arguments value human reproduction not for the infant that might be produced as the end result, but for the sheer reproduction of life that in turn reproduces more life. Thus Arendt's call to reenvision labor politics as something other than an endless cycle of production and consumption has the effect of also asking us to rethink the cycles of human fertility. Neither cycle should necessarily be considered "natural"; by imagining a new paradigm for labor or fertility, we might arrive at a politics that escapes the reification of the individual and the private.

Faulkner's 1939 *The Wild Palms* seems to anticipate this tension between private/public and individual/species in its foregrounded presentation of Charlotte's abortion. The novel is framed by the abortion: in the opening pages of the eponymously titled section "Wild Palms," Faulkner introduces Harry and Charlotte through the perspective of an older doctor, who leases a house to them and comes to help Harry treat Charlotte when she becomes deathly ill as a result of the abortion. The novel closes with Harry again, but this time he is imprisoned for performing the illegal abortion for Charlotte. Only later do we learn that Harry and Charlotte met at a party in New Orleans when Harry was still a celibate medical student and Charlotte was married with two young daughters. After only a few dates they decide to run off together; Harry leaves medical school, just a few months before his certification, and Charlotte leaves her husband and children. From there they travel to Chicago, a summer lake house, a mining community in Utah, and then back to the southern coastline, where Charlotte dies. Their travels are always motivated by an attempt to escape the social. Charlotte and Harry seem to believe that somewhere in the United States they can find a space where the division between the public and private hasn't collapsed, where they can retreat into a sphere outside the public/private to become bodies that resist the laboring and accumulation of capitalism.

In her insightful analysis of the novel, Cynthia Dobbs writes, "I also wonder about the notion of freedom as it applies to this novel. For the convict, prison is freedom; for Harry and Charlotte, their 'escape' from bourgeois respectability becomes its own sort of prison, as they remain on the run from an engagement with society that they can never escape."[8] Although Dobbs does not devote much of her argument to explaining how freedom works in *The Wild Palms*, understandably since the passage I cite above appears in an endnote to her article, the juxtaposition that she points to is key to my argument: Charlotte and Harry seek to carve a space of freedom outside of society, until they are ultimately confronted with the impossibility of their desire, while the tall convict (the main character in the "The Old Man") longs to return to prison for its freedom from the pressures of reproduction and accumulation.

Arendt argues that productivity places no value on the end product for its own sake but rather for its ability to reproduce itself.[9] Arendt's point is directed at the forces of capitalism in a modern world, but she also notes that the cycles of production are modeled on the cycles of fertility: the mandate to reproduce human life comes not from valuing life but from a drive to continue the endless cycle of human reproduction. It is precisely this drive that Harry and Charlotte attempt to escape. Before Harry meets Charlotte, when he is still a medical student laboring endlessly to finish his degree so he can continue to labor as a doctor, he reflects that his existence is "as if his life were to lie passively on his back as though he floated effortless and without volition upon an unreturning stream."[10] Harry envisions his future as a continuation of his sexless and laboring life: he sees himself as caught in a cycle of labor where he has no agential control as he drifts on producing and reproducing because it is what his father told him to do. Life happens to him, and he complies. That is, until he meets Charlotte. When they escape to Chicago, Harry attempts to find employment that will provide for their basic necessities. Yet after several failed interviews, he explains to himself that he can't find work because "I really dont try hard enough, dont really realise the need for trying because I have accepted completely her ideas about love."[11] Charlotte's chief idea about love, which Harry embraces more emphatically as the novel progresses, is that love will "clothe and feed me,"[12] as he explains. Yet Harry soon realizes that Charlotte's ideas are more complicated: they don't quite insist that love can clothe and feed human bodies, but that to live for love they must resist the entrapments of a capitalist society that thrusts them into its laboring cycles so that life becomes merely about ensuring food and clothing.

Harry comes to understand Charlotte's position when they spend the fall at a lake house owned by their friend McCord because Harry has lost his job and can't find another. When their food supplies start dwindling, Harry again begins worrying about their future. Charlotte stops him: "My God, I never in my life saw anybody try as hard to be a husband as you do. Listen to me, you lug. If it was just a successful husband and food and bed I wanted, why the hell do you think I am here instead of back there when I had them?" When Harry reminds her that they still have to eat and sleep, she continues: "Certainly we have. So why worry about it? That's like worrying about having to bathe just because the water in the bathroom is about to be cut off."[13] Here Charlotte articulates her position to Harry most directly; by worrying about food and sleep, by worrying about the cyclical needs of human life, they will fall into the entrapment of middle-class conventions and capitalist drives. Don't worry about food before you're hungry and sleep before you're tired, she tells him: the desire to accumulate the means that ensure food and sleep will lead to our destruction.

When they return to Chicago because the summer home becomes too cold to live in and indeed their food runs out, Harry begins writing and selling adolescent dime novels, and Charlotte finds stores that buy her sculptures for window dressings. Their life begins to get comfortable. This time Harry, having taken in Charlotte's lesson about love, puts an end to their lifestyle. He tells Charlotte that they are going to leave Chicago for good this time. He explains: "You're not going to work any more just for money. Wait . . . I know we have come to live like we had been married five years, but I am not coming the heavy husband on you. I know I catch myself thinking, 'I want my wife to have the best' but I'm not yet saying 'I dont approve of my women working.' It's not that. It's what we have come to work for, got into the habit of working for before we knew it, almost waited too late before we found it out."[14] In his essay on *The Wild Palms*, Joseph Urgo notes, "what Harry and Charlotte want above all else is to be disengaged from the sources of power that, initially, have assured their destinies."[15] Their destinies, which Urgo does not quite identify, are the constraints of laboring that are enforced through the desire for comfort, wealth, and security. Harry recognizes that despite Charlotte's insistence that they not end up like a married couple, their financial successes in Chicago all too easily managed to discipline them into a comfortable lifestyle where Harry begins to imagine Charlotte as his wife. Importantly, he tells her that he hasn't *yet* started thinking that his wife shouldn't work, but implicit in that "yet" is that if they continue their lives in Chicago, Harry will also eventually begin to think of Charlotte through conventional (for the 1930s) conjugal terms. Thus he tells her "you're not going to work any more *just for the money*" (italics mine) because he wants to disengage them from the cycles of laboring that entrap them in the desires of accumulation and capitalist norms. His solution is to move to a stark Utah mining community where he soon learns no one gets paid and respectability does not exist. Later in this chapter I will return to the Utah mines and connect their exceptional conditions to the 1927 Mississippi flood. However, first I would like to turn to the relationship between art and reproduction, noted by several critics of *The Wild Palms*, because of its connection to Charlotte and Harry's quest to elude laboring and to Charlotte's abortion.

In Arendt's denunciation of modern society, she makes one exception for the artist who is able to break free from laboring bonds. She explains, "Whatever we do, we are supposed to do for the sake of 'making a living';

such is the verdict of society, and the number of people, especially in the professions who might challenge it, has decreased rapidly. The only exception society is willing to grant is the artist, who strictly speaking, is the only 'worker' left in a laboring society. . . . As a result, all serious activities, irrespective of their fruits, are called labor, and every activity which is not necessary either for the life of the individual or for the life process of society is subsumed under playfulness."[16] In *The Human Condition*, Arendt makes an important distinction between work and labor, which she draws on in the above quotation. While labor, as I have been describing, is cyclical and geared toward reproduction and consumption, work values an end product that is lasting and has a use-value that is not inextricably tied to its exchange-value. In other words, the artist still produces objects that are valuable not only due to their worth on the market, their consumability, or their reproducibility. *The Wild Palms* engages in a similar valuation of art. When Harry first meets Charlotte and her friends, who define themselves as artists, he stares at the paintings on the walls and thinks "in bemusement without heat or envy at a condition which could supply a man with the obvious leisure and means to spend his days painting such as this and his evenings playing the piano and feeding liquor to people whom he ignored."[17] By the end of the novel, when Harry takes Charlotte to the Mississippi coast, where she will die, he introduces himself to the doctor as a painter of pictures, even though he quickly gave up painting after one brief attempt at the lake house. His mysterious answer echoes his response to the paintings he first encountered: in his new life, it is precisely the "leisure" of not laboring that he is trying to capture; both Harry and Charlotte search for a space that precludes endless labor and embraces work, which like Arendt they define as art.

Charlotte first articulates this philosophy of art when she explains, "That's what I make: something you can touch, pick up, something with weight in your hand that you can look at the behind side of, that displaces air and displaces water and when you drop it, it's your foot that breaks and not the shape."[18] Cynthia Dobbs reads Charlotte's claim as a desire "to create objects that are harder, more permanent than life, emphatically tougher than the body itself."[19] She argues that Charlotte desires "still-life," a term she borrows from Janet Carey Eldred's essay on the novel, because she wants to arrest "the flow of time." My reading borrows from this theory but expands it in a different direction: Charlotte wants to create objects that are tougher than the body because, like Arendt, she believes art is unconsumable. If Charlotte seeks to arrest the flow of time, it is because she wants to resist the time of capitalist reproduction. Her art should not be expendable, like a pair of shoes or a loaf of bread, which are bought, used up, and then rebought, but it should be lasting: in Arendt's words, a product of work.

Importantly, Charlotte connects her drive to make things with the pleasure she derives from sex; she pronounces, "I like bitching, and making things with my hands."[20] John Duvall reads this as Charlotte's "quest for subjectivity,"[21] but Charlotte never seems to long for subjectivity. In fact, she seems to be unconcerned with subjectivity as she tries to evade normative societal structures that would give her such legibility. Rather, by calling sex "bitching," she links the act to sheer pleasure and performance and not to reproduction or even love. Similarly, she suggests that as she wants to make art for the sake of art and not for potential profit, she also wants to have sex for the sake of sex and not because of its potential reproductive consequences. Given this context, Charlotte's insistence on aborting her pregnancy fits into her determination to escape laboring. As she tells Harry early in their relationship: she does not want a husband. Implicitly, she also tells him that she does not want children and the comforts of family. When she is pregnant—a consequence of a frozen douche bag that she could no longer use—she begs Harry to give her an abortion.

Harry had already performed an abortion on Bill, the wife of Buckner, who is the titular manager of the Utah mines. At first he refuses to comply with Buckner's request until Charlotte convinces him that the couple desperately needs his help because they can't have a baby given their financial conditions. When he finally agrees, he thinks to himself, "*I have thrown away lots, but apparently not this. Honesty about money, security, degree.*" While Harry's reflection might suggest that his discomfort with abortion is morally grounded, there is nothing in the novel that could explicitly confirm this position. When Harry considers how much he has thrown away, the immediate reason for his sacrifice might appear to be love, yet the above sentence continues with a narrative interruption before Harry resumes, " . . . and then for a terrible moment he thought *Maybe I would have thrown away love first too.*"[22] He and Charlotte have both attempted to escape the social by refusing to accumulate money and to gain legibility, and now Charlotte asks him to take things one step further by severing the cycle of reproduction that binds human bodies.

When Charlotte tells Harry she is pregnant and asks for an abortion, he adamantly refuses at first. She retorts, "You said it was simple. We have proof that it is, that it's nothing, no more than clipping an ingrowing toenail."[23] By comparing fetal life with an ingrown toenail—a dead and annoying piece of human matter—Charlotte refuses to recognize human life as beginning at conception. Yet even more significantly, the comparison suggests that Charlotte views her pregnancy as excessive reproduction. Elizabeth Grosz, in forming a nonaesthetic theory of art, writes, "Art and nature, art in nature, share a common structure: that of excessive and useless production—production for its own sake, production for the sake of profusion and differentiation."[24] Similarly, equating art and nature, Charlotte refuses to privilege virtual life over her own life. If production happens for its own sake, as Grosz contends, then its termination has no moral value. If artistic and natural productions are always excessive, then disrupting the process produces no guilt. Charlotte wants to escape the cycle of fertility just as much as she wanted to escape the cycle of laboring; both cycles entrap human bodies in a society that has collapsed the private and public into the social. However, ultimately, the pregnancy and botched abortion prove to both Charlotte and Harry that it is impossible to sever ourselves from the social. Once Charlotte is marked as still capable of reproduction, her body necessarily enters the realm of public regulations and laws. Charlotte tries to deal with her unwanted pregnancy privately by convincing Harry to give her an abortion, yet as Harry recognizes too late, the privitization of Charlotte's body once she became pregnant was impossible. After her death, he concludes that Charlotte died from his abortion while Bill survived hers because he loved Charlotte. When considering why Charlotte's abortion failed, he thinks, *"A miser would probably bungle the blowing of his own safe too. Should have called a professional, a cracksman who didn't care, didn't love the very iron flanks that held the money."*[25] In other words, Harry thinks that Charlotte died of her abortion because he was too close to her; he attempted to privately abort her pregnancy when it was a procedure that would always be subject to cold and distanced public code. By the end of the novel, Harry comes to terms with the fact that the private can never exist. The collapse of the private and public, as Arendt theorizes, is so consuming that even in an isolated mining community in Utah, it can't be escaped. We are always in the law, and it is a law that defines life even as it tries to contain nature and separate it from the forces of capital.

Life Expectancies and Exceptions: Harry and the Old Man

In April 1927 it rained so hard and for so long in Mississippi that the levees could not hold. The turn of events that caused the Mississippi

River floods did not come without warning. In the first four months of 1927 the midwestern and southern states saw an unprecedented amount of rain and snow. Farther north Pittsburgh and downtown Cincinnati flooded in early 1927 as a result of the overflowing Ohio River. State governments began forming armies of levee workers to help contain the massive torrent of water that was rushing into the Mississippi River and threatening to create catastrophic conditions in the South. The vast majority of these workers were black men, who were often forced into repairing the levees at gunpoint, especially as it became apparent that these efforts were often life threatening, while at the same time largely futile. Historian John M. Barry's carefully documented work on the Mississippi flood makes apparent how little the lives of black people were valued in the early twentieth-century South by white authorities in power. When the river came crashing through a crevasse in the levee with more force than had ever been documented, levee workers quickly climbed onto a barge to save their lives.[26] However, the force of the crevasse was actually pulling the barge and its tugboat upstream toward the crevasse and its uncontrollable power. One white man on the tugboat suggested that all blacks should be placed on the barge and then cut loose, so that the tugboat could more easily escape the crevasse.[27] In another example, Barry explains that as sandbags, which were used to cover gaps in the levee, were running out, an engineer ordered the black levee workers to use their bodies to fill gaps by lying on the levee in dangerous conditions until the sandbags arrived.[28] The flood was monstrous, uncontainable, and more powerful than any other natural force that had crossed the Mississippi Delta. Richard Washburn Child, writing for the *Saturday Evening Post*, described it as "the largest disaster in the history of our civilization."[29]

Yet before the 1927 Mississippi flood, the "'government' levees seemed immense, formidable, impregnable";[30] the levees were seen as a symbol of the human ability to control nature. Barry begins his project by asserting: "To control the Mississippi River—not simply to find a modus vivendi with it, but to control it, to dictate it, to make it conform—is a mighty task. It requires more than confidence; it requires hubris." He writes that finding the means to control the Mississippi River was "the perfect task for the nineteenth century" because it was "the century of iron and steel, certainty and progress, and the belief that physical laws as solid and rigid as iron and steel governed nature . . . and that man had only to discover these laws to truly rule the world."[31] The project of containing the Mississippi River is an apt metaphor for the capitalist forces of the nineteenth century for all the reasons Barry mentions but also because it is an example of both the power of capitalism and the precarious forces on which it rests. The 1927 Mississippi flood was one of the worst natural disasters in American history. Historians estimate that it left 1 percent of the national population homeless; it killed thousands of people, and it forced dramatic changes in American demographics.[32] It also shook the foundations of American power and wealth and the illusion that industrialization and sheer human power could control the forces of nature.

Many literary critics of *The Wild Palms* have struggled to understand cohesively why Faulkner drew these two narratives together.[33] I propose that the conditions of bare life brought about by the state of exception and the individualizing and endless cycles of laboring, which try to stabilize natural forces, are all interwoven in the modern human condition and the two narratives of Faulkner's novel. In other words, in *The Wild Palms* the convict's desire to return to the stabilizing and disciplining space of the prison and Charlotte and Harry's peripatetic existence, which unsuccessfully tries to escape the alienating cycles of labor and fertility, are two parts of a narrative about the modern forces that shape life. It is no coincidence that Charlotte's abortion frames *The Wild Palms*; the novel, like Arendt's *The Human Condition* and Agamben's *State of Exception*, asks us to reconsider what constitutes life and what might be the implications of granting certain forms of life more legibility than others. By attempting to answer this question, this chapter rethinks why antiabortion activists and politicians place such an emphasis on prenatal life.

The Wild Palms ends with Harry in jail and Charlotte dead; their experiment has failed because of Charlotte's unsuccessful abortion. The extreme conditions of the Utah mines pushed their experiment to its limit and exposed its impossibility. There, as Buckner readily tells them on their arrival, no one gets paid for their labor. The Polish miners stay working because they believe that eventually they will be compensated, and the mine keeps running so its owner can continue selling stock. Harry was brought to the mine because the law required a doctor on staff, but as Buckner tells him, medical inspectors will never come by to make sure he is properly certified. The mine exists on the edge of law, which is its appeal for Harry; he will never be paid for his services there, which is why, before he leaves for Utah, while drinking beer with his friend McCord, he toasts, "To freedom,"[34] even as McCord mocks him. Harry and Charlotte revel in the freedom from society at the mines because they have escaped from middle-class norms, but they eventually come to realize their entrapment by recognizing themselves in the Polish miners. As they seek to communicate with the miners once Buckner and Bill have left, they observe that among the group of miners there are five women, some with young children who were obviously born at the mine. Harry thinks, "My God. They dont even know I'm a doctor. They dont even know that they are supposed to have a doctor, that the law requires that they have one."[35] Watching the Polish miners, Charlotte and Harry come to realize that the abject conditions of the mine, where the miners continuously labor without compensation and under horrible conditions, is not a form of freedom. The exposure to bare life is frightening, and Charlotte and Harry quickly give up their plan to help the miners. Shortly after, Charlotte discovers she is pregnant.

Charlotte's pregnancy dramatically changes the course of the novel and her ability to live with Harry somewhat beyond the rules governing American society. Writing about *The Wild Palms* and Charlotte's pregnancy, Eldred explains, "Faulkner uses realism in the scenes at the mines in Utah to link childbirth with oppression and to present a powerful visual argument *against* procreation as a 'natural' end to female sexuality."[36] If childbirth is linked to oppression, it is because it entraps the female body in the cycles of fertility. If *The Wild Palms* argues against procreation as natural, it is because the snare of reproduction does not have to be the only course for women's bodies. Yet the novel also suggests that escaping the cycle of fertility—as Charlotte attempts through her abortion—is difficult in a capitalist and chaotic world where human life has become premised on cyclical laboring.

The intertwining narrative in *The Wild Palms*, "The Old Man," punctuates this point by drawing attention to the precarious forces of nature that capital attempts to rein in and control.[37] In "The Old Man" the tall convict, whose name we never learn, is caught in the Mississippi flood after he rescues a pregnant woman and then mistakenly rows his boat in the wrong direction because the force of the flood has shifted the current of the river. While taking responsibility for the well-being of the pregnant woman, who eventually gives birth when they manage to briefly dock on dry land, he spends most of the narrative desperately trying to return to prison with his boat and prison clothes intact. As they travel through various towns on the river, they pass though a chaotic landscape where everything has gone awry. Law has been suspended; yet in this state of exception the tall convict does not find himself exposed to freedom but to a brutality that threatens to strip away his human legibility.

The state of exception, as Agamben describes it, is a suspension of the juridical order, which at the same time works to uphold the forces of sovereignty.[38] He writes, "If the law employs the exception—that is the suspension of law itself—as its original means of referring to and encompassing life, then a theory of the state of exception is the preliminary condition for any definition of the relation that binds and, at the same time abandons the living being to law."[39] The paradox Agamben points to is that only law—the sovereign—can suspend law; at the same time this exceptionalism is based on a power that constructs life through law. In other words, through the state of exception, the sovereign can decide what is recognizable life and what is bare life—life that threatens the law and should therefore be excluded from it and banished to the margins. In "The Old Man" sections of *The Wild Palms* it is this confrontation with illegible life that the tall convict finds so frightening. However, unlike Agamben's theoretical conception of exceptionalism, Faulkner's novel recognizes the gendered nature of the state of exception. The pregnant woman's body scares the convict because it reveals how life becomes reproduced and how, in turn, that life becomes recognized or dismissed.

Trapped in a small boat with the laboring pregnant woman, the convict frantically searches for land and any sign of human settlement where the pregnant woman could give birth. Days have passed, and he has no orientation of where to go next because the changing flows of the river have misdirected him. As he proceeds to feel even more lost and more insignificant in the chaotic landscape, the narration shifts to focalize through him:

> Now he believed that all he had to do would be to paddle far
> enough and he would come to something horizontal and above
> water even if not dry and perhaps even populated; and, if fast
> enough, in time, and that his only other crying urgency was to
> refrain from looking at the woman who, as vision, the incontro-
> vertible and apparently inescapable presence of his passenger,
> returned with dawn, had ceased to be a human being and . . . had
> become instead *one single inert monstrous sentient womb* from
> which, he now believed, if he could turn his gaze away and keep it
> away, would disappear.[40]

The tall convict finds the pregnant woman's body terrifying because in the chaotic landscape it becomes another marker of an excess of life. The convict desires containment and restraint; he wants to be legible within the law, but in the exceptional conditions of the Mississippi flood he does not know what to do with the "monstrous" body of the woman that is about to labor under incoherent conditions. Like antiabortion laws that seek to define life at conception, the convict more than anything is intent on drawing the boundaries of life. He looks away from the pregnant woman and hopes for her miraculous disappearance because he longs for the reestablished order of his prison life. Without the constraining forces of capitalism, the pregnant body becomes frightening because it contains a reproductive power that exceeds the capacities of the tall convict and has no legibility in the chaotic world caused by the flooding river. It has the potential power to threaten the structures holding the state of exception that orders his life, for better or worse.

When the tall convict and the woman (now no longer pregnant because she successfully gave birth with the convict's help) first encounter other human beings on a boat, rather than feeling relief, more confusion arises. First, the tall convict does not understand where the boat is headed. When the people on the boat try to rescue them, the tall convict first wants to ascertain where they are going because he wants to move closer to Parchman, his prison, rather than farther away. A voice "foreign and out of place" coming from the boat begins the following conversation:

> "Where is it you are trying to go?"
> "I aint trying," the convict said. "I'm going to Parchman."
> . . .
> "Carnarvon?"
> "What?" the convict said. "Parchman?"[41]

After this jumbled exchange, where neither man seems to understand the other, the foreign voice concedes and tells the convict they're going his way, although it soon becomes apparent that this is not true as the woman admits that it never sounded like the man said "Parchman" but that "it sounded like he said something else." Once on the boat, he notices something else: "the other refugees who crowded the deck . . . were not white people."[42] In telling this story to the other convicts in retrospect, once he is safely back in prison, the incomprehensibility of the convict's experience becomes more apparent. His cellmate, the plump convict, responds, and they have the following dialogue:

> "You mean niggers?"
> "No. Not Americans."
> "Not Americans? You was clean out of *America* even?"

"I don't know," the tall one said. "They called it Atchafalaya."—
because after a while he said "What?" to the man and man did it
again, gobble-gobble——"Gobble-gobble?" the plump convict said.

"That's the way they talked," the tall one said. "Gobble-gobble,
whang, caw-caw-to-to."[43]

In retelling his story to his cellmates, the tall convict emphasizes the
illegibility of his world. Although Atchafalaya is within US borders—
in the southwestern corner of Louisiana—and the people on the boat
are most likely speaking French, given Atchafalaya's proximity to New
Orleans, he can only register these strangers as foreigners because in
his world their difference has no place. The chaotic, upside-down environment the convict finds himself in is terrifying because he does not
recognize its order and its will. Shortly before the convict becomes lost
on the river, he looks out across the Mississippi and sees far on the hori-
zon another levee. At first he does not recognize what he sees because it
looks so small compared to the looming landscape around him. Then a
moment of realization comes to him, and he thinks, "*That's what we look
like from there. That's what I am standing on looks like from there.*"[44] A
prodding guard immediately interrupts his thoughts by urging him to
walk on. Yet what this brief moment intimates is the convict's smallness
in a large world where the forces that organize his life are just one order
among many and that once he is lost in this larger world those forces no
longer sustain their legibility.

In prison the tall convict's life was constrained yet fully legible to the
law. The prisoners spend their days farming, performing labor for the
sake of labor because the profits of their work will never be represented
monetarily to them. The narrative notes, "It could have been pebbles they
put into the ground and papier-mâché cotton and corn sprouts which
they thinned."[45] The convicts engage in endless labor with no remunera-
tion; they are the epitome of Arendt's cyclical laborers because their
efforts never can have value in terms of the lasting products of work.
Yet when the convict finds "freedom," in the days after the flood, when
he is lost on the Mississippi River and his prison files him as dead, he
longs to return to his labor. He thinks, "All in the world I want is just
to surrender."[46] He begins fantasizing about his mule Henry, who serves
as a comforting and safe memory. Henry, bound by his hybrid birth, is
incapable of reproducing and spends his days in endless labor. Dobbs
argues that the mule's separation from the laws of reproduction "serves
as a figure for a crucial purity and 'freedom' within the world of this

novel, a world in which reproduction (central to both women's 'maternal function' and to capitalism) is equivalent to a site of frightening contamination."[47] Dobbs's description ironically denotes the space of the prison as "freedom" because, as Dobbs does not state, in prison the convict is freed *from* the chaos of nature. In prison, he can mindlessly labor and have his needs attended to. The world of excess and art is safely on the other side of the bars.

Ten years later Harry finds himself in Parchman as well, the same prison that presumably still holds the tall convict. To connect the pregnant woman to Charlotte's abortion, I would like to turn to Grosz again and her theorization of chaos. She writes, "Chaos here may be understood not as absolute disorder but rather as a plethora of orders, forms, wills—forces that cannot be distinguished or differentiated from each other, both matter and its conditions for being otherwise, *both the actual and the virtual indistinguishable.*"[48] The world Grosz describes is precisely the flooded environment surrounding the convict, and it is also the world Harry and Charlotte try to construct for themselves. In insisting that her abortion is no more than clipping an ingrown toenail, Charlotte articulates the potential sameness of actual and virtual life. If virtual life in this case is a yet-to-be-born cellular mass growing in Charlotte, it is a life that it not yet individuated and personified. Similarly, Charlotte and Harry both want to live their lives against the individualizing and privatizing forces of capitalism. Until they meet the Polish workers who quite literally and abjectly embody the notion of life as an unindividuated organism, they too want to be able to strip away their individuality. Thus, when Charlotte insists on an abortion, she is not expressing an anti-life position. On the contrary, she is resisting the privileging of so-called individuated life. The fetus that grows inside her has as much worth as all potential and virtual life forms around her, and thus either to abort it or to nurture it amounts to a reshaping of life, potential or already there.

In the last chapter of "Wild Palms," the doctor and his wife, who rent Charlotte and Harry a dilapidated shack in Mississippi as Charlotte is slowly dying of her abortion, argue over how to respond to the strange couple living on their property. The wife wants to call a taxi and get them off her property, while the doctor wants to call an ambulance and the police. He shouts that Harry "must suffer for this." She retorts, "Suffer fiddlesticks. You're mad because he used a scalpel without having a diploma. Or did something with it the Medical Association said he mustn't."[49] As the "foreign" doctor the tall convict encounters tells him, the American Medical Association confers "the power to bind and to loose,"[50] a sentiment obviously heeded by the Mississippi doctor. In other words, Harry broke the Law; he violated not the law of a god or a religious order, or even the law of the state, but the law of the AMA and its disciplinary apparatus. His transgression in the eyes of the doctor is not immoral, treasonous, or sacrilegious, but it simply defies his established order and authority. Harry and Charlotte have acted with little regard for the order of things, and now they must pay: Charlotte with her life and Harry with his freedom. Thus, in an act that mirrors the tall convict's return to prison, Harry surrenders by insisting that the officer called to arrest him for performing an illegal abortion put handcuffs on him.

He willingly enters prison, where separations between the private and public no longer exist even in name. His experiment with Charlotte has failed not because of the abortion but because they realized the impossibility of their ambitions: to make a living not premised on endless labor and its individuating tendencies, but to live life as life, in its actual and virtual possibilities. What they tragically discover once Charlotte becomes pregnant is that there is no outside to capital and its organizing technologies.

Abortion and the Politics of Life

I end this chapter with a turn to the late twentieth and early twenty-first century to think about how Faulkner's *The Wild Palms* gives antiabortion life rhetoric a different valence. In *Life's Domain*, legal philosopher Ronald Dworkin takes on a project similar to this one in that he seeks to demonstrate a shared ideology between pro-life and pro-choice advocates. Yet his conclusions are startlingly different, and his unacknowledged assumptions point to the complicated constructions of human life that Faulkner's *The Wild Palms* explores. Dworkin asserts that most objections to abortion are based on either a *derivative* objection or a *detached* objection. The first takes an antiabortion position because it believes that the fetus has a right to life, which it shares with all human beings. The second contends that abortion is wrong because life has an intrinsic, sacred value. Dworkin quickly dismisses the first objection by arguing that even people who say they object to abortion on this basis don't really believe that a fetus can have rights because it does not yet have a consciousness and thus a volitional will. He therefore concludes that the real reason why people insist that abortion is wrong lies in their belief that terminating any human life is reprehensible.

Dworkin takes a decisively pro-choice stance in *Life's Domain*; he believes that abortion should be legal and accessible as put forth by the terms of *Roe v. Wade*. At the same time, he also argues that fetal life, like all individuated human life, is sacred and inviolable. In fact, the phrase "human life is sacred" functions as the refrain of his work and is repeated at least once in almost every chapter. He contends that the belief that "individual human life is sacred" is an idea that "we almost all share in some form."[51] Occasionally Dworkin replaces "sacred" with "inviolable" to make clear that this conception is not based in religious belief but also has secular interpretations.[52] Before I go on to critique Dworkin's assertions, I would like to emphasize that he makes clear that his arguments primarily apply along a conservative-liberal spectrum. While he acknowledges that some people might hold views outside this spectrum, he decides to limit his arguments to this field because it "will make it easier to describe my main points."[53] This decision ultimately limits the power of his argument, but it also demonstrates the similarities between the liberal and conservative positions on abortion, which brings it in line with my aims here. However, as I will soon show, Dworkin and I reach strikingly different conclusions.[54]

Dworkin begins by contending that both liberal and conservative thinkers can agree that human life "has intrinsic moral significance";[55] the two sides diverge in how they apply that conviction to their position on abortion. Ultimately, his argument settles on explaining that liberal and conservative positions on abortion don't differ in how they value life but in how they judge waste. He explains, "The real argument against abortion is that it is *irresponsible to waste human life* without a justification of appropriate importance."[56] The real difference between the two positions, Dworkin then concludes, is that conservatives view the termination of a pregnancy at any stage as a waste of life, while liberals are more likely to contend that if a woman does not abort a pregnancy when carrying it to term would mean that her quality of life would be severely impacted, then her life is wasted. Yet he also asserts that liberals agree with conservatives because as the fetus develops, "[as] this natural investment continues [in life], and the fetus develops toward the shape and capacity of an infant, abortion, which wastes that investment, is progressively an event more to be avoided or regretted."[57] Similarly, he argues that conservatives, no matter how much they insist that life begins at conception and therefore that any abortion is in violation of that life, would still agree that human life has more value the further along in fetal development.[58] Dworkin and I agree that the liberal and conservative stances on abortion are based in a similar ideological platform. However, Dworkin attempts to reconcile these positions to promote a rights-based platform for abortion. Yet, by deconstructing the language of the pro-choice and pro-life positions, his argument deconstructs itself. I would like to point to three flaws in his assertions that nevertheless might lead toward developing an epistemological framework for abortion rhetoric that privileges neither a pro-life nor a pro-choice ideology and emphasizes the need for abortion's accessibility.

The most vexing assumption Dworkin makes is that most people view all human life as sacred and inviolable. If asked, many people, across cultures, ethnicities, and religions, might undoubtedly agree with this view, but in practice upholding this assertion as truth becomes more problematic. If human life were so sacred, how could the atrocities of the twentieth and twenty-first centuries have happened and with such little protest? If all people believed in the inviolability of human life, how could the killings in Auschwitz, the bombing of Hiroshima, the genocide in Bosnia, the massacres in Rwanda, have happened? Were lives not wasted then? Crucially missing from Dworkin's analysis is a differentiation between bare life and vested human life. Timothy Campbell notes this elision in Dworkin's work when he writes, "Such a conflation of bare life and *bios* accounts for his failure to think life across different forms."[59] Campbell points to Dworkin's incapacity to think of human life beyond the individual and beyond the subject who is legible to the state and its laws. Yet Dworkin's oversight also raises the question: If abortion politics in the United States are not rooted in a shared belief that all human life is inviolable, then how did the association between abortion and life politics arise?

Dworkin emphasizes that both liberals and conservatives share the view that it is "irresponsible to waste human life." This stress on waste, which Dworkin returns to several times, echoes Arendt's critique of the capitalist ethic that guides our modern conceptualization of life and labor. Explaining her position, which she identifies as one shared by Marx, she writes:

> If any human activity was to be involved in the process at all [of accumulating wealth], it could only be bodily "activity" whose natural functioning could not be checked even if one wanted to do so. To check these "activities" is indeed to destroy nature, and for the modern age, whether it holds fast to the institution of private property or considers it to be an impediment to the growth of wealth, a check or control of the process of wealth was equivalent to an attempt to destroy the very life of society.[60]

Dworkin's rhetoric, seen through Arendt's argument, reveals itself to be rooted in a capitalist logic of accumulation and reproduction. If pro-life ideologies view abortion as "wasteful" and pro-choice positions view women who can't afford to have children but do so anyway as "wasteful," it is because they are enmeshed in a capitalist rhetoric that perceives the checking of any productive or reproductive activity as an impediment to the natural forces of profit and accumulation, and thus this checking will "destroy the very life of society." In this way the cycle of fertility is linked to the cycle of laboring not only in that they both emphasize reproduction for the sake of reproduction, as Faulkner's *The Wild Palms* shows, but also because they both generate an ideology of proliferation without regulation or impediment. Just as wealth must be allowed to grow without check, so too must individual human life be preserved for the sake of letting "nature" fulfill its cycles.

Added to his capitalist and individualizing rhetoric, Dworkin also suggests that the real reason people might be antiabortion is because they view wasting human life as "irresponsible," thus echoing the language of Margaret Sanger and Anthony Comstock, as I describe in chapter 2. Although he disagrees with this position, he does not discredit the rhetoric of responsibility, but rather uses this point to argue that antiabortion ideology is more at issue with the irresponsible action of wasting life than with actually believing that fetuses have rights. Ultimately, he agrees that since human life is sacred, we must make responsible choices, even if, as he concludes, that means deciding to abort a pregnancy. Yet by emphasizing this rhetoric of responsibility, his argument rests on certain normative assumptions: as discussed in previous chapters, discourses of responsibilization work to interpellate subjects into a liberal ethics that stabilizes norms that in turn work to demarcate populations by racial, class, and other identity-based markers. As Campbell explains in his critique, "ethic individualism quickly becomes the norm that transcends life; it is a norm of life that limits life to the confines of an individual subject and individual body."[61] Campbell points to a key problem with Dworkin's argument: it assumes an individuated life that is already formed through liberal epistemologies. Dworkin cannot seem to imagine life that is not static, not individual, and not already made legible through the recognition of the liberal state.

In *Time Travels*, Grosz asks feminists to reconsider Charles Darwin's theories of evolution and what they might have to offer to feminist conceptions of life, culture, and sexual differentiation. She explains Darwin's contribution to the life sciences as offering an ontology "in which life is now construed as an open and generative force of self-organization and growing material complexity, where life grows according to a materiality, a reality, that is itself dynamic, that has features of its own which, rather than being seen as responsive or reactive, are as readily understood in terms of the active forces of interaction that generate and sustain change."[62] Grosz's turn to Darwin has the potential to radically alter the status of life in abortion rhetoric.[63] Through her reading of Darwin she presents life as dynamic and unindividuated matter, as always having the potential for change and movement. She positions this view of life in contrast to that of feminists who have posited that nature is static and fixed.[64] One of her main interventions is to undo the nature/culture binary that has structured feminist debates for more than thirty years by contending that to argue that human behavior is formed by nature is not to say that it is fixed and therefore unchangeable, but rather that nature and the natural are as constantly changing and moving as cultural forces. Her argument has much to offer abortion rhetoric because it opens up a new understanding of life that is much larger than the individual or even the human. Grosz argues that "what the humanities may learn from Darwin is that human products and practices—institutions, languages, knowledges—are never adequate to the real of life and matter, but are always attempts to contain them, to slow them down, to place them in a position of retrospective reconstruction in the service of life's provisional interests."[65] Similarly, current American abortion rhetoric attempts to contain life by reducing it to an individuated and static form. Instead, I suggest here that if the emergence of fetal life were viewed within the larger, more complex network of all life, then we might come to realize that the valuing of human life in pro-life abortion rhetoric has nothing to do with the intrinsic value of individuated human life, but with the valuing of capitalist ideals that drive an economy based on reproduction. Perhaps once we recognize that neither the pro-life nor the pro-choice position actually values *zoe*, human life that has not been granted legibility and individuation, then we might begin to move toward abortion rhetoric that does not work through biopolitical technologies that are founded on the reification of norms and the management of populations through racial demarcations.

Epilogue: 1944 and Beyond

"White women get pregnant—plenty." His voice was harsh and angry.
"They wouldn't want it—they'd be too shamed to want it."

−LILLIAN SMITH, *STRANGE FRUIT*

The above conversation takes place between Dr. Sam Perry and Bess Anderson, friends with a professional relationship, given that Sam is also the town's only African American doctor. Bess has come to tell him that her sister, Nonnie, is pregnant as a result of a love affair with a white man, Tracy Deen, and she wants to keep the baby even though marriage is impossible given race relations in rural Georgia in the 1940s. Bess, however, insists that her sister must have an abortion. Both women are college educated, an accomplishment they achieved in part because of their mother's hard work and savings. They are, as a white character notes, the town's most respected black family. Yet when Nonnie becomes pregnant, their fragile relationship with the small and deeply segregated Maxwell begins to unravel. When Nonnie admits to Bess, her older sister, that she is pregnant, Bess immediately suggests an abortion, and her rationale reflects the popular discourse about reproduction. She tells Nonnie, "We've got to follow American ways. We've got to be respectable. We *are* respectable, Non. Our folks were decent people— fine good people."[1] Bess's admonishment might seem hypocritical: she recommends that her sister obtain an abortion—an illegal procedure, as Bess is aware—in order to "follow American ways" and "be respectable." However, Bess also knows that while she is having this conversation with her sister, Grace Stephenson, the fifteen-year-old daughter of another respectable white family in town, is struggling with the same question. Grace had a fling with another white boy—a boy her father calls "white trash"[2]—and now her father is seeking an abortion for her. Unlike Nonnie, Grace is complying, and after Tut Deen, the town's white doctor and Tracy's father, refuses to provide his friend's daughter with an abortion, he refers him to a doctor in Atlanta who will do the procedure. Bess wants the same for her sister.

As previous chapters already noted, historical records show that white women with financial means most commonly resorted to abortion. Even when abortion was outlawed, most wealthy women could still find a doctor willing to provide an abortion for the right sum.[3] Bess is disgusted that her sister would agree to live as Tracy's mistress, to have his child out of wedlock, and to live, according to her and most of the town's residents, in disgrace. Those practices, she explains to her sister, were understandable "in slavery maybe" and "in those bad years afterward," when "folks had to find back ways,"[4] but in an era when she and Nonnie can legally marry other black men and be educated, Bess cannot understand her sister's decision. Yet, despite her desire to follow respectable standards, obtaining an abortion was by no means respectable according to state law. In the 1940s government crackdowns on abortion were as strong as ever, if not at their peak. Leslie Reagan has documented that through the 1940s and 1950s authorities focused much of their energy on prosecuting not only abortionists but also women who sought abortions.[5] Kristen Luker notes that beginning in the early 1950s hospitals responded to rather lax standards about what constitutes a therapeutic abortion by creating boards that scrutinized women's reasons for seeking the procedure, and some boards even created yearly quotas that could not be surpassed.[6] Despite this harsh new legislation, women still turned to abortion to control their reproduction, and as Bess's position documents, many women preferred risking the illegal procedure to the alternative: humiliation and rejection by a community that condemned any woman who had a child out of wedlock.

Strange Fruit anticipates the movement to liberalize abortion laws that would only really begin in the 1960s and that would most famously end with *Roe v. Wade*. The novel neither condones nor condemns abortion, although Bess's last description of the fetus as "simply a mass of pulp, which could be quickly removed, were it not for Non's stubbornness,"[7] does privilege Nonnie's life over the fetus she carries. Yet *Strange Fruit* admits what few other public discussions of abortion published after 1900 would: abortion has always been available regardless of its legal status, but access to it is a marker of class, privilege, and, ironically, public respectability. The novel also dramatizes how lines of class and status often cross with race, as the Anderson family has tried to conform to white standards of living in order to gain a recognized position in their community. *Strange Fruit* was Lillian Smith's first novel; it was both acclaimed and decried. In Boston and Detroit it was banned from bookstores for its explicit sexuality, for its interracial relations, and presumably for its discussions of abortion (and lesbianism), yet in other cities it was declared a best seller. In 1944 another novel would be published that made a similar splash: Kathleen Winsor's *Forever Amber*. Winsor's novel takes place in the seventeenth century, which allows it some distance from Amber, the protagonist of the novel, who engages in licentious behavior to make her way into the arms of the king. Amber also has one abortion after another with no consequence, and the novel does little to condemn the procedure, which she often resorts to as her only method of birth control. Like *Strange Fruit, Forever Amber* was a best seller, although on a much larger scale.[8]

The decades leading up to *Roe v. Wade* continued to see the publication of novels, poems, memoirs, and plays that represent abortion. If anything, as abortion once again became a public topic of debate, it appeared everywhere. In the years just before 1973 works such as Sidney Kingsley's *Detective Story* (1949), Grace Metalious's *Peyton Place* (1956), John Barth's *The End of the Road* (1958), Lorraine Hansberry's *A Raisin in the Sun* (1959), John Updike's *Rabbit Run* (1960), Richard Yates's *Revolutionary Road* (1961), Richard Brautigan's *The Abortion: An Historical Romance* (1966), and Joan Didion's *Play It as It Lays* (1970) dealt with abortion.[9] Judith Wilt has written about the representation of abortion in late twentieth-century literature, and more recently Heather Latimer's *Reproductive Acts* looks at both fiction and film to question contemporary abortion rhetoric.

The latter half of the twentieth century and the beginning of the twenty-first century saw even more novels and films deal with women's reproductive issues. Yet as we enter an era that seems to treat every topic as fair game for public consumption, and TV shows and movies continue to push more boundaries in their depiction of sexuality and once-taboo sexual issues, abortion, ironically enough, seems to have become the unutterable word.[10] Latimer has noted that late twentieth-century representations of abortion have demonstrated "how insidious the terms of anti-abortion politics have become; it is completely routine now to be both pro-choice and to embrace foetal personhood, or to argue for a woman's reproductive freedom, but be uncomfortable with the 'A' word."[11] Latimer specifically refers to the 2007 films *Juno* and *Knocked*

Up, both of which deal with the unwanted pregnancies of young, single women. She notes that the directors of both films have publicly claimed that they are pro-choice even as their films foreclose abortion as a legitimate—and potentially more appropriate—possibility for their characters. Another stark example demonstrating shifting American attitudes toward abortion in the twentieth century comes from a comparison between Yates's brutal *Revolutionary Road*, first published in 1961, and its 2008 film adaptation. In both novel and film, April, the disillusioned suburban housewife, dies of an abortion after she realizes that her husband has no desire to change the course of their lives in order to escape rigid gender roles and bourgeois values. When April learns she is pregnant, she worries that the news will disrupt their plans to move to Paris. In the novel, Frank, her husband, opposes her suggestion of an abortion in order to make their move to Paris feasible (since she plans to work as a secretary once they arrive there). He suggests that her desire to abort isn't rational and reminds her that she has had three pregnancies and "wanted to abort two of them."[12] Yet the novel emphasizes that Frank's desire to have another child is also rooted in his promotion at work and the fact that he gains satisfaction from being a relatively mobile head of his household. The film likewise acknowledges his hidden motives for opposing the abortion, but it also twists the words of the novel to give voice to the antiabortion rhetoric that infiltrates twenty-first-century America. He tells April, "A normal woman, a normal, sane mother doesn't buy a piece of rubber tubing to give herself an abortion so she can live out some kind of a goddamn fantasy." Rather than suggesting, as he does in the novel, that April's desire to have an abortion might be rooted in her unstable childhood (a problematic accusation to be sure), in the film Frank goes a step further to accuse April of not conforming to normative standards of womanhood and motherhood, a much more far-reaching claim that suggests that abortion can never be reconciled with being a "proper woman." Even if the film is constructed to resist Frank's aggressive sentiments, the words still hang there, giving credence to the position that many Americans currently hold.

Beyond these current representations of abortion, the procedure still remains in a contested state in American politics. In March 2006 South Dakota passed a law outlawing abortion, except in rare cases of rape. While the law has been subsequently overturned, the political climate surrounding abortion politics is still charged. In the 2007 case *Gonzales v. Carhart*, the US Supreme Court ruled to outlaw a form of abortion medically known as dilation and extraction, now popularly referred to by the antiabortion movement as "partial-birth abortion." While the outlawing of this type of abortion did not make third-trimester abortion illegal in the United States, it did chip away at abortion's accessibility and, more important, created an environment of fear for both proabortion activists and medical workers. More recently, in the summer of 2013 legislators in Texas passed a law that would require any doctor who performs abortions at a freestanding women's health clinic to have hospital privileges. The US Supreme Court refused to block the law, with a five to four vote. Until a more formal appeal is presented to the court, there will be fewer than twenty clinics providing abortions for a state with more than twenty million people. South Dakota passed a law that takes a different antiabortion approach. Its most recent antiabortion measure now has the longest waiting period for women who seek abortions: after examination they must wait at least seventy-two hours before they can have the procedure. Safe and legal access to abortion is under attack in a way unseen since the late nineteenth century. Even presidential nominee and former secretary of state Hilary Clinton, historically a supporter of abortion rights, was quoted as saying, "I think abortion should remain legal, but it needs to be safe and rare. And I have spent many years now, as a private citizen, as first lady, and now as senator, trying to make it rare, trying to create the conditions where women had other choices."[13] In a speech she delivered to NARAL on January 22, 1999, she also explained, "I have never met anyone who is pro-abortion. Being pro-choice is not being pro-abortion."[14] Similarly, Wilt, in her monograph on abortion in American literature, begins her work by stating that abortion is a "monstrous, a tyrannous, but a *necessary* freedom in a fallen world."[15] Both Clinton and Wilt approach abortion as a necessary evil; both assume that the best approach to abortion is eliminating the conditions that cause women to seek ways to terminate their unwanted pregnancies or to prevent these accidental pregnancies.

As the subtitle of this book suggests, I take an unapologetic proabortion position that insists both on the relativity of life and on the problematic use of "choice" in the contemporary debate. For those of us committed to easy and affordable access to abortion, giving in to the terms of the current debate will only curtail, not open, access. Rather, I suggest we look backward to see *how* this conversation began and to learn from its genealogical unfolding. Although it is difficult to find a contemporary conversation about abortion that is not framed as a conflict between life and choice, I would argue that the rhetoric that framed abortion in the first half of the last century subtends much of our current conversation. The biopoliticization of women's bodies—of all bodies, but especially those that have been historically oppressed—is as strong as ever. We are still bound by a liberal discourse that valorizes individuality, self-reliance, responsibilization, and autonomy over any sense of collective responsibility and caretaking. Dorothy Roberts's work has eloquently argued for the ways in which reproduction, including abortion, is tied to racial issues and racism. In *Killing the Black Body* she describes a comment she once received after giving a talk on Supreme Court cases regarding reproduction and race. The commenter, a black man, advised her that abortion and reproductive rights were white women's issues and that she should "stick to traditional civil rights concerns."[16] Her work has since sought to demonstrate that reproduction is an important topic for blacks as it is intimately linked to black oppression and black women's loss of reproductive freedom. Roberts's work covers a period from colonial slavery to the twentieth century. In *Abortion in the American Imagination*, I focus on a shorter period of time to demonstrate that the eugenics movement sought to control the reproduction of black Americans (as well as that of immigrants and working-class women) and that the rhetoric that did this doubly worked to coerce white, middle- and upper-class women to reproduce.

However, just as Roberts traces a historical continuum that connects black women's reproductive conditions during slavery to the Norplant controversy in the 1990s, I believe that the eugenic rhetoric that inflected antiabortion sentiments in the early twentieth century still lingers today. In February 2011 an antiabortion group from Texas called Life Always put up a billboard in Manhattan showing a young black girl, with the message "The most dangerous place for an African American is in the womb" above her head and a URL with the words "that's abortion" below.[17] While the message actually inverts early twentieth-century rhetoric about abortion by suggesting that abortion is genocidal for black people—not Anglo-Saxons—the antiabortion tactic shares much with Horatio Storer's grandiloquent 1868 plea, "Shall [the West and the South] be filled by our own children or by those of aliens? This is a question our women must answer; upon their loins depends the future destiny of the nation."[18] The twenty-first-century billboard shares a rhetorical legacy with Storer's threat, for both appeal to fears that a particular population will be eradicated or disempowered through depopulation. Yet neither the Life Always billboard nor Storer's plea considers the woman seeking abortion and the conditions that might motivate her to end a pregnancy. Their antiabortion rhetoric is ensconced in racial politics meant to incite fear, resentment, and an insular population politics.

Luker argues that *Roe v. Wade* marked a change in the way Americans discussed abortion. For her the pre-1973 debate "merely echoes . . . the issue as the nineteenth century defined it: a debate about the medical profession's right to make life-and-death decisions." Once abortion became legal in the United States, she sees the debate as encompassing wholly new terms that bring "the issue of the moral status of the embryo to the fore" to focus on "the relative rights of women and embryos."[19] While public discussions of abortion may have changed, I believe that at the core the debate is much the same: it's still about race and eugenics; it's still about capital and economics; it's also still about liberal notions of responsibility and autonomy. Examining the early twentieth century can show us that; now it's time for us to realize that our twenty-first-century discussions about abortion are still bound in these issues. The literature and culture of the early twentieth century allow us to see these issues as inextricably connected. In order to situate the contemporary abortion debate within a rhetoric that takes into account racial, liberal, economic, and of course gendered factors, a similar study needs to be done that examines not only contemporary literature but the popular culture that has infiltrated our lives: today we have films, TV shows, and websites that represent abortion. I believe that such a study would similarly reveal a more nuanced contemporary rhetoric of abortion that could be used to gain women more access to the practice. I'll end with a sentiment that began this book: abortion does not have to be a moral issue. By looking backward to an era before life and choice framed abortion rhetoric, I hope that we can develop a new discourse for abortion that looks forward in new ways—one that is finally beyond life and choice.

Notes

Introduction

1. See Mohr, *Abortion in America,* for more of this history; see A. M. Mauriceau's *The Married Woman's Private Medical Companion* (1848) for an example of one such guide. Mauriceau is believed to be a pseudonym for Madame Restell's husband, discussed in chapter 4.

2. Jewett, *Country of the Pointed Firs,* 11.

3. Ibid., 4. The rest of the passage reads: "but with certain vials she gave cautions, standing in the doorway, and there were other doses which had to be accompanied on their healing way as far as the gate, while she muttered long chapters of directions, and kept up an air of secrecy and importance to the last. It may not have been only the common ails of humanity with which she tried to cope; it seemed sometimes as if love and hate and jealousy and adverse winds at sea might also find their proper remedies among the curious wild-looking plants in Mrs. Todd's garden." Although this passage is elusive, Mrs. Todd's work does seem to deal with matters of life and death, love and reproduction.

4. Examples of nineteenth-century dime novels that discuss abortion are the anonymously penned *Anna, Louisa, and Nannie; or, The Three Victims* (1859); Andrew Jackson Davis's *Tale of a Physician; or, The Seeds and Fruits of Crime* (1869), which featured a villainous abortionist, Madame LeStelle, ostensibly modeled on the real-life Madame Restell; and *The Great "Trunk Mystery" of New York City* (1871), also based on a true case. Davis's novel and the Trunk Mystery are discussed in more detail in chapter 1. In nineteenth-century novels *abortion* is more commonly used to refer to a living monstrosity, as in *Moby-Dick,* in which Melville calls the albino "more strangely hideous than the ugliest abortion" (211).

5. When I began my research, the number of fictional works written before 1945 that incorporate an abortion or the possibility of an abortion in their plots surprised me. Some works by more canonical or recognized authors that include abortion are

Gertrude Stein's "The Good Anna" (1909), which implies that a character operates an abortion clinic; Eugene O'Neill's plays *The Abortion* (1914) and *Strange Interlude* (1928); Edith Wharton's *Summer* (1917); F. Scott Fitzgerald's *The Beautiful and Damned* (1922); Edith Summers Kelley's *Weeds* (1923); Floyd Dell's *Janet March* (1923); Dorothy Parker's "Mr. Durant" (1924) and "Lady with a Lamp" (1932); Theodore Dreiser's *An American Tragedy* (1925); John Dos Passos's *Manhattan Transfer* (1925); Ernest Hemingway's "Hills like White Elephants" (1927); Josephine Herbst's *Money for Love* (1929) and *The Executioner Waits* (1934); Margery Latimer's *This Is My Body* (1930); William Faulkner's *As I Lay Dying* (1930) and *The Wild Palms* (1939); Sinclair Lewis's *Ann Vickers* (1932); Kay Boyle's *My Next Bride* (1934); Tess Slesinger's *The Unpossessed* (1934); Langston Hughes's "Cora Unashamed" (1936); and Lillian Smith's *Strange Fruit* (1944). By the mid- to late twentieth century the number of authors who incorporate abortion as a component of plot are far more numerous.

6. Carlson, *Crimes of Womanhood*, 8.

7. Dell, *Janet March*, 211.

8. Doyle, *Bordering on the Body*, 232.

9. Mao and Walkowitz, "Expanding Modernism." See also Friedman, "Planetarity," for an expanded reading of Mao and Walkowitz's arguments on modernism.

10. Trask, *Cruising Modernism*, 14.

11. Doyle, *Bordering on the Body*, ix.

12. Seitler, *Atavistic Tendencies*, 15.

13. Luker, *Abortion and the Politics of Motherhood*, 2.

14. Brown, *Edgework*, 39.

15. Pateman would not have called herself a "radical liberal"; Jane Mansbridge plays with applying the term to her as a means to investigate certain themes in her writing, although she admits that the label has an uneasy fit. See Mansbridge, "Carole Pateman: Radical Liberal?"

16. Brown, *States of Injury*, 164.

17. Deutscher, "Inversion of Exceptionality," 56.

18. Doyle, *Bordering on the Body*, 4.

19. Weinbaum, *Wayward Reproductions*, 1.

20. The research group Advancing New Studies in Reproductive Health (ANSIRH) recently began a study to trace how women who are denied abortions fare compared to those who have them. More information and some preliminary results of that study can be found here: http://www.ansirh.org/research/turnaway.php (accessed Nov. 26, 2013).

21. LeSueur, *Girl*, 94.

22. Ibid., 97.

23. Ibid., 158.

24. See Schoen, *Choice and Coercion*.

25. Nikolas Rose describes the shift thusly: "In the processes of nation-building in European states and their colonies, from at least the mid-nineteenth century, ideas and practices of citizenship involved ways in which citizens should conduct themselves in relation to their health and reproduction. And for the biopolitics of the first half of the twentieth century—whether in its eugenic or welfarist forms—the body of the citizen, the individual citizen and the collective citizen body of the people, the nation or the Volk, was a prime value" (*Politics of Life Itself*, 24).

26. For histories of abortion regulation in the United States, see Mohr, *Abortion in America*; Reagan, *When Abortion Was a Crime*; Brodie, *Contraception and Abortion*; Smith-Rosenberg, *Disorderly Conduct*; Beisel and Kay, "Abortion, Race, and Gender"; L. Gordon, *Woman's Body, Woman's Right*; Luker, *Abortion and the Politics of Motherhood*; Roberts, *Killing the Black Body*; Solinger, *Wake Up Little Susie*; and Schoen, *Choice and Coercion*. For works that focus on a critique of abortion discourse, see Petchesky, *Abortion and Woman's Choice*; Poovey, "Abortion Question and the Death of Man"; Cornell, *Imaginary Domain*; Solinger, *Beggars and Choosers*; and Stormer, *Articulating Life's Memory*.

1 / The Biopolitics of Abortion as the Century Turns

1. Surprisingly, little has been written in peer-reviewed publications about this short story. In 2000, PBS produced a made-for-TV movie based on the story.

2. Hughes, "Cora Unashamed," 3.

3. Ibid., 4.

4. Ibid., 12.

5. Ibid., 13.

6. Ibid., 15.

7. Ibid., 18.

8. Ibid., 7.

9. Ibid., 4.

10. The term *bare life*, as I'm using it here, comes from Agamben's *Homo Sacer*, drawing on a notion that has its roots in Roman law. According to this law, *Homo sacer* is a man who can be killed but cannot be sacrificed. Agamben reads this law into more contemporary politics, suggesting that today life, or in Judith Butler's terms a livable life, only exists with state law. Thus the subject that exists outside the law is bare life, abject, perhaps homeless—like the Rwandan child pictured on American TV begging for money yet perhaps no longer alive on Rwandan soil, Agamben tells us. Butler also has an interesting discussion of this kind of life, which she terms "merely life." See Butler, *Undoing Gender*.

11. Agamben, *Homo Sacer*, 131.

12. Ibid., 132.

13. Ibid., 6.

14. See Aristotle, *Nicomachean Ethics, Eudemian Ethics*, and *Politics*.

15. Latimer, "Bio-reproductive Futurism," 53.

16. Ibid., 53.

17. Weinbaum, *Wayward Reproduction*, 20.

18. Harris, "Whiteness as Property."

19. James Mohr, in *Abortion in America*, one of the first histories of abortion regulation in the United States, argues that in a span of less than fifty years abortion was villainized as a working-class practice. He suggests that many elite white women began thinking of abortion as only sought by nonwhite and poor women. See chapter 3 for more discussion of Mohr's argument.

20. See Beisel and Kay, "Abortion, Race, and Gender," for a review of how race has been discussed by historians of abortion practice in the United States. While Beisel and Kay's literature review is quite comprehensive, they overlook Nathan Stormer's

Articulating Life's Memory, which was published two years prior to their article and is the only monograph on American abortion politics that commits several chapters to the racist and eugenic beginnings of American antiabortion laws. For a fuller discussion of their work and how it differs from this project, see chapter 3.

21. Reagan, *When Abortion Was a Crime*, 11, 13.

22. See Mohr, *Abortion in America*; L. Gordon, *Woman's Body, Woman's Right*; Smith-Rosenberg, *Disorderly Conduct*.

23. "A Terrible Mystery," *New York Times*, Aug. 27, 1871.

24. "The Evil of the Age," *New York Times*, Aug. 29, 1871.

25. Ibid.

26. Although the novel was published anonymously, its author was mostly likely Augustus St. Clair, who was hired by the *New York Times* to cover stories like the one described in this chapter. Many of the quotations in the novel attributed to Dr. Rosenzweig and other characters in the trial were lifted directly from the paper's reporting of the case.

27. Anonymous, Great *"Trunk Mystery,"* 20.

28. Ibid., 22.

29. Ibid., 52.

30. "The Trunk Murder," *New York Times*, Sept. 2, 1871.

31. Anonymous, Great *"Trunk Mystery,"* 34, 44, 67.

32. Ibid., 35.

33. That Rosenzweig performed abortions is likely. The *Times* reported that police found instruments of abortion and recipes for herbal mixtures at his offices that would likely produce abortion. Whether Rosenzweig was responsible for the death of Alice Bowlsby is questionable, as the evidence provided for the connection is based on the word of the trunkman and a handkerchief found in Rosenzweig's home that had the faint initials and name "A. A. Bowlsby," according to police investigators. In fact, a family friend of Rosenzweig's, Cornelia Bowlsby of Brooklyn, testified in court, after hearing in the news that the handkerchief was a key piece of evidence in the case, that it actually belonged to her daughter, Anna Martine Bowlsby, who had accidentally left it there after using it to wipe up some spilled wine. She claimed that upon close scrutiny the faded and miniscule middle initial would reveal itself to be an "M," not an "A." Her testimony did not influence the jury. See "The Terrible Crimes," *New York Times*, Aug. 31, 1871; "Rosenzweig's Trial," *New York Times*, Oct. 27, 1871. The *New York Times* carried extensive and detailed coverage of this case.

34. Kassanoff, *Edith Wharton*, 145.

35. The economics of this transaction are discussed in more detail in chapter 4.

36. Mohr, *Abortion in America*, 147.

37. Ibid., 124.

38. Ibid., 218. New York was one of the first states to completely outlaw abortion, and then in 1970, along with Hawai'i and Alaska, it was one of the first states to repeal nearly all its antiabortion laws.

39. A. J. Davis, *Tale of a Physician*, 122.

40. Ibid., 185.

41. Ibid., 241–242.

42. Ibid., 195.

43. Mary Rogers, commonly known as the "Beautiful Cigar Girl," was found dead in the Hudson in the summer of 1841. The marks on her body indicated murder, although

the case was never solved. The story was widely publicized in the New York media, and it was speculated that the abortionist Madame Restell was involved, although no conclusive evidence was discovered. In 1842 Edgar Allan Poe published a serialized detective story that loosely fictionalized Rogers's story, although he changed her name to Marie Roget and set the story in Paris. His story concludes that Mary's death was the result of an abortion, although this is obliquely alluded to. Besides Molly Ruciel sharing the initials of Mary Rogers, Davis's description of her death resonates with how Mary Rogers's death was received by the media. Additionally, as if to confirm this connection, in one place Davis slips and calls his character Mary Ruciel instead (202). For more on Mary Rogers's history and its connection to Poe's story, see Srebnick, *Mysterious Death of Mary Rogers*.

44. Storer, *On Criminal Abortion*, 1.

45. Ibid., 8.

46. Ibid., 11.

47. Ibid., 14.

48. Ibid., 14.

49. Kristin Luker calls nineteenth-century antiabortion activists, like Storer, the first "right-to-life" movement and places them as most active between 1850 and 1890. She refutes previous historians' claims that antiabortion physicians were actually most concerned with the life of the fetus. Rather, she argues that in trying to professionalize medicine, doctors latched on to "pro-life" rhetoric in order to emphasize that they were somehow on a higher moral plane than quacks and midwives who allowed abortion (*Abortion and the Politics of Motherhood*, 14, 29).

50. By the late twentieth century antiabortion activists would make this link even more explicit, even calling those born after 1972 survivors of the abortion holocaust. This gruesome antiabortion website is a prime example: http://www.survivors.la/ (accessed Nov. 26, 2013).

51. E. H. Parker, "Relation of the Medical and Legal Professions," 468.

52. Bacon, "Duty of the Medical Profession," 19.

53. Ibid., 19.

54. Biever, "Moral Aspect of Race Suicide," 257.

55. Storer, *On Criminal Abortion*, 115.

56. Ibid., 4.

57. Unfortunately, some recent histories of abortion, such as Joseph Dellapenna's work, which argues that nineteenth-century activists were motivated by a respect for life above all, rather than by misogynist desires to control women's reproduction and eliminate midwives and other alternative practitioners, have been given credence in respected law reviews discussing contemporary abortion law and its historical precedents. See also, as an example, Gorski, "Author of Her Trouble."

58. Wharton, *Summer*, 145.

59. Ibid., 235.

60. Ibid., 236.

61. Ibid., 248.

62. Ibid., 167, 176, 184, 185.

63. Ibid., 71.

64. Ibid., 170.

65. Arendt, *Origins of Totalitarianism*, 302.

66. These are precisely the conditions and breakages that Wharton would have noticed in her intimate and often frustrating work trying to obtain a decent standard of living for refugees during World War I.

67. Wharton, *Summer*, 72 (italics mine).

68. Ibid.,184.

69. Ibid., 260.

70. Ibid., 269, 273.

71. Brown, *States of Injury*, 171.

72. Wharton, *Summer*, 271.

73. The phrase "state of exception" as I'm using it here implies a state of emergency where the law has been suspended indefinitely. See chapter 5 for definition of this term and its relation to abortion law. Here I'm arguing that Charity lives in a state of exception both in North Dormer and on the Mountain, or rather in the relational existence of the two places; in North Dormer the crisis is always in the town's fear and disdain of the Mountain, which it claims threatens with its lawlessness but where the threat of being banished to the Mountain also always exists. On the Mountain law is always suspended and relational to the conditions of the town.

74. Bauer, *Edith Wharton's Brave New Politics*. Numerous essays have by now documented the conversations about race, eugenics, reproduction, and gender in *Summer*, including those by Bauer, Kassanoff, and Allison Berg.

2 / The Inadvertent Alliance of Anthony Comstock and Margaret Sanger

1. For more on this history see Brodie, *Contraception and Abortion*; Mohr, *Abortion in America*; Reagan, *When Abortion Was a Crime*.

2. I see the rhetorics of rights and choice as related because they are both grounded in a liberal and individuated understanding of law. Both assume a universal, ahistoricized subject with no attention to particularities that often make access to a right or choice impossible or even more oppressive. There is a rich scholarship of writing critiquing the legalization of abortion through rights and choice. For a critique of choice but a defense of rights, see Cornell, *Imaginary Domain*; Solinger, *Beggars and Choosers*. For a critique of choice that avoids valorizing rights, see Petchesky, *Abortion and Woman's Choice*. For a critique of both rights and choice, which the argument made here follows most closely, see Poovey, "Abortion Question and the Death of Man." In the following pages I will briefly summarize these arguments.

3. One of the most well-regarded and thorough texts critiquing the rhetoric of choice in abortion politics is Solinger's *Beggars and Choosers*. Solinger calls choice a watered-down version of rights and strongly advocates for a more rights-based abortion politics.

4. In *Roe v. Wade*, the rhetoric of "freedom to" appears in Justice Blackmun's opinion as follows: "This right of privacy, whether it be founded in the Fourteenth Amendment's concept of personal liberty and restrictions upon state action, as we feel it is, or, as the District Court determined, in the Ninth Amendment's reservation of rights to the people, is broad enough to encompass a woman's decision whether or not to terminate her pregnancy." "Freedom from" is also represented in the case's decision: "We repeat, however, that the State does have an important and legitimate interest in preserving and protecting the health of the pregnant woman, whether she be a

resident of the State or a nonresident who seeks medical consultation and treatment there, and that it has still another important and legitimate interest in protecting the potentiality of human life."

5. The Apr. 2007 Supreme Court Case decision on abortion rights, *Gonzales v. Carhart*, made this point even more explicit when Justice Anthony Kennedy argued that "partial-birth" abortion must be outlawed to protect women from making a harmful decision for themselves.

6. Crenshaw begins her article by asserting that the era of civil rights is dead. She notes, for example, that whenever "civil rights" are invoked in bills, the words often signal a reactionary attack on gains made during the civil rights era, such as affirmative action, thus demonstrating the slipperiness of rights language. See Crenshaw, "Were the Critics Right about Rights?"

7. In tracing the history of critiques of rights, Crenshaw identifies the critics of rights as "Crits"—those who during the civil rights movement opposed the rights-based attempts to overcome American racism (ibid.).

8. Ibid., 67, 70.

9. In Marx the critique is focused on how in the nascent United States the separation of church and state grants the individual the right to freedom of religion, thereby actually sedimenting the practice of religion by relegating it to the realm of individual choice and expression.

10. Lisa Duggan critiques Brown's analysis of rights-based leftist activism because it doesn't acknowledge that using a rights-based approach can be strategic in a system where change often happens through rights. She also thinks that Brown overgeneralizes her characterization of leftist organizations. See Duggan, *Twilight of Equality?* 79–80. Yet Duggan also agrees with the importance of Brown's argument against using rights to advance antioppression movements.

11. Ruhl, "Dilemmas of the Will," 643.

12. Cornell, *Imaginary Domain*, 35.

13. Ibid., 46.

14. For example, in the 1992 Supreme Court Case *Planned Parenthood v. Casey*, which did uphold *Roe v. Wade*, state laws requiring twenty-four-hour waiting periods, "informed consent" (meaning, in many cases, that a doctor had to inform the patient that she was terminating a life), and parental notification were deemed constitutional. All of these clauses were supported by antiabortion activists, who believed that they would mitigate the harm women caused themselves (and the fetus).

15. Solinger, *Beggars and Choosers*, 5.

16. Petchesky, *Abortion and Woman's Choice*, xxv.

17. Ibid., 2.

18. Ibid., 7.

19. Poovey, "Abortion Question and the Death of Man," 243.

20. Ibid., 249.

21. Berlant, "America, 'Fat,' the Fetus," 153.

22. Foucault, *History of Sexuality*, 145.

23. The subtitle for this section is a "Nietzschean Incident." Earlier in the novel, Fitzgerald associates the philosopher's ideologies with selfishness and egotism. For example, Gloria is described as a "practicing Nietzschean" because "of her outrageous and commendable independence of judgment" and because "of her arrogant

consciousness that she had never seen a girl as beautiful as herself" (*Beautiful and Damned*, 131). By titling this section with such an allusion to Nietzsche, Fitzgerald implies that Gloria is about to commit the supposedly most selfish (and independent) of all acts—aborting motherhood.

24. Ibid., 135.

25. When Gloria informs Anthony of her plan, her decision seems cryptic. However, in the novel's ironic spirit, perhaps Fitzgerald was alluding to Clinton Levi Merriam, US senator from 1871 to 1875, who pushed the Comstock Laws forward because he saw them as "saving the outraged manhood of our day." Merriam argued that obscene material circulating through respectable homes was the largest threat society faced because it challenged "the purity and beauty of womanhood." See Dennett, *Birth Control Laws*.

26. Fitzgerald, *Beautiful and Damned*, 135.

27. Ibid., 138.

28. Ibid., 139.

29. Ibid., 149.

30. The official title of the law is "An Act for the Suppression of Trade in, and Circulation of, Obscene Literature and Articles of Immoral Use." Comstock objected to the colloquial reference of this law by his name. In *Frauds Exposed* he tries to show that he was not responsible for its passing but that several members of Congress strongly supported antiobscenity laws and pushed their passage. However, with the law's passing, Comstock was made a special agent of the US Postal Service, which inextricably associated him with its enforcement.

31. These laws would not be federally overturned until the 1965 Supreme Court case *Griswold v. Connecticut*.

32. Consumption of alcohol was his first target. Before he became a moral reformer, he opened up a small dry goods store and was soon shocked by the amount of alcohol consumed by his male customers.

33. 18 USC Section 1461. An earlier version of this law included the phrase "for preventing conception" in front of "producing abortion."

34. *Frauds Exposed* is descriptively subtitled *How the People Are Deceived and Robbed, and Youth Corrupted*.

35. Comstock, *Frauds Exposed*, 43.

36. Her given name was Ann Lohman. An immigrant from England, Madame Restell sold pills that were claimed to abort fetuses. Her business was so successful, she moved to Fifth Avenue in New York City and worked among the most elite New Yorkers, many of whom were her clients. See chapter 4 for more of Restell's history.

37. Beisel, *Imperiled Innocents*, 47 (italics mine).

38. Brodie, *Contraception and Abortion*, 273.

39. In 1872 Woodhull organized the People's Party and ran for president with Frederick Douglass as her running mate. She was also the first woman to become a stockbroker on Wall Street. See ibid., 273.

40. Brodie notes that the case reflected so poorly on Comstock that both the YMCA and his sympathetic biographer made no note of the incident in their records (ibid.).

41. Comstock, *Frauds Exposed*, 417.

42. Ibid., 416.

43. The concept of "responsibilization" comes from Michel Foucault's *History of Sexuality*. Foucault also adds that procreative behavior is socialized as one means to

construct sexuality, which he writes should "not be thought of as a kind of natural given which power tries to hold in check, or as an obscure domain which knowledge tries to gradually uncover." In other words, there are no normative sexualities, as Comstock and Sanger wanted their audiences to believe; rather, they both constructed narrative sexualities that fit into their political agendas (*History of Sexuality,* 104–105).

44. Shuttleworth, "Female Circulation," 55.

45. My point here about how autonomous and self-willed men are a middle-class construction is also reflected in Comstock's temperance crusades in the late nineteenth century. See Beisel's conclusion to *Imperiled Innocents,* where she argues that temperance movements were based in preserving class divisions and maintaining a well-disciplined middle class.

46. This chapter focuses on Comstock's book *Frauds Exposed.* His other three books were also polemical texts, as the titles explicitly state: *Traps for the Young* (1883), *Gambling Outrages* (1887), and *Morals versus Art* (1887).

47. As an anonymous bystander observing Gloria in the closing page of the novel comments, "She seems sort of—sort of dyed and unclean, if you know what I mean. Some people just have that look about them whether they are or not" (Fitzgerald, *Beautiful and Damned,* 366).

48. For example, a Google search for "Margaret Sanger" turns up Planned Parenthood sites praising their founder for work to make birth control accessible, as well as feminist organizations holding Sanger up as a role model for women, while also revealing sites that villainize Sanger, accusing her of racial genocide for her involvement in the American eugenics movement.

49. Blount, "Large Families and Human Waste," 3.

50. Sanger, "Birth Control and Racial Betterment," 11.

51. Ibid., 12.

52. Sanger, "Birth Control or Abortion?" 3.

53. Ibid., 3.

54. Ibid., 4.

55. Sanger, *Woman and the New Race,* 122.

56. Ibid., 129.

57. Mohr, *Abortion in America,* 86. Here Mohr documents that it was primarily white, middle-class women who sought abortion during its era of illegality.

58. Sanger, *Margaret Sanger,* 286.

59. Ibid., 449.

60. Ibid., 451.

61. Ibid., 449.

62. Chesler, *Woman of Valor,* 300.

63. Ibid., 271.

64. See J. M. Jensen, "Evolution of Margaret Sanger's 'Family Limitation.'" *Family limitation* was Sanger's early description for what she later named birth control.

65. Sanger, *Selected Papers,* 1: 88–89, 359.

66. J. M. Jensen acknowledges that her theory is speculative since the eighth and ninth editions of "Family Limitation" are missing, perhaps with important clues to Sanger's seemingly new position on abortion.

67. Stopes was one of the leading birth control activists in early twentieth-century England.

68. Sanger, *Selected Papers*, 1: 164–166.

69. The editors of *The Selected Papers of Margaret Sanger* include a different reading in their notes. They argue, "since MS never strongly reprimanded BCCRB [Birth Control Clinical Research Bureau] workers Marjorie Prevost and Anna Lifshiz for referring patients for abortions, her private views may not have changed much since 1914" (2: 154 n21), referring to Sanger's earlier, more lenient view of abortion. However, as I demonstrate here, almost all of her writings, including personal letters, suggest that she did view abortion as personally irresponsible behavior, even if she was occasionally forgiving of women who sought the procedure.

70. Sanger, *Selected Papers*, 1: 199. Allowing women access to abortion if pregnancy presented a risk to the health of the woman (physical or mental) gave rise to the term *therapeutic abortion*, which was legal in the United States until *Roe v. Wade* made all abortions legal.

71. See Sanger, *Woman and the New Race*, 126–127.

72. Sanger, *Selected Papers*, 1: 381. The editors of *The Selected Papers of Margaret Sanger* note that the figures Sanger cites are miscalculated in the note to the cited quotation (92 n1).

73. Ruhl, "Dilemmas of the Will," 654.

74. Ibid., 656.

75. Angelina Weld Grimké published two short stories in the *Birth Control Review*, the second entitled "Goldie." Named after her somewhat more famous aunt, Angelina Grimké Weld, the nineteenth-century feminist and abolitionist, the younger Grimké has an unusual history, given the conditions of early twentieth-century America. Her father was Angelina Weld's half-brother, the child of their shared father and his slave. Weld invited her half-brother to live with her up north and provided for his education. He eventually married a white woman, Grimké's mother. However, when Grimké was still a child, her mother abandoned her and returned to live with her family, leaving Grimké to be raised by her father.

76. Owen, "Women and Children of the South," 9.

77. Burrill, "They That Sit in Darkness," 6.

78. Ibid., 7.

79. Ibid., 7.

80. Meier, "Refusal of Motherhood," 117.

81. Ibid., 120.

82. Dawkins, "From Madonna to Medea," 225–226.

83. Grimké, "Closing Door," part 1, 12.

84. Ibid., 135.

85. Ibid., 138.

86. Hartman, *Scenes of Subjection*, 117.

87. Grimké, "Closing Door," part 2, 10.

88. Dawkins, "From Madonna to Medea," 230.

89. English, *Unnatural Selections*, 125.

90. See Fleissner, *Women, Compulsion, Modernity*, 267–272, for more speculation on why Grimké might have submitted her stories to the *Birth Control Review*.

91. Ibid., 132.

92. In fact, W. E. B. Du Bois advocated this position. He publicly supported the *Birth Control Review* and even published in it on a few occasions. See English, *Unnatural*

Selections, for more information on Du Bois's involvement in eugenics and the ways in which it influenced his work and life choices.

93. Chesler, *Woman of Valor,* 66.

94. Sanger, *Selected Papers,* 1: 165.

95. Brown, *States of Injury,* 96.

3 / The Eugenics of Bad Girls

1. Mills, "Biopolitics, Liberal Eugenics, and Nihilism," 187.

2. Admittedly, abortion laws, attitudes, and ideologies have been used to shape women's reproductive functions in myriad ways. In our contemporary moment, for example, disability rights groups often argue that proabortion laws allow potential parents to discriminate against fetuses diagnosed with abnormalities as a means to privilege only those children who conform to society's expectations of what a healthy child is and what it means to parent that child.

3. Bauer, *Sex Expression,* 230.

4. See Morrow, *Great War.*

5. In *The Passing of the Great Race; or, The Racial Basis of European History* Grant makes some very unscientific claims about the different white races that make up Europe. The entire thrust of the book is to demonstrate how Nordics, a group he sees as originating in northern Europe, are superior to all other whites. While Stoddard concedes to this claim in *Rising Tide,* he makes it in a more minor passing point.

6. Stoddard, *Rising Tide of Color,* 162.

7. If there were fewer than one hundred residents of a given national population, then one hundred was used as the minimum number. Therefore, from that country two people would be allowed to immigrate per year. A maximum quota was also determined that used a complicated ratio. See Trevor, *Analysis of the American Immigration Act of 1924,* for the complete act and its rules.

8. Galton coined the term *eugenics* from the Greek root meaning "good in birth."

9. Numerous books have been published on the history of eugenics. See, e.g., Bruinius, *Better for All the World;* Roberts, *Killing the Black Body;* and English, *Unnatural Selections.* I'm particularly referring here to the eugenics movement that gained strength after World War I and encouraged the ideology that intelligence was inherited, that class and race position was genetically coded, and thus that certain populations needed to be managed through limiting their ability to reproduce, often through forced sterilization. A 1927 Supreme Court case, *Buck v. Bell,* provides an infamous example of these policies; Carrie Buck was sterilized without her consent because her "lower intelligence" made her an unsuitable candidate for reproduction, according to the Court.

10. Beisel and Kay, "Abortion, Race, and Gender," 499.

11. Other historians of abortion in the United States have similarly argued that abortion was mostly sought by white women. See Brodie, *Contraception and Abortion;* Reagan, *When Abortion Was a Crime;* Mohr, *Abortion in America.*

12. I share Wendy Brown's critique in "The Impossibility of Women's Studies," where she argues that a model of intersectionality for understanding the cross-section of gender, race, and class is problematic. This model often assumes, including in the way Beisel and Kay employ it, that all three categories of identity function on different

axes that can be analyzed separately. Instead, Brown suggests we understand the construction of identity as a tight weave that is constantly reified and resisted through various technologies. See Brown, "Impossibility of Women's Studies," for more.

13. When the American Medical Association unanimously passed the resolution that abortion should be outlawed from the moment of conception, it gave the following justification: "We are the physical guardians of women; we, alone, thus far, of their offspring in utero. The case here is life or death—the life or death of thousands—and it depends, almost wholly, upon ourselves." See "Report on Criminal Abortion," 76.

14. Lockwood, "Criminal Abortion," 220.

15. Taussig, "Control of Criminal Abortion," 772.

16. Beckman, "Abortion, and Some Suggestions," 447.

17. Foucault, *Security, Territory, Population*, 95.

18. Ibid., 93.

19. A *New York Times* article reported that bookstores in Boston refused to sell *Bad Girl* because of "one pretty strong chapter in it." See "Boston Bans Delmar Book," *New York Times*, May 4, 1928. Presumably, the *Times* article, which was published shortly after the novel's debut, refers to the chapter where Dot visits the abortionist and is molested by him.

20. Viña Delmar's *Bad Girl* was the fifth-best-selling novel in 1928, according to the *Publishers Weekly* list of the top ten best-selling works of fiction. *Ann Vickers* was the third-best-selling novel in 1933. And Christopher Morley's 1939 *Kitty Foyle* was the second most widely read novel in 1940. Second-wave feminist criticism in the late 1970s to the early 1990s brought attention to women's popular fiction—novels and stories that were written specifically with a female audience in mind and sometimes by women writers. Critics such as Tania Modleski, Madonne Miner, and Jennifer Scanlon have argued that genre fiction aimed at women provides them a space for connection, or as Scanlon puts it, opportunities for "identification, escape, and catharsis" ("Inarticulate Longings," 139). While I certainly think it might have invoked these emotions in many women, particularly if they were white women with leisure time and access to books, popular fiction is also a place to tell women stories about themselves and a means to circulate dominant ideologies, in particular those regarding the ties among reproduction, race, and class.

21. Gillette, "Making Modern Parents," 58. For more details see Gillette's essay, where she carefully documents the novel's reception in its time. Bauer also incisively argues that Dot's sexuality is "more about bourgeois possibility and geographic location than it is about racial stereotypes of black promiscuity and Jewish greed" (*Sex Expression*, 161). I agree with Bauer's first two points, but I argue here that the novel equates racial identity with the first two categories.

22. In a *New York Times* review of books published in first six months of 1928, John R. Chamberlain writes of *Bad Girl*, "If the novel had been written before the wars commenced to rage over Zola back in the last century it would have marked a great date in literary history; as it is, it marks a minor date in the history of contemporary manners. The story is skilful, observant, and captures a mood in the life of a section of the metropolis that will be invaluable 100 years hence for those seeking bygone atmosphere." While in the same review Chamberlain dismisses Claude McKay's *Home to Harlem*, his observation of *Bad Girl* feels quite prescient to me, as a reader who sought the novel precisely because of its portrayal of early twentieth-century American life.

See John R. Chamberlain, "Six Months in the Field of Fiction," *New York Times*, June 24, 1928.

23. Delmar, *Bad Girl*, 34.

24. Ibid., 221.

25. Ibid., 239.

26. Ibid., 25.

27. Ibid., 37.

28. Ibid., 233.

29. Mohr, *Abortion in America*, 240.

30. Bauer, *Sex Expression*, 159.

31. Weinbaum argues that race and reproduction form a bind that make the two terms inextricable, so that one cannot discuss race without conjuring reproduction and vice versa. Weinbaum is interested in how "race and reproduction are bound together within transatlantic modernity's central intellectual and political formations" (*Wayward Reproductions*, 6). See chapter 1 for further discussion of her work. This chapter takes Weinbaum's argument to be central, so that any discussion of abortion must then be subtended by racial undertones. Similarly, Berg's *Mothering the Race* and Doyle's *Bordering on the Body* argue that modernist discussions of motherhood are always racially imbued, and thus I further their claim here to include abortion. Doyle, e.g., has argued that "mothers reproduce bodies not in a social vacuum but for either a dominant or a subordinate group" (*Bordering on the Body*, 5). I also further discuss her argument in the introduction.

32. Berg, *Mothering the Race*, 18.

33. Rabinowitz, "End Results of Criminal Abortion," 809.

34. Buckingham, "Criminal Abortion," 141.

35. Michinard, "Medical Aspect of Criminal Abortion," 262.

36. Delmar, *Bad Girl*, 119.

37. Ibid., 106.

38. Ibid., 117.

39. Ibid., 125.

40. Ibid., 111–112.

41. Ibid., 114.

42. The subheading is from Morley, *Kitty Foyle*, 262.

43. For more on the effects of the women's movement beginning in the 1940s, see L. Gordon, *Woman's Body, Woman's Right*, which argues that the backlash against feminist gains in the 1920s began in the 1940s, not the 1950s, as previous historians have argued.

44. Some states, including New York, even instituted laws that forced women who had had abortions to testify against their providers. If they refused, they risked being incarcerated until they testified. See Reagan, *When Abortion Was a Crime*, 165.

45. Ibid., 163.

46. To stress the difference in population between Kitty and Wyn, a 1939 *New York Times* review of the novel states, "Translated into local terms, it is almost as though a girl from Brooklyn had fallen in love with a gentleman from Westbury or Sands Point. Almost, but not quite; actually there is no parallel anywhere in the East for the suburban elegance that clusters along the main line of Pennsylvania this side of Paoli." See Ralph Thompson, "Books of the Times," *New York Times*, December 5, 1939.

47. Stetz, "Christopher Morley's *Kitty Foyle*," 135.

48. Morley, *Kitty Foyle*, 18.

49. Ibid., 17.

50. Kitty and Myrtle's position in the novel as outsiders could be encapsulated by what Nietzsche has termed *ressentiment*. He writes: "in order to exist, slave morality always first needs a hostile external world [most often constructed]; it needs, physiologically speaking, external stimuli in order to act at all—its action is fundamentally reaction" (*On the Genealogy of Morals*, 37). For Myrtle and Kitty, the Main Liners, who can supposedly trace their ancestors back seven generations in Philadelphia and even further in England, are posited as the hostile external world against which they construct their identities.

51. Foucault, *History of Sexuality*, 37.

52. Morley, *Kitty Foyle*, 46.

53. Foucault, *Security, Territory, Population*, 42.

54. I realize that my language here suggests a fairly static formulation of the population. Therefore, I want to stress that while populations are meant to be static, the continuation of their existence actually depends on a more fluid categorization. For example, in the early twentieth century, whiteness only constituted people of Anglo-Saxon heritage, but by the middle of that century that categorization had already shifted to include Jews, Italians, Irish, and other previously excluded groups. This shift was necessary to maintain whiteness as a construction of population.

55. In 1947 Milton M. Gordan published an article in the *American Journal of Sociology*, using *Kitty Foyle* to demonstrate his argument that "class is culture." Margaret Stetz's article, which I cite, was published in 2008 in an anthology on periodicals and mass culture. Beyond those two works, most of the attention *Kitty Foyle* received was in the form of reviews in the year of its publication.

56. Morley, *Kitty Foyle*, 27.

57. Ibid., 280.

58. Ibid., 336.

59. By comparing Mark's race to Fedor's missing leg, Kitty is defining race as consisting of lack. In a similar vein, the German Nazi-era eugenicist Otmar Freiherr von Verschuer understands "inferior" races as "a group of human beings who manifest a certain combination of homzygotic genes that are lacking in other groups" (Agamben, *Homo Sacer*, 88). For Verschuer racism is pseudo-scientifically based on the lacking of key genes in certain population categories, whereas for Kitty race is formed through an inverse process—Mark's racial difference is due to an incompleteness in his genetic makeup.

60. I should note that the end of the novel is ambiguous. Kitty never tells her reader what she decides, although she does answer Mark's phone call and calls him "darling."

61. Kühl, *Nazi Connection*, 29.

62. Ibid., 31.

63. Ibid., 37.

64. Morley, *Kitty Foyle*, 306.

65. Ibid., 325–326.

66. Kitty's reference to a "cross-pattern of the genes," explained to her by Mark, who is also a doctor, suggests that Morley was familiar with the work of geneticists such as Hugo de Vries and August Weismann, whose work in the early twentieth

century rediscovered Mendelian genetics and helped establish in the scientific community that heredity in genetically inscribed.

67. Morley, *Kitty Foyle*, 270.
68. Ibid., 270.
69. Ibid., 269.
70. Ibid., 65.
71. Ibid., 263.
72. Donald Adams, "A New Novel," *New York Times*, Jan. 29, 1933.
73. Cass, "*Ann Vickers* by Sinclair Lewis Book Review," 814.
74. Adams, "New Novel."
75. For a reading of the novel as feminist see Fleming, "Lewis's Two 'Feminist Novels'"; and Parry, "Boundary Ambiguity and the Politics of Abortion."
76. Lewis, *Ann Vickers*, 16, 17.
77. Ibid., 59.
78. Ibid., 79.
79. Ibid., 163.
80. Ibid., 170.
81. Ibid., 186.
82. Ibid., 191.
83. Ibid., 194.
84. Ibid., 196.
85. Ibid., 195.
86. Taussig, "Control of Criminal Abortion," 777.
87. Lewis, *Ann Vickers*, 197.
88. Ibid., 198–199.
89. Ibid., 209–210.
90. Ibid., 215.
91. Ibid., 218.
92. Ibid., 324.
93. The film adaptation of *Kitty Foyle*, which was first released in 1940, is easily accessible on DVD and available for mainstream viewing. *Bad Girl* in its 1931 film version is available only through the UCLA Film Archives. At the time of writing, *Ann Vickers* was available for purchase only in VHS format.
94. See Miller, *Censored Hollywood*, for more on the Hays Code and its influence on Hollywood productions.
95. Joy, letter, Nov. 28, 1928, Production Code Administration (PCA) Archive, Margaret Herrick Library, Los Angeles.
96. *Bad Girl* was also made into a Broadway play, scripted by Lincoln Osborn, and was first performed off-Broadway in a Bronx theater in Sept. 1930. Surprisingly, the dramatic script for this version is frank and direct about Dot and Eddie's premarital sex and the discussion of abortion after their marriage. Whereas the film deleted most of the novel's discussion of birth control, the play uses these lines word for word and in some cases even elaborates on them. During its opening night both the district attorney and several local policemen attended the performance, ostensibly because they suspected it might depict unsavory scenes. A *New York Times* article ("'Bad Girl' Hearing Delayed," Sept. 21, 1930) reports that they filed a complaint against the play and that the action would have prevented the show from its upcoming scheduled run

on Broadway. However, the producer, Robert Newman, insisted that the inappropriate scenes would be deleted before the Broadway opening.

97. Breen, letter, May 5, 1933, PCA Archive.

98. Sergel, *Christopher's Morley's "Kitty Foyle."*

99. Ibid, 123.

100. Ibid., 128–129.

4 / Economies of Abortion

1. Smedley, *Daughter of Earth*, 205.

2. Josephine Herbst's *Money for Love* (1929) provides another example of the intersection of abortion and economy. The protagonist, Harriet, pays for her own abortion but then tries to bribe her former lover for thousands of dollars with the threat that she'll otherwise tell his wife.

3. Matthews, *"As I Lay Dying* in the Machine Age," 72.

4. Faulkner, *As I Lay Dying*, 73.

5. Ibid., 62.

6. Matthews cites James Mohr's study, which focuses on abortion history in the nineteenth century. While both Matthews and Mohr are correct in noting that over-the-counter distribution of abortifacients declined in the early twentieth century, when Faulkner's novel is set, Lafe was not completely outdated in suggesting to Dewey Dell that she could find a way to abort with the help of a pharmacist.

7. Reagan, *When Abortion Was a Crime*, 44.

8. Sanger, *Selected Papers*, 2: 258. Apiol was one of the chemicals often found in abortifacients from the early twentieth century, although if it produced abortion there were often also toxic effects. See Shorter, *History of Women's Bodies*, 217–221.

9. See *The Propaganda for Reform in Proprietary Medicines*, published by the AMA Press in 1922. The book is a collection of articles published in the AMA journal that document a long list of drugs that in many cases do not list ingredients or make impossible claims for cures.

10. Faulkner, *As I Lay Dying*, 201–202.

11. Ibid., 201.

12. Marx, *Grundisse*, 91.

13. Ibid., 92.

14. Faulkner, *As I Lay Dying*, 176.

15. Haag, *Consent*, 38.

16. Faulkner, *As I Lay Dying*, 176.

17. Ibid., 247.

18. Haag, *Consent*, 5.

19. Ibid., 19.

20. Faulkner, *As I Lay Dying*, 257.

21. Dreiser, *Sister Carrie*, 48.

22. Benn Michaels, *Our America*, 33.

23. Ibid., 35.

24. Ibid., 48.

25. Bauer, *Sex Expression*, 43.

26. Dreiser, *American Tragedy*, 105.

27. Ibid., 261.

28. Ibid., 317.

29. Ibid., 349.

30. Benn Michaels, *Our America*, 57.

31. Capo documents that Dreiser was interested in birth control politics and wrote in support of birth control in the Apr. 1921 issue of the *Birth Control Review*. She quotes him: "I sometimes suspect the wealthy and powerful of various persuasions and interests, especially those who might hope to profit from the presence here of vast and docile hordes, of having more of an interest in blind, unregulated reproduction on the part of the masses that they would care to admit." See Capo, *Textual Contraception*, 26. I argue that just as Dreiser saw birth control as inextricably linked to economy and class, he also saw abortion as part of this economy.

32. Dreiser, *American Tragedy*, 387.

33. Ibid., 392.

34. Ibid., 722.

35. Stix, "Study of Pregnancy Wastage," 361. A reprint of this article was found in Margaret Sanger's papers at the Sophia Smith Collection, Women's History Archives at Smith College.

36. O'Reilly, "Abortion and Birth Control," 9.

37. Dreiser, *American Tragedy*, 388.

38. Ibid., 395.

39. Ibid., 400.

40. Ibid., 416.

41. Ibid., 425.

42. Dreiser basically acknowledges this point in his essay "I Find the Real American Tragedy," published ten years after *An American Tragedy* in *Mystery Magazine*. He writes, "If at the moment when [Chester] stood in the boat and was ready to strike Billy Brown [Roberta's real-life counterpart] with the tennis racket, a voice had called, 'Stop! You don't have to do that in order to escape. Take the girl to a doctor. Have an operation performed. Give her this money and tell her how deeply you desire to be released and why, and she will release you!'—there is no question in my mind, and none in yours, that he would have dropped the racket and gladly gone about the business of giving this girl her life and freedom." See Dreiser, "I Find the Real American Tragedy," 299.

43. Trask, *Cruising Modernism*, 19.

44. Karaganis, "Naturalism's Nation," 156.

45. Besides Dreiser's fictional account of the trial, two films were made based on the novel. The 1931 film *An American Tragedy*, which Dreiser felt butchered his novel, and the 1951 *A Place in the Sun*, starring Elizabeth Taylor. In 1986 Craig Brandon published a nonfictional account of the trial and its characters' histories. Interestingly, Brandon writes that there is no evidence that Chester Gillette, the character that Dreiser modeled Clyde Griffiths on, sought an abortion for Grace Brown, Roberta's nonfictional equivalent, before her drowning. See Brandon, *Murder in the Adirondacks*, 78.

46. For a more comprehensive history of Madame Restell's involvement with abortion and contraception, see Horowitz, *Rereading Sex*; Carlson, *Crimes of Womanhood*; Homberger, *Scenes from the Life*; and Keller, *Scandalous Lady*.

47. Born in England as Ann Trow Summers, she moved to New York City in the early nineteenth century with her husband, who died shortly after leaving her with a

young daughter. In order to support herself she began making and selling contraceptive potions. She then met and married Charles Lohman, a printer for the *New York Herald*. He also published tracts related to contraception and was in a circle of "free thinkers" that included Robert Dale Owen and Frances Wright. Together the couple created the alias for her—Madame Restell, which was supposedly the name of the French doctor that trained her.

48. Carlson, *Crimes of Womanhood*, 111.

49. The exposé is entitled *Lights and Shadows of New York Life; or, the Sights and Sensations of the Great City* and contains the disclaimer that "it is not safe for a stranger to undertake to explore these places for himself." See McCabe, *Lights and Shadows*, 15.

50. Madame Restell is actually never explicitly named. Rather, McCabe writes that he will focus on "Madam——" and explains that she "is well known and needs no comment" (*Lights and Shadows*, 623). The proceeding details make it clear that it is indeed Restell whom he describes.

51. Ibid., 623.

52. Ibid., 621.

53. Ibid., 623–624.

54. Ibid., 627.

55. The actual price for the book was twelve cents, and it was intended to be "sold by all the dealers in cheap books."

56. Anonymous, *Madame Restell*, 6.

57. Ibid., 8.

58. Ibid., 8.

59. Homberger, *Scenes from the Life*, 89.

60. Horowitz, *Rereading Sex*, 198.

61. *Sun*, Mar. 28, 1839. The ad then appeals to readers to visit Madame Restell's clinic.

62. Marvin Olasky chronicles Madame Restell's advertising history in his article and estimates that Madame Restell's annual advertising bill in the *Sun* would have amounted to about $650 a year and in the *Herald* to about $420 a year, unless she received a discount for publishing regularly. See Olasky, "Advertising Abortion," 51.

63. Homberger, *Scenes from the Life*, 102. The physician-author of *Madame Restell: Her Life* acknowledges that Madame Restell saw herself as aiding the public. Rebutting her idea of herself as a benefactoress, he sarcastically notes, "No—Madame Restell is, in her own estimation, a philosopher, a philanthropist, and in more ways than one, a public benefactor. She has the most serene and complacent ideas of her importance to society, and she really don't [sic] see how the community could possibly get along without her. She would tell you, in a very affecting way, no doubt, of the fears she had allayed, the agonies she has removed, and the sorrows and misfortunes concealed. In all this she has the most unbounded confidence. She positively thinks that she is one of the nicest, best, bravest little women in the world; and she would be very indignant, if any one should offer to dispute it. . . . It does not seem to occur to her that she is the horrible wretch they think her" (Anonymous, *Madame Restell*, 19). According to the transcripts for the trial of Maria Bodine in 1847, published by the *Police Gazette*, there is much evidence that Madame Restell cared deeply for her patients. She slept in the same bed with Maria until she fully recovered from her abortion, gave her money out of her pocket for train fare and food for the ride home, and affectionately kissed her goodbye.

64. *New York Tribune*, Aug. 26, 1847, quoted in Homberger, *Scenes from the Life*, 107. The *Tribune* did not publish Madame Restell's advertisements for abortion, which, among New York City papers, could only be found in the *Sun* and the *Herald*.

65. Homberger, *Scenes from the Life*, 116.

66. Horowitz, *Rereading Sex*, 206.

67. Carlson, *Crimes of Womanhood*, 130.

68. Horowitz, *Rereading Sex*, 206.

69. "End of a Criminal Life," *New York Times*, Apr. 2, 1878.

70. See, e.g., Piercy, *Sex Wars*, a fictionalized account of Madame Restell.

71. Meridel LeSueur's *The Girl*, written in 1939 and discussed in the introduction, was as radical in many ways, but LeSueur wasn't able to find her novel a publisher until 1978.

72. Smedley, *Daughter of Earth*, 193.

73. Ibid., 205.

74. Ibid., 207.

75. Ibid., 216.

76. Ibid., 217.

77. Capo, *Textual Contraception*, 158, 166.

78. See Rubin, "Traffic in Women"; Butler, "Merely Cultural"; and Duggan, *Twilight of Equality?* for discussions of how sexuality is critically connected to political economy under liberal and neoliberal governments.

5 / Making a Living

1. Another way to understand this critique of human value is through Martin Heidegger's "Letter on Humanism." In his essay Heidegger writes, "To think against 'values' is not to maintain that everything interpreted as 'a value' . . . is valueless. Rather, it is important finally to realize that precisely through the characterization of something as 'a value' what is so valued is robbed of its worth. That is to say, by the assessment of something as a value what is valued is admitted only as an object for man's estimation. . . . Every valuing, even when it values positively, is a subjectivizing" (*Basic Writings*, 251). Heidegger's point is similar to the one I make here: by proclaiming that human life has value, we turn that life into a "thing" that can be measured, encapsulated, and individuated. We actually devalue the value of that life by only viewing it as a subjectivized, individuated form and not as part of a larger species of life or as part of other nonhuman conditions.

2. Arendt, *Human Condition*, 313.

3. I will use the term *pro-life* here to designate the belief that abortion equals the killing of a human because that it is the recognized terminology for the movement. However, as my argument will suggest, I think this description is a misnomer.

4. See *Samford Crimson*, http://media.www.samfordcrimson.com/media/storage/paper1166/news/2007/09/05/Opinion/ProLife.until.Birth-2954202-page2.shtml (accessed July 15, 2009).

5. While this chapter focuses mostly on Agamben's explanation of the state of exception, the concept is not original to him and can be found in the work of the conservative political thinker Carl Schmitt and in Walter Benjamin's writings. See Schmitt, *Political Theology*; Benjamin, *Theses on the Philosophy of History*.

6. Importantly, Arendt critiques Marx here for his own valorization of labor in his economic theories. Arendt instead suggests that labor and work be seen as distinct categories, where labor is entrapment in endless cycles of reproduction and work values the end product. By separating these two categories, Arendt envisions a world where production is not always reproduction and where all products are just viewed as consumable objects (*Human Condition*, 89).

7. Ibid., 88.

8. Dobbs, "Flooded," 834.

9. Arendt, *Human Condition*, 93.

10. Faulkner, *Wild Palms*, 29.

11. Ibid., 72.

12. Ibid., 72.

13. Ibid., 99.

14. Ibid., 107.

15. Urgo, "Faulkner Unplugged," 254.

16. Arendt, *Human Condition*, 127.

17. Faulkner, *Wild Palms*, 33.

18. Ibid., 35.

19. Dobbs, "Flooded," 827.

20. Faulkner, *Wild Palms*, 88.

21. Duvall, *Faulkner's Marginal Couple*, 46.

22. Faulkner, *Wild Palms*, 46.

23. Ibid., 173.

24. Grosz, *Chaos, Territory, Art*, 9.

25. Faulkner, *Wild Palms*, 250.

26. Barry describes this crevasse as pouring out 468,000 second-feet into the delta. This amount of water at such speed would in ten days cover almost one million acres with water ten feet deep. See Barry, *Rising Tide*, 203.

27. Ibid., 203.

28. Ibid., 131.

29. Richard Washburn Child, "The Battle of the Levees," *Saturday Evening Post* 199 no. 52 (June 25, 1927): 8.

30. Barry, *Rising Tide*, 190.

31. Ibid., 21.

32. Barry cites this statistic in "The Prologue, and Maybe the Coda," *New York Times*, Sept. 4, 2005, where he compares the 1927 Mississippi flood to Katrina and the flood it caused in 2005. Barry also argues that the flood was one of the precipitating factors that caused thousands of African Americans to leave the South and move to northern cities like Chicago and New York.

33. Faulkner wrote the two sections continuously; he started with "Wild Palms" and then continued with "The Old Man," switching between the sections until he finished the story. However, after the novel's initial publication, some publishers excerpted "Wild Palms" or "The Old Man" as though they were separate stories. In one version of the novel, the two sections are printed together side by side as though the publisher had just happened to decide to anthologize them together. See McHaney's *William Faulkner's "The Wild Palms"* for more about the novel's publication history.

34. Faulkner, *Wild Palms*, 111.

35. Ibid., 168.

36. Eldred, "Faulkner's Still Life," 141.

37. In writing about his novel, Faulkner explained that he saw "The Old Man" as a contrapuntal narrative that emphasized certain themes present in "Wild Palms."

38. In American history, notable moments when the state of exception was visibly declared were in 1861, when President Abraham Lincoln suspended habeas corpus when he declared war on the South, and in 2001, when President George W. Bush enacted a similar suspension of law after the attacks of Sept. 11. See Agamben, *State of Exception*, for more on this history.

39. Ibid., 1.

40. Faulkner, *Wild Palms*, 137 (italics mine).

41. Ibid., 200.

42. Ibid., 204, 201.

43. Ibid., 201.

44. Ibid., 62.

45. Ibid., 26.

46. Ibid., 146.

47. Dobbs, "Flooded," 822.

48. Grosz, *Chaos, Territory, Art*, 5 (italics mine).

49. Faulkner, *Wild Palms*, 243–244.

50. Ibid., 209.

51. Dworkin, *Life's Domain*, 13.

52. Ibid., 25.

53. Ibid., 31. Even more problematically, when Dworkin ventures to address feminist critiques of legalizing abortion on the basis of a right to privacy, he draws on Catharine MacKinnon's reactionary assertions. Dworkin takes issue with MacKinnon's argument that granting abortion on the basis of privacy frees the government from responsibility to aid women who cannot afford abortions. Additionally, by protecting women's privacy, the law could then also insist that the government cannot interfere with what happens behind private doors, even in cases of domestic abuse and rape. He does draw on MacKinnon's assertion that the fetus is a form of human life to demonstrate that the liberal position also views human life as inviolable. Dworkin does not address critiques of rights and choice by such feminist thinkers as Mary Poovey, Rosalind Petchesky, and Carroll Rosenberg-Smith, who were publishing their critiques by the mid-1990s.

54. Drucilla Cornell has also critiqued Dworkin's defense of abortion in terms of life's sanctity. Cornell's critique is powerful, but it ultimately rests on a rights-based paradigm, which I critique in chapter 2. For more of her argument, see *Imaginary Domain*.

55. Dworkin, *Life's Domain*, 34.

56. Ibid., 58 (italics mine).

57. Ibid., 94.

58. Ibid., 94.

59. Campbell, introduction, xxxvii.

60. Arendt, *Human Condition*, 112.

61. Campbell, introduction, xxxviii.

62. Grosz, *Time Travels*, 37.

63. I acknowledge that implicit in accepting Grosz's understanding of life as dynamic and its implications for a life politics of abortion is agreement that evolution, as Darwin observed it, does exist and informs life on earth.

64. Another way to understand Grosz's argument is through Keith Ansell-Pearson's reading of Henri Bergson. Ansell-Pearson writes, "If our consciousness were eliminated the material universe would continue to subsist as it was and matter would resolve itself into numberless vibrations linked together in an uninterrupted continuity 'and traveling in every direction like shivers through an immense body'" (*Philosophy and the Adventure of the Virtual*, 165). In other words, we only perceive matter as formed and, in some cases, in its individuated state because our human brains have been structured to do so. If we can imagine life without the organizing functions of our consciousness, then we might begin to perceive a very different material world and a very different understanding of life within that world.

65. Grosz, *Time Travels*. 42.

Epilogue

1. Smith, *Strange Fruit*, 292.

2. Ibid., 151.

3. See Luker, *Abortion and the Politics of Motherhood*, 44.

4. Smith, *Strange Fruit*, 124.

5. Reagan, *When Abortion Was a Crime*, 161.

6. Luker, *Abortion and the Politics of Motherhood*, 56.

7. Smith, *Strange Fruit*, 369.

8. Barbara Taylor Bradford, in a foreword to an edition of the novel published in 2000, reports that in its first week *Forever Amber* sold one hundred thousand copies and that by the end of its run in hardcover two million copies had been sold. See Bradford, introduction, i.

9. Some of these texts are discussed in Judith Wilt's study of twentieth-century representations of abortion in literature (*Abortion, Choice, and Contemporary Fiction*). Wilt primarily focuses on both American and British texts from the latter half of the twentieth century.

10. Latimer also notes that in the 1980s popular films such as *Dirty Dancing* (1987) and *Fast Times at Ridgemont High* (1982) were willing to seriously grapple with and represent abortion ("Popular Culture," 223).

11. Ibid., 213.

12. Yates, *Revolutionary Road*, 195.

13. From the Democratic Compassion Forum, Messiah College, Apr. 13, 2008.

14. "NARAL" formerly stood for the National Abortion Rights Action League. However, in 2003 its name was changed to NARAL: Pro-Choice America, removing any visible association with the word *abortion*. This move in itself signifies the growing antiabortion sentiment in the United States; even organizations that support women's reproductive rights want to dissociate themselves from abortion.

15. Wilt, *Abortion, Choice, and Contemporary Fiction*, xii.

16. Roberts, *Killing the Black Body*, 5.
17. See the following *New York Times* opinion piece from Mar. 1, 2011: http://www.nytimes.com/2011/03/01/nyregion/01nyc.html.
18. Storer, *Why Not!* 85.
19. Luker, *Abortion and the Politics of Motherhood*, 193.

Works Cited

"An Act for the Suppression of Trade in, and Circulation of, Obscene Literature and Articles of Immoral Use" ("Comstock Law"). March 3, 1873, ch. 258, § 2, 17 Stat. 599.

Agamben, Giorgio. *Homo Sacer: Sovereign Power and Bare Life.* Translated by Daniel Heller-Roazen. Stanford: Stanford University Press, 1998.

———. *Means without Ends: Notes on Politics.* Translated by Vincenzo Binetti and Cesare Cesarino. Minneapolis: University of Minnesota Press, 2000.

———. *State of Exception.* Translated by Kevin Attell. Chicago: University of Chicago Press, 2005.

Anonymous. *Anna, Louisa, and Nannie; or, The Three Victims: With Full and Correct Statements of the Intrigue, Deception, Conspiracy, and Murder Committed by Daniel Longrave, the Accomplished Accomplice of Mother Higgins.* Philadelphia: M. A. Milliette, 1859.

Anonymous. *The Great "Trunk Mystery" of New York.* Philadelphia: Barclay, 1871.

Anonymous. *Madame Restell: An Account of Her Life and Horrible Practices Together with Prostitution in New York.* New York: Self-published, 1847.

Ansell-Pearson, Keith. *Philosophy and the Adventure of the Virtual: Bergson and the Time of Life.* New York: Routledge, 2002.

Arendt, Hannah. *The Human Condition.* Chicago: University of Chicago Press, 1958.

———. *The Origins of Totalitarianism.* New York: Harcourt, 1951.

Aristotle. *The Eudemian Ethics.* Translated by Anthony Kenny. New York: Oxford University Press, 2011.

172 / WORKS CITED

———. *The Nicomachean Ethics*. Translated by J. A. K. Thomson. New York: Penguin, 2003.

———. *Politics*. Translated by Ernest Barker. New York: Oxford University Press, 2009.

Ann Vickers. Directed by John Cromwell. Los Angeles: RKO, 1933.

Atwood, Margaret. *The Handmaid's Tale*. 1985. New York: Anchor, 1998.

Bacon, C. S. "The Duty of the Medical Profession in Relation to Criminal Abortion." *Illinois Medical Journal* 7 (1905): 18–24.

Bad Girl. Directed by Frank Borzage. Los Angeles: Motion Pictures, 1931.

Balay, Anne. "'Hands Full of Living': Birth Control, Nostalgia, and Kathleen Norris." *American Literary History* 8, no. 3 (Autumn 1996): 471–495.

Balibar, Etienne, and Immanuel Wallerstein. *Race, Nation, Class: Ambiguous Identities*. Translated by Chris Turner. New York: Verso, 1991.

Barry, John M. *Rising Tide: The Great Mississippi Flood of 1927 and How It Changed America*. New York: Simon and Schuster, 1998.

Bauer, Dale M. *Edith Wharton's Brave New Politics*. Madison: University of Wisconsin Press, 1994.

———. *Sex Expression and American Women Writers, 1860–1940*. Chapel Hill: University of North Carolina Press, 2009.

Beckman, Oswald. H. "Abortion, and Some Suggestions How to Lessen Criminal Abortion." *California State Journal of Medicine* 14 (1916): 447–450.

Beisel, Nicola. *Imperiled Innocents: Anthony Comstock and Family Reproduction in Victorian America*. Princeton: Princeton University Press, 1997.

Beisel, Nicola, and Tamara Kay. "Abortion, Race, and Gender in Nineteenth-Century America." *American Sociological Review* 69, no. 4 (August 2004): 498–518.

Benjamin, Walter. "Theses on the Philosophy of History." In *Illuminations: Essays and Reflections*, translated by Harry Zohn, 253–264. New York: Shocken Books, 1968.

Benn Michaels, Walter. *The Gold Standard and the Logic of Naturalism: American Literature at the Turn of the Century*. Berkeley: University of California Press, 1987.

———. *Our America: Nativism, Modernism, and Pluralism*. Durham: Duke University Press, 1997.

Berg, Allison. *Mothering the Race: Women's Narratives of Reproduction, 1890–1930*. Urbana: University of Illinois Press, 2001.

Berlant, Lauren. "America, 'Fat,' the Fetus." *boundary 2* 21, no. 3 (Autumn 1994): 145–195.

Biever, Albert. "Moral Aspect of Race Suicide and Criminal Abortion." *New Orleans Medical and Surgical Journal* 61 (1908–1909): 251–260.

Blount, Anna. "Large Families and Human Waste." *Birth Control Review* 2, no. 1 (1918): 3.

Bradford, Barbara. Introduction to *Forever Amber*, by Kathleen Winsor (1944), i–iii. Chicago: Chicago Review Press, 2000.

Brandon, Craig. *Murder in the Adirondacks: "An American Tragedy" Revisited.* Utica: North Country Books, 1986.

Briggs, Laura. "The Race of Hysteria: 'Overcivilization,' and the 'Savage' in Late Nineteenth-Century Obstetrics and Gynecology." *American Quarterly* 52, no. 2 (2000): 246–273.

Brodhead, Richard. *Cultures of Letters: Scenes of Reading and Writing in Nineteenth-Century America.* Chicago: University of Chicago Press, 1995.

Brodie, Janet Farrell. *Contraception and Abortion in Nineteenth-Century America.* Ithaca: Cornell University Press, 1994.

Brown, Wendy. *Edgework: Critical Essays on Knowledge and Politics.* Princeton: Princeton University Press, 2005.

———. "The Impossibility of Women's Studies." *differences: A Journal of Feminist Cultural Studies* 9, no. 3 (1997): 79–102.

———. *States of Injury: Power and Freedom in Late Modernity.* Princeton: Princeton University Press, 1995.

Bruinius, Harry. *Better for All the World: The Secret History of Forced Sterilization and America's Quest for Racial Purity.* New York: Knopf, 2006.

Buckingham. E. M. "Criminal Abortion." *Cincinnati Lancet and Observer* 10, no. 3 (March 1867): 139–143.

Burrill, Mary. "They That Sit in Darkness: A One-Act Play." *Birth Control Review* 3, no. 9 (September 1919): 5–8.

Butler, Judith. "Merely Cultural." *New Left Review* 227 (1998): 33–44.

———. *Precarious Life: The Powers of Mourning and Violence.* New York: Verso, 2004.

———. *Undoing Gender.* New York: Routledge, 2004.

Butler, Judith, and Gayatri Chakravorty Spivak. *Who Sings the Nation-State? Language, Politics, Belonging.* London: Seagull Books, 2007.

Campbell, Timothy. "*Bios*, Immunity, Life: The Thought of Robert Esposito." Introduction to *Bios: Biopolitics and Philosophy*, by Roberto Esposito, translated by Timothy Campbell, vii–xlii. Minneapolis: University of Minnesota Press, 2004.

Capo, Beth Widmaier. *Textual Contraception: Birth Control and Modern American Fiction.* Columbus: Ohio State University Press, 2007.

Carlson, A. Cheree. *The Crimes of Womanhood: Defining Femininity in a Court of Law.* Urbana: University of Illinois Press, 2009.

Cass, E. R. "*Ann Vickers* by Sinclair Lewis Book Review." *Journal of Criminal Law and Criminology* 24, no. 4 (1933): 814–817.

Castro, Joy. "'My Little Illegality': Abortion, Resistance, and Women Writers on the Left." In *The Novel and the American Left: Critical Essays on Depression-Era Fiction*, edited by Janet Galligani Casey, 16–34. Iowa City: University of Iowa Press, 2004.

Chanock, Martin. "'Culture' and Human Rights: Orientalising, Occidentalising, and Authenicty." In Mamdani, *Beyond Rights Talk and Culture Talk*, 15–36.

Chesler, Ellen. *Woman of Valor: Margaret Sanger and the Birth Control Movement in America*. New York: Doubleday, 1992.

Cheah, Pheng. "Mattering." *Diacritics* 26, no. 1 (Spring 1996): 108–139.

Comstock, Anthony. *Frauds Exposed; or, How the People Are Deceived and Robbed, and Youth Corrupted*. Montclair, NJ: Patterson Smith, [1880] 1969.

———. *Traps for the Young*. New York: Funk and Wagnalls, c. 1883.

Cornell, Drucilla. *The Imaginary Domain: Abortion, Pornography, and Sexual Harassment*. New York: Routledge, 1995.

Crenshaw, Kimberlé. "Were the Critics Right about Rights? Reassessing the American Debate about Rights in the Post-Reform Era." In Mamdani, *Beyond Rights Talk and Culture Talk*, 61–74.

Crewe, Jonathan. "Baby Killers." *differences: A Journal of Feminist Cultural Studies* 7, no. 3 (1995): 1–23.

Dash, Irene. "The Literature of Birth and Abortion." *Regionalism and the Female Imagination* 3, no. 1 (1977): 8–13.

Davis, Andrew Jackson. *Tale of a Physician; or, The Seeds and Fruits of Crime*. New York: American News Company [distributor], 1869.

Davis, Angela. *Women, Race, Class*. New York: Random House, 1981.

Dawkins, Laura. "From Madonna to Medea: Maternal Infanticide in African American Women's Literature of the Harlem Renaissance." *Literature Interpretation Theory* 15 (2004): 223–240.

Dearborn, Ella K. "Birth Control and a Bugaboo." *Birth Control Review* 4, no. 5 (1920): 14–15.

Deleuze, Gilles. *Negotiations*. Translated by Martin Joughin. New York: Columbia University Press, 1995.

Dell, Floyd. *Janet March*. New York: Knopf, 1923.

Dellapenna, Joseph. *Dispelling the Myths of Abortion History*. Durham: Carolina Academic Press, 2006.

Delmar, Viña. *Bad Girl*. New York: Harcourt, Brace, and Co., 1928.

Dennett, Mary Ware. *Birth Control Laws: Shall We Keep Them, Change Them, or Abolish Them?* New York: F. H. Hitchcock, 1926.

Deutscher, Penelope. "The Inversion of Exceptionality: Foucault, Agamben, and 'Reproductive Rights.'" *South Atlantic Quarterly* 107, no. 1 (Winter 2008): 55–70.

Dobbs, Cynthia. "Flooded: The Excesses of Geography, Gender, and Capitalism in Faulkner's *If I Forget Thee, Jerusalem*." *American Literature* 73, no. 4 (December 2001): 811–835.

Doyle, Laura. *Bordering on the Body: The Racial Matrix of Modern Fiction and Culture*. New York: Oxford University Press, 1994.

Dreiser, Theodore. *An American Tragedy*. 1925. New York: Signet, 2000.

———. "I Find the Real American Tragedy." In *Theodore Dreiser: A Selection of Uncollected Prose,* edited by Donald Pizer, 291–299. Detroit: Wayne State University Press, 1977.

———. *Sister Carrie.* New York: Oxford University Press, 2009.

Duggan, Lisa. *The Twilight of Equality? Neoliberalism, Cultural Politics, and the Attack on Democracy.* Boston: Beacon Press, 2004.

Duvall, John. *Faulkner's Marginal Couple: Invisible, Outlaw, and Unspeakable Communities.* Austin: University of Texas Press, 1990.

Dworkin, Ronald. *Life's Domain: An Argument about Abortion, Euthanasia, and Individual Freedom.* New York: Vintage, 1994.

Edelman, Helen Susan. "Safe to Talk: Abortion Narratives as a Rite of Return." *Journal of American Culture* 19, no. 4 (1996): 29–39.

Eldred, Janet Carey. "Faulkner's Still Life: Art and Abortion in *The Wild Palms.*" *Faulkner Journal* 4, nos. 1–2 (Autumn 1988–Spring 1989): 139–158.

Engels, Friedrich. *The Origin of the Family, Private Property, and the State.* New York: Penguin, 2009.

English, Daylanne. *Unnatural Selections: Eugenics in American Modernism and the Harlem Renaissance.* Chapel Hill: University of North Carolina Press, 2004.

Esposito, Roberto. *Bios: Biopolitics and Philosophy.* Translated and with an introduction by Timothy Campbell. Minneapolis: University of Minnesota Press, 2004.

Faulkner, William. *As I Lay Dying.* 1930. New York: Vintage Books, 1990.

———. *Wild Palms.* 1939. New York: Vintage Books, 1990.

Fedorko, Kathy A. *Gender and the Gothic in the Fiction of Edith Wharton.* Tuscaloosa: University of Alabama Press, 1995.

Fitzgerald, F. Scott. *The Beautiful and Damned.* 1922. New York: Penguin Books, 1998.

———. *The Great Gatsby.* 1925. New York: Scribner, 1999.

Fleissner, Jennifer L. *Women, Compulsion, Modernity: The Moment of American Naturalism.* Chicago: University of Chicago Press, 2004.

Fleming, Robert E. "Lewis's Two Feminist Novels: *The Job* and *Ann Vickers.*" In *Sinclair Lewis: New Essays in Criticism,* edited by James M. Hutchisson, 52–67. Athens: University of Georgia Press, 1995.

Foucault, Michel. *Discipline and Punish: The Birth of the Prison.* Translated by Alan Sheridan. New York: Vintage, 1977.

———. "Governmentality." In *The Foucault Effect: Studies in Governmentality,* edited by Graham Burchell, Colin Gordon, and Peter Miller, 87–104. Chicago: University of Chicago Press, 1991.

———. *History of Sexuality: An Introduction: Volume 1.* Translated by Robert Hurley. New York: Vintage, 1978.

———. "Nietzsche, Genealogy, History." In *Language, Counter-Memory, Practice,* translated by Donald F. Bouchard, 139–164. Ithaca: Cornell University Press, 1977.

———. *Security, Territory, Population: Lectures at the Collège de France, 1977–1978.* Translated by Graham Burchell. New York: Palgrave Macmillan, 2007.

———. *Society Must Be Defended: Lectures at the Collège de France, 1975–1976.* Translated by David Macey. New York: Picador, 2003.

Friedman, Susan Stanford. "Planetarity: Musing Modernist Studies." *Modernism/modernity* 17, no. 3 (September 2012): 471–491.

Galton, Francis. *Hereditary Genius: An Inquiry into Its Laws and Consequences.* 1869. New York: St. Martin's Press, 1978.

Gillette, Meg. "Making Modern Parents in Ernest Hemingway's 'Hills like White Elephants' and Viña Delmar's *Bad Girl.*" *Modern Fiction Studies* 53, no. 1 (Spring 2007): 50–69.

Goldsmith, Meredith. "White Skin, White Mask: Passing, Posing, and Performing in the *The Great Gatsby.*" *Modern Fiction Studies* 49, no. 3 (Autumn 2003): 443–468.

Gonzales v. Carhart. April 2007. Public Law 108–105, HR 760, S 3, 18 US Code 1531 (US Supreme Court Case).

Gordon, Linda. *Woman's Body, Woman's Right: Birth Control in America.* New York: Penguin, 1990.

Gordon, Milton M. "Kitty Foyle and the Concept of Class as Culture." *American Journal of Sociology* 53, no. 3 (1947): 210–217.

Gorski, Ashley. "The Author of Her Trouble: Abortion in Nineteenth- and Early Twentieth-Century Judicial Discourses." *Harvard Journal of Law and Gender* 32 (2009): 431–462.

Grafton, Kathy. "Degradation and Forbidden Love in Edith Wharton's *Summer.*" *Twentieth Century Literature* 41, no. 4 (Winter 1995): 350–366.

Grant, Madison. *The Passing of the Great Race; or, The Racial Basis of European History.* New York: C. Scribner's Sons, 1916.

Grimké, Angelina Weld. "The Closing Door." Part I. *Birth Control Review* 3, no. 9 (September 1919): 10–14.

———. "The Closing Door." Part II. *Birth Control Review* 3, no. 10 (October 1919): 8–12.

Griswold v. Connecticut. June 1965. 381 US 479 (US Supreme Court Case).

Grosz, Elizabeth. *Chaos, Territory, Art: Deleuze and the Framing of the Earth.* New York: Columbia University Press, 2008.

———. *Time Travels: Feminism, Nature, Power.* Durham: Duke University Press, 2005.

Haag, Pamela. *Consent: Sexual Rights and the Transformation of American Liberalism.* Ithaca: Cornell University Press, 1999.

Hardt, Michael. "Affective Labour." *boundary 2* 26, no. 2 (Summer 2009): 89–100.

Harris, Cheryl I. "Whiteness as Property." *Harvard Law Review* 106, no. 8 (June 1993): 1707–1791.

Hartman, Saidiya. *Scenes of Subjection: Terror, Slavery, and Self-Making in Nineteenth-Century America*. New York: Oxford University Press, 1997.

Hemingway, Ernest. "Hills like White Elephants." In *The Complete Short Stories of Ernest Hemingway*, 211–214. New York: Scribner, 1998.

Heidegger, Martin. *Basic Writings*. New York: Harper, 2008.

Herbst, Josephine. *Money for Love*. 1929. New York: Arno Press, 1977.

Hobsbawm, Eric. *The Age of Extremes: A History of the World, 1914–1991*. New York: Vintage Books, 1994.

Holloway, Karla. *Private Bodies, Public Texts: Race, Gender, and a Cultural Bioethics*. Durham: Duke University Press, 2011.

Homberger, Eric. *Scenes from the Life of a City: Corruption and Conscience in Old NewYork*. New Haven: Yale University Press, 1994.

Honig, Bonnie, editor. *Feminist Interpretations of Hannah Arendt*. University Park: Pennsylvania State Press, 1995.

Horowitz, Helen Lefkowitz. *Rereading Sex: Battles over Sexual Knowledge and Suppression in Nineteenth-Century America*. New York: Knopf, 2002.

Hughes, Langston. "Cora Unashamed." In *The Ways of White Folks*, 3–18. 1934. New York: Vintage, 1969.

Jacobs, Harriet. *Incidents in the Life of a Slave Girl*. Mineola, NY: Dover, 2001.

Jensen, Joan M. "The Evolution of Margaret Sanger's 'Family Limitation' Pamphlet, 1914–1921." *Signs: Journal of Women in Culture and Society* 6, no. 3 (1981): 548–567.

Jensen, Robin E. *Dirty Words: The Rhetoric of Public Sex Education, 1870–1924*. Urbana: University of Illinois Press, 2010.

Jewett, Sarah Orne. *The Country of the Pointed Firs and Other Stories*. 1896. New York: W. W. Norton & Co., 1968.

Johnson, Barbara. "Apostrophe, Animation, and Abortion." *Diacritics* 16, no. 1 (Spring 1986): 29–47.

Kaplan, Amy. *The Social Construction of American Realism*. Chicago: University of Chicago Press, 1992.

Karaganis, Joseph. "Naturalism's Nation: Toward an American Tragedy." *American Literature* 72, no. 1 (March 2000): 153–180.

Kassanoff, Jennie A. *Edith Wharton and the Politics of Race*. Cambridge: Cambridge University Press, 2004.

Keller, Allan. *Scandalous Lady: The Life and Times of Madame Restell, New York's Most Notorious Abortionist*. New York: Atheneum, 1981.

Kelly, Edith Summers. *Weeds*. 1923. New York: Feminist Press, 1996.

Kitty Foyle. Directed by Sam Wood. Los Angeles: RKO Radio Pictures, 1940.

Korda, Michael. *Making the List: A Cultural History of the American Bestseller 1900–1999*. New York: Barnes & Noble Publishing, Inc., 2001.

Kühl, Stefan. *The Nazi Connection: Eugenics, American Racism, and German National Socialism*. New York: Oxford University Press, 2002.

Latimer, Heather. "Bio-reproductive Futurism: The Pregnant Refugee in Alfonso Cuaron's Children of Men." *Social Text 108* 29, no. 3 (2011): 51–72.

———."Popular Culture and Reproductive Politics: *Juno, Knocked Up,* and the Enduring Legacy of the *Handmaid's Tale.*" *Feminist Theory* 10, no. 2 (2009): 211–226.

———. *Reproductive Acts: Sexual Politics in North American Fiction and Film.* Montreal: McGill-Queen's University Press, 2013.

Lee, Hermione. *Edith Wharton.* New York: Knopf, 2007.

LeSueur, Meridel. *The Girl.* 1978 (written 1939). Albuquerque: West End Press, 2006.

Lewis, R. W. B. *Edith Wharton: A Biography.* New York: Harper & Row Publishers, 1975.

Lewis, Sinclair. *Ann Vickers.* New York: P. F. Collier & Son Corporation, 1932.

Liber, Benzion. "As the Doctor Sees It." *Birth Control Review* 1, no. 3 (1917): 7.

Livingston, Ira. *Between Science and Literature: An Introduction to Autopoetics.* Urbana: University of Illinois Press, 2005.

Lock, Robert Heath. *Variation, Heredity, and Evolution.* New York: E. P. Dutton and Company, 1906.

Locke, John. *Second Treatise of Government.* Indianapolis: Hackett Publishing Co., 1980.

Lockwood, T. F. "Criminal Abortion; A Prevailing Evil against the Unborn Generation; a National Crime Committed for Mere Social Promotion." *Journal of Missouri Medical Association* 3 (1906–1907): 220–231.

Lovett, Laura L. *Conceiving the Future: Pronatalism, Reproduction, and the Family in the United States, 1890–1938.* Chapel Hill: University of North Carolina Press, 2007.

Luker, Kristin. *Abortion and the Politics of Motherhood.* Berkeley: University of California Press, 1984.

Mahmood, Saba. *Politics of Piety: The Islamic Revival and the Feminist Subject.* Princeton: Princeton University Press, 2005.

Mamdani, Mahmood, editor. *Beyond Rights Talk and Culture Talk: Comparative Essays on the Politics of Rights and Culture.* New York: St. Martin's Press, 2000.

Mansbridge, Jane. "Carole Pateman: Radical Liberal?" In *Illusion of Consent: Engaging with Carole Pateman,* edited by Daniel I. O'Neill, Mary Lyndon Shanley, and Iris Marion Young, 17–30. University Park: Pennsylvania State University Press, 2008.

Mao, Douglas, and Rebecca Walkowitz. "Expanding Modernism." *PMLA* 123, no. 3 (May 2008): 737–748.

Matthews, John T. "*As I Lay Dying* in the Machine Age." *boundary 2* 19, no. 1 (Spring 1992): 69–94.

Marx, Karl. *Capital.* Volume 1. Translated by Ben Fowkes. New York: Penguin Books, 1990.

———. *Grundrisse.* Translated by Martin Nicolaus. New York: Penguin Books, 1993.

———. "On the Jewish Question." In *Early Writings,* translated by Rodney Livingston and Gregor Benton, 211–242. New York: Penguin Books, 1992.

Mauriceau, A. M. *The Married Woman's Private Medical Companion.* New York: Self-published, 1848.

McCabe, James D., Jr. *Lights and Shadows of New York Life; or, The Sights and Sensations of the Great City.* Philadelphia: National Publishing Co., 1872.

McGarry, Molly. "Spectral Sexualities: Nineteenth-Century Spiritualism, Moral Panics, and the Making of U.S. Obscenity Law." *Journal of Women's History* 12, no. 2 (2000): 8–29.

McHaney, Thomas L. *William Faulkner's "The Wild Palms": A Study.* Jackson: University Press of Mississippi, 1975.

Meier, Joyce. "The Refusal of Motherhood in African American Women's Theater." *MELUS* 25, nos. 3–4 (Autumn–Winter 2000): 117–139.

Melville, Herman. *Moby-Dick.* New York: Oxford University Press, 2000.

Michinard, P. "Medical Aspect of Criminal Abortion." *New Orleans Medical and Surgical Journal* 61, no. 4 (October 1908): 260–263.

Miller, Frank. *Censored Hollywood: Sex, Sin, and Violence on Screen.* Atlanta: Turner Publishing, 1994.

Mills, Catherine. "Biopolitics, Liberal Eugenics, and Nihilism." In *Giorgio Agamben: Sovereignty and Life,* edited by Matthew Calarco and Steven DeCaroli, 180–202. Stanford: Stanford University Press, 2007.

Mohr, James. *Abortion in America.* New York: Oxford University Press, 1978.

Morley, Christopher. *Kitty Foyle.* New York: Grosset & Dunlap, 1939.

Morrow, John Howard. *The Great War: An Imperial History.* New York: Routledge, 2003.

Newman, Karen. *Fetal Imagery: Individualism, Science, Visuality.* Stanford: Stanford University Press, 1996.

Nhlapo, Thandabantu. "The African Customary Law of Marriage and the Rights Conundrum." In Mamdani, *Beyond Rights Talk and Culture Talk,* 136–148.

Nietzsche, Friedrich. *On the Genealogy of Morals.* Translated by Walter Kaufmann. New York: Vintage Books, 1967.

Nussbaum, Martha C. *Sex and Social Justice.* New York: Oxford University Press, 1999.

Olasky, Marvin. "Advertising Abortion during the 1830s and 1840s: Madame Restell Builds a Business." *Journalism History* 13, no. 2 (Summer 1986): 49–55.

Olin-Ammentorp, Julia. *Edith Wharton's Writings from the Great War.* Gainesville: University Press of Florida, 2004.

O'Neill, Eugene. *The Abortion.* In *Complete Plays 1913–1920,* 201–220. New York: Library of America, 1988.

O'Reilly, John J. A. "Abortion and Birth Control: A Critical Study of 'A Critical Study.'" *American Medicine* 27, no. 12 (December 1931): 9, 20–24.

Osborn, Lincoln A. *Bad Girl: A Dramatic Comedy in Three Acts.* New York, n.d.

Owen, Chandler. "Women and Children of the South." *Birth Control Review* 3, no. 9 (September 1919): 9.

Parker, Dorothy. "Lady with a Lamp." In *The Portable Dorothy Parker*, 246–253. New York: Viking Press, 1973.

———. "Mr. Durant." In *The Portable Dorothy Parker*, 35–46. New York: Viking Press, 1973.

Parker, Edward H. "The Relation of the Medical and Legal Professions to Criminal Abortion." *Transactions of the American Medical Association* 31 (1880): 465–471.

Parry, Sally E. "Boundary Ambiguity and the Politics of Abortion: Women's Choices in *Ann Vickers* and *Kingsblood Royal*." In *Sinclair Lewis: New Essays in Criticism*, edited by James M. Hutchisson, 68–79. Troy, NY: Whitson, 1997.

Petchesky, Rosalind. *Abortion and Woman's Choice: The State, Sexuality, and Reproductive Freedom.* Boston: Northeastern University Press, 1990.

Piercy, Marge. *Sex Wars: A Novel of Gilded Age New York.* New York: Harper Perennial, 2006.

Pitkin, Hanna Fenichel. *The Attack of the Blob: Hannah Arendt's Concept of the Social.* Chicago: University of Chicago Press, 2000.

Poe, Edgar Allen. "The Mystery of Marie Roget." In *Tales*, 151–199. New York: Wiley and Putnam, 1845.

Poovey, Mary. "The Abortion Question and the Death of Man." In *Feminists Theorize the Political*, edited by Judith Butler and Joan W. Scott, 239–256. New York: Routledge, 1992.

Price, Alan. *The End of the Age of Innocence: Edith Wharton and the First World War.* New York: St. Martin's Press, 1996.

Price, Ruth. *The Lives of Agnes Smedley.* New York: Oxford University Press, 2005.

Propaganda for Reform in Proprietary Medicines, Volume 2. Chicago: Press of American Medical Association, 1922.

Rabinowitz, M. "End Results of Criminal Abortion: With Comments on Its Present Status." *New York Medical Journal* 100, no. 17 (October 24, 1914): 808–811.

Reagan, Leslie J. *When Abortion Was a Crime.* Berkeley: University of California Press, 1997.

"Report on Criminal Abortion." *Transactions of the American Medical Association* 12, no. 6 (1859): 75-78.

Revolutionary Road. Directed by Sam Mendes. Los Angeles: Dreamworks, SKG, 2008.

Richardson, Anna Steese. "Birth Control and the War." *Birth Control Review* 2, no. 4 (1918): 3–4.

Roberts, Dorothy. *Killing the Black Body: Race, Reproduction, and the Meaning of Liberty.* New York: Vintage, 1997.

———. "Race, Gender, and Genetic Technologies: A New Reproductive Dystopia?" *Signs* 34, no. 4 (Summer 2009): 783–804.

Roe v. Wade. January 1973. 410 US 113 (US Supreme Court Case).

Rose, Nikolas. *The Politics of Life Itself: Biomedicine, Power, and Subjectivity in the Twenty-first Century.* Princeton: Princeton University Press, 2007.

Rousseau, Jean-Jacques. *The Social Contract and Other Later Political Writings.* Edited by Victor Gourevitch. Cambridge: Cambridge University Press, 2007.

Rubin, Gayle. "The Traffic in Women: Notes of the 'Political Economy' of Sex." In *Toward an Anthropology of Women,* edited by Rayna Reiter, 157–210. New York: Monthly Review Press, 1975.

Ruhl, Lealle. "Dilemmas of the Will: Uncertainty, Reproduction, and the Rhetoric of Control." *Signs: Journal of Women in Culture and Society* 27, no. 3 (2002): 641–663.

Sanger, Margaret. "Birth Control and Racial Betterment." *Birth Control Review* 3, no. 2 (1919): 11–12.

———. "Birth Control or Abortion—Which Shall It Be?" *Birth Control Review* 2, no. 11 (1918): 3–4.

———. "The Eugenic Value of Birth Control Propaganda." *Birth Control Review* 5, no. 10 (1921): 5.

———. *Margaret Sanger: An Autobiography.* New York: W. W. Norton & Company, 1938.

———. *The Selected Papers of Margaret Sanger.* Volume 1, *The Woman Rebel, 1900–1928.* Edited by Esther Katz. Urbana: University of Illinois Press, 2003.

———. *The Selected Papers of Margaret Sanger.* Volume 2, *Birth Control Comes of Age, 1928–1939.* Edited by Esther Katz. Urbana: University of Illinois Press, 2006.

———. *Woman and the New Race.* New York: Blue Ribbon Books, 1920.

Scanlon, Jennifer. *Inarticulate Longings: "The Ladies' Home Journal," Gender, and the Promises of Consumer Culture.* New York: Routledge, 1995.

Schmitt, Carl. *Political Theology: Four Chapters on the Concept of Sovereignty.* Translated by George Schwab. Chicago: University of Chicago Press, 2006.

Schoen, Johanna. *Choice and Coercion: Birth Control, Sterilization, and Abortion in Public Health.* Chapel Hill: University of North Carolina Press, 2005.

Seitler, Dana. *Atavistic Tendencies: The Culture of Science in American Modernity.* Minneapolis: University of Minnesota Press, 2008.

Sergel, Christopher. *Christopher Morley's "Kitty Foyle, A Comedy in Three Acts."* Chicago: Dramatic Publishing Company, 1942.

Shorter, Edward. *A History of Women's Bodies.* New York: Basic Books, 1983.

Shuttleworth, Sally. "Female Circulation: Medical Discourse and Popular Advertising in the Mid-Victorian Era." In *Body/Politics: Women and the*

Discourses of Science, edited by Mary Jacobus, Evelyn Fox Keller, and Sally Shuttleworth, 47–68. New York: Routledge, 1990.

Smedley, Agnes. *Daughter of Earth.* 1929. New York: Feminist Press, 1987.

Smith, Lillian. *Strange Fruit.* New York: Harcourt, 1944.

Smith-Rosenberg, Carroll. *Disorderly Conduct: Visions of Gender in Victorian America.* New York: Oxford University Press, 1985.

Solinger, Rickie. *Beggars and Choosers: How the Politics of Choice Shapes Adoption, Abortion, and Welfare in the United States.* New York: Hill and Wang, 2002.

———. *Wake Up Little Susie: Single Pregnancy and Race Before "Roe v. Wade."* New York: Routledge, 2000.

Spivak, Gayatri. "Righting Wrongs." *South Atlantic Quarterly* 103, nos. 2–3 (2004): 523–581.

Srebnick, Amy Gilman. *The Mysterious Death of Mary Rogers: Sex and Culture in Nineteenth-Century New York.* New York: Oxford University Press, 1995.

Stein, Gertrude. *Three Lives.* 1909. New York: Penguin Classics, 1990.

Stetz, Margaret D. "Christopher's Morley's Kitty Foyle: (Em)Bedded in Print." In *Transatlantic Print Culture, 1880–1940: Emerging Media, Emerging Modernisms,* edited by Ann L. Ardis and Patrick Collier, 134–147. New York: Palgrave Macmillan, 2008.

Stix, Regine K. "A Study of Pregnancy Wastage." *Milbank Fund Quarterly* 13 (October 1935): 349–365.

Stoddard, Lothrop. *The Rising Tide of Color against White World-Supremacy.* 1922. Honolulu: University of the Pacific Press, 2003.

Stoler, Laura. *Race and the Education of Desire: Foucault's History of Sexuality and the Colonial Order of Things.* Durham: Duke University Press, 1995.

Storer, Horatio. *On Criminal Abortion in America.* Philadelphia: J. B. Lippincott & Co., 1860.

———. *Why Not! A Book for Every Woman.* Boston: Lee and Shepard, 1868.

Storer, Horatio, and Franklin Fiske Heard. *On Criminal Abortion in America: Its Nature, Its Evidence, and Its Law.* Boston: Little, Brown, and Company, 1868.

Stormer, Nathan. *Articulating Life's Memory: U.S. Medical Rhetoric about Abortion in the Nineteenth Century.* Boston: Lexington Books, 2003.

Taussig, Fred J. "The Control of Criminal Abortion as Influenced by the Present War." *Interstate Medical Journal* 23, no. 8 (August 1916): 772–778.

Trask, Michael. *Cruising Modernism: Class and Sexuality in American Literature and Thought.* Ithaca: Cornell University Press, 2003.

Trevor, John Bond. *An Analysis of the American Immigration Act of 1924.* New York: Carnegie Endowment for International Peace, Division of Intercourse and Education, 1924.

Turlish, Lewis A. "The Rising Tide of Color: A Note on the Historicism of *The Great Gatsby.*" *American Literature* 43, no. 3 (November 1971): 442–444.

Urgo, Joseph R. "Faulkner Unplugged: Abortopoesis and *The Wild Palms*." In *Faulkner and Gender,* edited by Donald M. Kartiganer and Ann J. Abadie, 252–272. Jackson: University of Mississippi Press, 1996.

Weinbaum, Alys Eve. *Wayward Reproductions: Genealogies of Race and Nation in Transatlantic Thought.* Durham: Duke University Press, 2004.

Wharton, Edith. *A Backward Glance.* New York: Simon & Schuster, 1998.

———. *Summer.* New York: D. Appleton and Company, 1917.

Where Are My Children? Directed by Lois Weber. 1916. National Film Preservation Foundation, 2007.

Williams, Patricia. *Alchemy of Race and Rights.* Cambridge: Harvard University Press, 1992.

Wilt, Judith. *Abortion, Choice, and Contemporary Fiction: The Armageddon of the American Literature.* Bloomington: Indiana University Press, 2004.

Winsor, Kathleen. *Forever Amber.* 1944. Chicago: Chicago Review Press, 2000.

Wolff, Cynthia Griffin. *A Feast of Words: The Triumph of Edith Wharton.* New York: Oxford University Press, 1977.

Yates, Richard. *Revolutionary Road.* 1961. New York: Knopf, 2009.

Zerilli, Linda. *Feminism and the Abyss of Freedom.* Chicago: University of Chicago Press, 2005.

INDEX

Abortifacients, 1, 57, 98, 100–101, 104, 107, 115, 162n6, 162n9

Abortion: comparison to birth control, 11, 38, 53–55, 64, 116; controversy, 5, 134–136, 142; cost of, 98, 104–105, 111; discussions in medical journals, 30, 69, 74, 82, 87, 105; feminist interpretations of, 28, 41–43; historical cases of, 21–23, 47–48, 108, 150n33, 150–151n43, 164n63; history of, 10, 12, 20, 54, 76, 140; infanticide as form of, 27, 60; laws about, 8–10, 19, 23, 25, 38, 39, 46–47, 50, 112, 140, 142–143, 150n38, 159n44; nineteenth-century attitudes towards, 28, 31, 37; politics of, 5, 8, 13, 22, 35, 147n4; relationship to class, 15, 24, 31, 38, 46, 49–50, 53–54, 64, 73–74, 83, 86–87, 139, 149n19; relationship to citizenship, 9, 11, 18–19, 22, 33, 36–37, 41, 50–51, 74, 116; representations in film, 2, 24, 89–95; representations in literature, 1–2, 3, 9–10, 12, 14–16, 22–23, 27–28, 31–37, 44–46, 58–63, 73–76, 81–83, 85–89, 96–101, 104–107, 115–116, 121, 125–126, 133–134, 139–141, 147n5; shame of, 3, 15, 71, 151n50

The Abortion (O'Neill), 2

Abortionists, 2, 21–24, 27–28, 48, 75–76, 81–82, 86, 96, 108–113

Advancing New Studies in Reproductive Health, 148n20

Agamben, Giorgio, 7, 12, 16–17, 21, 33, 120, 128, 130, 160n59

American Medical Association, 10, 22, 25, 29–30, 38, 68–69, 88, 98, 133–134, 158n13, 162n9

An American Tragedy (Dreiser), 12, 99, 102–108, 115, 117

Ann Vickers (Lewis), 11–12, 70–71, 83–89, 158n20

Ann Vickers (film), 91–93

Ansell-Pearson, Keith, 168n64

Arendt, Hannah, 12, 16, 33–34, 118–121, 124, 128, 132, 136, 165n6

As I Lay Dying (Faulkner), 11, 97–101, 115, 117

Atwood, Margaret, 38

Bad Girl (Delmar), 11, 71–76, 97, 99, 158n19, 158n20, 158n22

Bad Girl (film), 89

Bad Girl (play), 161n96

Bare life, 16–17, 19, 21, 25, 33–34, 120, 128–130, 149n10. *See also* Biopolitics

Barry, John M., 127, 166n26, 166n32

Bauer, Dale, 24, 36–37, 67, 74, 102, 158n21

The Beautiful and Damned (Fitzgerald), 11, 44–46, 51, 153n23, 154n25, 155n47

Beisel, Nicola, 19, 48, 68–69, 149–150n20, 155n45

Benn Michaels, Walter, 102–104, 107

Berg, Allison, 74, 159n31